Governance of the Divinely-Sanctioned Social Order
under Conditions of Religious Solidarity
Volume 3: The Just Ruler
by Ayatollāh Sayyed Alī Khāmeneī

An Interpolative Rendition into English with Annotations
by Blake Archer Williams

LANTERN
PUBLICATIONS

Lantern Publications
info@lanternpublications.com
www.lanternpublications.com

Ordering Information:

Quantity sales. Special discounts are available on quantity purchases by corporations, associations, and others. For details, contact the distributor at the address below.

Shia Books Australia
www.shiabooks.com.au
info@shiabooks.com.au

ISBN-978-1-922583-58-1

First Edition

In the Name of God,
the Most Compassionate, the Most Merciful

Table of Contents

The Names and Dates of the Twelve Imams

No	Konya (Patronimic)	Name	Dates of Birth-Death Islamic	Christian
1	Ab'al-Hasan	Ali b.AbuTalib	-23 to 40	600–661
2	Abu Md.	Hasan ibn Ali	3–50	624–670
3	Abu Abdillah	Husain b. Ali	4–61	626–680
4	Abu Md.	Ali b. Husain	38–95	658–712
5	Abu Ja'far	Md. ibn Ali	57–114	677–732
6	Abu Abdillah	Ja'far ibn Md.	83–148	702–765
7	Ab'al-Hasan	Musa b. Ja'far	128–183	744–799
8	Ab'al-Hasan	Ali ibn Musa	148–203	765–817
9	Abu Ja'far	Md. ibn Ali	195–220	810–835
10	Ab'al-Hasan	Ali ibn Md.	212–254	827–868
11	Abu Md.	Hasan ibn Ali	232–260	846–874
12	Ab'al-Qasim	Md. B. Hasan	255–Present	868–Present

Acknowledgments

All translations of verses of the Quran are Muhammad Asad's, with the occasional minor change.

Prayers of God's Peace and Blessings

In keeping with the Islamic practice of showing respect for the name of God, and sending prayers of God's peace and blessings whenever the name of His blessed Prophet, Lady Fātema, and the Twelve Imams is mentioned, as well as for asking God to hasten the reappearance of the Lord of the Age on the Earthly plane, one or more of the following Arabic symbols have been employed throughout the text. They are repeated for their great rewards.

عَزَّوَجَلَّ Used exclusively after the name of God, meaning "the Sublimely Exalted", or, as a prayer, "[May His name be] Sublimely Exalted".

صَلَّى اللهُ عَلَيْهِ وَآلِهِ Used exclusively after the name of the Prophet, meaning "May the peace and blessings of God be unto him and unto [the purified and inerrant members of] his family"

عَلَيْهِ السَّلَامُ Used for any of the Twelve Imams or past prophets of God, meaning "May God's peace be unto him".

عَلَيْهِمُ السَّلَامُ Used for two or more of the Twelve Imams or past prophets of God, meaning "May God's peace be unto them".

عَلَيْهَا السَّلَامُ Used for Lady Fātema, meaning "May God's peace be unto her".

عَلَيْهِمُ الصَّلَاةُ أَجْمَعِين Used for a plurality of the Fourteen Immaculates, meaning "May God's peace be unto them all collectively".

عَجَّلَ اللهُ تَعَالَى فَرَجَهُ الشَّرِيف Used for the Master of the Age (the Twelfth Imam), meaning "May God hasten the advent of his noble person".

A Note on Transliteration

The Persian words and Persian words of Arabic origin referred to in this book have been transliterated as they are pronounced (as opposed to all standard academic transliteration systems that transliterate words as they are written). As such, there is no 'system' of transliteration, such as that used by the Library of Congress, because pronunciations vary from region to region. Nevertheless, the reason this approach was preferred is that, while it is necessarily somewhat subjective, it has the advantage of accurately representing the sounds of words as they are meant to be pronounced. This might not be a factor among a group of orientalist scholars who already know how the words are pronounced and will pronounce the words correctly, despite their transliteration. Still, the intelligent general reader who is the target audience of this book is not in a position to be able to differentiate between the 'solar' (*shamsī*) and 'lunar' (*qamarī*) letters of the Arabic alphabet, and thus, unlike the orientalist scholar, will mispronounce an-Najaf as al-Najaf. The matter becomes even more complicated when it comes to the name of the august daughter of the Most Noble Prophet, Lady Fātemat oz-Zahrā, the correct pronunciation of whose name is an essential consideration for the Shī'a faithful. It is the preclusion of these kinds of pronunciation errors that have motivated us to use the 'as pronounced' as opposed to the 'as written' approach.

That having been said, there are several Arabic words whose transliterations based on the as-written system(s) has become so prevalent that seeing a transliteration other than what has unfortunately become the standard fare would seem awkward and out of place. To preclude this, we have chosen to use what has become standard in such cases. Instances of these cases include the words Quran (rather than Qoran or Koran), Muslim (rather than Moslem), and Muhammad (rather than Muhammad, using the letter 'o' to designate the dhamma over the *mīm*, this being the correct English equivalent symbol for the phoneme that is symbolised by the *dhamma*).

Translator's Preface

I had already translated *Imam Husain's Brothers in Arms* when my esteemed friend and colleague Mr. Shaykhlar, the publisher of Sahbā Publications (who produced *The 250-Year Old Person*, a highly successful and important work by Ayatollah Khāmeneī), released another seminal work by him entitled *Velāyat va Hokūmat* (*Welāya* and Governance). When I finished the translation of this second book (which was sponsored and made possible by the generous support of Mr. Vahīd Jalīlī and Mr. Malekī of The Cultural Front of the Islamic Revolution), I realized that in order to provide a complete picture of the concept that is at the core of the Islamic Revolution of Iran (which I ended up rendering as 'Governance of the Divinely-Sanctioned Social Order under Conditions of Religious Solidarity'), I had to add certain sections from *Imam Husain's Brothers in Arms*, as well as to translate an important essay that Ayatollah Khāmeneī had written in the early 1970's which dealt with the central concept of what I have called 'The Exclusivity of Providential Lordship' (*tawhīd-e rubūbīat*), which is the idea that no one other than God has a right of sovereignty over anyone else, and that it is to Him and His revealed dispensational order that people must submit to, and to no one and nothing else (including, of course, the arbitrary will of a majority of the populace arrived at by conventional rather than revealed means). The inclusion of this important essay was necessary as the concept it explicates is at the crux of the issue of the imamate or the Shi'a vision of how the community of those who have attained to faith must necessarily be governed. (The three intertwined strands of the rope of the imamate are *hojja* (see below), *esma* (immaculacy, inerrancy), and *afdalīa* (primacy or preeminence), all three of which are based on the fact that the right to legitimate sovereignty is the exclusive domain and province of God, and upon whose grace, therefore, it is incumbent to provide inerrant guidance that will act at one and the same time as (1) an exemplary model for emulation for mankind, as well as (2) as testamentary and evidentiary proof against those who fail to model their lives on the basis of that Divinely-provided Proof (*hojja*)).

Ayatollah Khāmeneï is the only scholar that I know of who has written extensively on this key concept of the Exclusivity of Providential Lordship. And as good as his treatment is, I felt that there was still a gap that existed between the conceptual framework that he provides in the essay (that is based on the presuppositional framework of the Islamic mindset), and the Western mindset. And so I decided that it was necessary to bridge that gap, which I have done by borrowing a chapter from my own *Creedal Foundations of Walīyic Islam*, which is a book that I wrote in 2016 as an introduction to the seminal work by Ayatollah Javādī-e Āmolī which I had just translated at that time and rendered as *The Regency of the Magisterium*. And so, with the addition of all of this material, the book turned into a four-volume work which begins with my own introductory remarks on the Exclusivity of Providential Lordship, continues with Ayatollah Khāmeneï's essay *The Spirit of Tawhīd: the Denial of Submission to Anyone and Anything other than God*, and continues with the translation of Ayatollah Khāmeneï's *Welāyat va Hokūmat*, supplemented by sections from his *Imam Husain's Brothers in Arms* interspersed throughout the work where deemed necessary. In this way, this four-volume work became a comprehensive and definitive treatment of the concept of the 'Governance of the Divinely-Sanctioned Social Order under Conditions of Religious Solidarity', by one of its most important advocates and practitioners, who is Imam Khomeinī's most talented student and successor; a concept which is, as I have already stated, at the core of the Islamic intellectual and political movement that gave rise to the Islamic Revolution of Iran.

The only thing that remains to be added is that almost without exception, the entirety of the content of all four volumes predate the Islamic revolution, being either written by Ayatollah Khāmeneï in the early 1970's (as is the case with the essay *The Spirit of Tawhīd: the Denial of Submission to Anyone and Anything other than God*), or are redactions of speeches and lectures that he delivered in the early to mid-1970's, the recordings of which were then redacted and edited, and which are the basis of *Welāyat va Hokūmat*, as well as of *Imam Husain's Brothers in Arms*.

And lastly, it might be of interest to point out that the main thesis that Ayatollah Khāmeneī espouses in these pages is that of the politicism of all of the Shī'a Imams; that they all acted in a coordinated if covert way (under conditions where precautionary dissimulation (*taqīya*) had to be used), to bring about their project of active political resistance against the usurping Umayyad and Abbāsid powers of their day). This thesis is highly controversial among the senior seminarians in Qom (let alone Najaf), mainly because it is believed that the Imams knew that such a project was bound to come to naught (and that conditions would degenerate for the community to such an extent that the Twelfth Imam would be occulted by God in order to ensure his survival). But be that as it may, it can be said that the possession of such knowledge is by no means necessarily incompatible with Ayatollah Khāmeneī's averred position concerning the political activity of the Imam's, just as today we know that all of our efforts at trying to establish just, legitimate, and equitable governance is bound ultimately to fail absent the advent of the Mahdi ﷻ, but that this knowledge does not and should not prevent us from doing our utmost to strive to bring such conditions about. To the contrary, this is indeed the correct position of 'active awaiting', i.e. an active pursual of the establishment of Islamic tenets and ideals, tempered by the knowledge of our limited ability (and ultimate inability) to do so, which temperance is the key to ensuring that these efforts will not fall into the error of what the late Eric Voegelin used to call an 'immanentization of the eschaton'.[1] The reason for this is that if all that is incumbent on us is to twiddle our political

---

[1] The belief that the disorder of the world can be transcended through special knowledge (or what Voegelin called a 'Gnostic Speculation') that is then implemented in order to actualize the speculation on earth within history, replacing the Kingdom of God with a humanist form of salvation.

thumbs while waiting for the advent of the Mahdi ﷺ, then whyever did God bother to commission Abraham ﷺ to go up against Nimrod's iniquities and waywardness? Why not have Moses ﷺ leave Pharaoh alone to do his worst? Why did Jesus ﷺ cast out the moneylenders from the temple? And why did the Prophet Muhammad ﷺ go up against the Quraysh idolaters? These great prophets were commissioned and sent down from on high for a reason.[2]

But whatever the case might be, Ayatollah Khāmeneī's claim must be judged on its own merits, namely, on the scriptural and rational proofs and exegesis and reasoning that Ayatollah Khāmeneī brings to bear in making his argument. And whether he is right or wrong, suffice it to say that the cogency of his argumentation is such that its rejection is by no means an open and shut case. To the contrary: the question remains an open one, and its settlement is one of the most pressing issues of our time.

---

2 As Allāma Sayyed Mortaḍa Askarī has stated (In *naqsh-e a'emme dar ehyā-ye dīn*, 1:52), "The aim of all the prophets through the ages has been to bring humanity under the dominion of the Providential Lordship of Almighty God and to raise humanity up to a point where only God's commands are obeyed, and to take guidance and instruction as to what is licit and illicit exclusively from God. The entirety of the spirit and substance of religion is naught but this very goal."

1 The Islamic Ruler

1.1 The Demeanour of the Prophets, Rulers of the Islamic Social Order

God ۞ the All-Knowing and All-Wise, has stated in His Sacred Writ:

وَجَعَلْنَاهُمْ أَئِمَّةً يَهْدُونَ بِأَمْرِنَا وَأَوْحَيْنَا إِلَيْهِمْ فِعْلَ الْخَيْرَاتِ وَإِقَامَ الصَّلَاةِ وَإِيتَاءَ الزَّكَاةِۖ
وَكَانُوا لَنَا عَابِدِينَ ﴿٧٣﴾

[21:73] and We made them Imāms (*a'immat^{an}*) [= leaders] who guided [others] in accordance with Our command, and We revealed to them [ordinances concerning] the performance of good deeds, the establishment and maintenance (*15qama*) of prayers, and the giving of the charity due (*zakā'*); and Us [alone] did they worship.

Two alternate images of the ruler have been envisaged in the Quran and in the *hadīth* report corpus, particularly in the *Nahj al-Balāgha*: a positive one and a negative one. The positive image is presented as a leader who guides (*imām-e hudā*) [his people] to the right path, i.e. to that which is true, real, and just, *al-haqq*; [in other words, to God ۞]. And the negative

15

image is presented as the leader who guides people to error and to the fire [of everlasting perdition]. The leaders who guide [their people to the right path] are the prophets and the *awliā*[3] and the rulers who rule in accordance with what is considered to be right and just by Islam (*ḥukkām be ḥaqq-e islāmī*); rulers who serve God 🌸 and who are deserving [of investiture into the office of rulership] on the basis of the conformance [of their reigns] with criteria [revealed by the] Divine. And the *bāṭil* leaders, [i.e. leaders who guide people away from the right path], are those who lead [people] to the Fire – these are [what the Quran refers to as] the *ṭāghūt*. This is the basic distinction that is depicted in the Quran. On one hand there is the demeanor of the Prophet 🌸, which is highly luminous, and is beloved and cherished and transcendent. Now the question might arise as to why we use the example of the prophets when we are talking about Islamic rulers, and whether the prophets were indeed examples of Islamic rulers? The answer is affirmative insofar as all of the prophets who have been commissioned [by God 🌸] were so commissioned in order to administer the societies in which they lived. And it so happened that at times, the society in question was limited to a city or to a nation, or even to a village; and at other times – with respect to certain prophets – the society [to which the prophet was commissioned from on high] did not have any geographical limits and included the entirety of the world; and the commissions of [all of] the great prophets were of this sort. But irrespective [of the scope of their respective commissions], there is no difference between the prophets in that *all* of them were commissioned to uproot the illegitimate and unjust social orders (*ḥukūmat-e ṭāghūt*) that existed in various parts of the world, and to replace them with a divine[ly-inspired] order which they were [commissioned] to establish. And this is why it is stated in the Quran "[4:64] ... *for We have never sent any apostle save that he should be obeyed by God's 🌸 leave* {= in accordance with the will of God}."

---

[3] See footnotes 13 and 35.

Thus, the nature of the prophets' encounters with the societies to which they were commissioned was for them to bid the populace not to obey the dictates of the illegitimate rulers who oppressed them and ruled over them with injustice: "[26:151] *and do not obey the dictates of the transgressors* – [26:152] *those who spread corruption on earth instead of setting things to rights!*" What this means is that there was a ruler or a king ruling over the society to which a prophet had been commissioned. Or [look at] the slogan of all of the divinely-commissioned prophets throughout the course of history, as it is related in the Quran: [26:108] *Therefore guard against {the punishment of} God* ✥ *by paying heed unto me!* This verse (108) is spoken by the prophet Noah, but if you look at the chapter of The Poets (*ash-Shu'arā*), you will see that there are seven different instances of this same utterance repeated by others prophets, such as the prophets Lut, Sāleh, Shu'ayb, Moses and other divinely-inspired prophets, where these prophets bid their people to obey them rather than obeying [the dictates of] the illegitimate rulers (*tāghūt*). And it was for this reason that the illegitimate rulers were the first people to feel threatened when a prophet [who] was commissioned [by God ✥] started to call people [to himself]; which is why they would go up against the prophets and send them to their martyrdom, or imprison or exile them; examples of all of which can be found in the Quran. Or, alternately, it could be that a given prophet would be able to attain to victory after a long battle and to establish a government which he would either head personally (as was the case of the Seal of the Prophets, the prophet Muhammad, unto whom be God's ✥ peace and blessings); and, as it was the case of the prophets Solomon, David, and other prophets whose [reigns] have been recorded in history or which have been alluded to in the Quran. Or, it could be the case that the prophet would not head the government personally but would appoint someone in his stead, instances of which also appear in the Quran: [2:246] "*Art thou not aware of those elders of the children of Israel, after the time of Moses, how they said unto a prophet of theirs, "Raise up a king for us, [and] we shall fight in God's* ✥ *cause"?*" [And in the foregoing verse, we see that] a people came to a prophet and bade him to "raise up a king or ruler" for them, so that they could wage holy battle (*jihād*) in his ranks and under his aegis in God's ✦ cause.

We can thus conclude that all of the prophets were commissioned [and sent down from on high] as rulers and governors over communities which had submitted to God's ✦ will (*jāme'e-ye islāmī*); and that the attributes which are ascribed to the prophets in the Quran are in fact attributes of a righteous divinely-appointed ruler. Now, let us depict these characteristics as a whole. The Quranic image of a divinely-inspired prophet is a highly luminous one. There are certain attributes that I have mentioned here, relying on verses of the Quran, each of which I will now proceed to enumerate in turn.

The first thing that catches one's eye concerning [the attributes of] the prophets is that they have been honored by God ✦ acting in His capacity as the Guide and Manager of the affairs of mankind (*parvardegār*, Arabic: *rabb*), Who has bestowed wisdom and knowledge on them, as well as having purified them [of all] moral [impurities] – these being the highest accolades which can be bestowed on a person. Numerous verses in the Quran tell us this with respect to various prophets:

وَلَمَّا بَلَغَ أَشُدَّهُ وَاسْتَوَىٰ آتَيْنَاهُ حُكْمًا وَعِلْمًا ۚ وَكَذَٰلِكَ نَجْزِي الْمُحْسِنِينَ ﴿١٤﴾

[28:14] Now when [Moses] reached full manhood and had become mature [of mind], We bestowed upon him [innate] knowledge [of right and wrong] as well as [the ability and right to legitimate i.e. divinely-sanctioned] rule (*hukm*)[4].

---

[4] I have chosen to render the word *hukm* as ruler here, while most translators of the Quran have rendered it as "wisdom", which is incorrect. Muhammad Asad which is usually head and shoulders above the rest of the translators (though he is not without his shortcomings, too, of course), renders this key phrase as follows: "We bestowed upon him *the ability to judge* [between right and wrong]" (my

18

The same wording is used regarding the prophets Joseph, Lot, and Solomon. [Here, what is meant by the word] "knowledge" is that knowledge which is necessary to administer society, [i.e.] *tawḥīdic*[5] knowledge, religious knowledge. When a prophet administers a given

---

emphasis). This is an improvement, but it does not go far enough. The word *ḥukm* as used here does indeed mean to judge, but not to judge in the usual sense (i.e. 'between right and wrong"). Rather, it means to judge in the archaic or Biblical sense of to rule. The fifth definition of the transitive verb to judge of the American Heritage dictionary provides the following definition: "5. Bible: To govern; rule. Used of an ancient Israelite leader". The second definition of the same dictionary under the nounal form of the same word provides the following definition: "A leader of the Israelites during a period of about 400 years between the death of Joshua and the accession of Saul". The 4th and 12th definitions provided by the Random House Kernerman Webster's College Dictionary gives us the same thing: "4. an administrative head of Israel in the period between the death of Joshua and the accession to the throne by Saul; 12. (of the ancient Hebrew judges) to govern." Traditional Persian translations render the word as "the [office of] governance" (مقام حکمفرمایی), as in Elāhī-e Qomshe'ī, or simply as "governance" (حکومت) in Makārem-e Shīrāzī's translation; whereas the translations of, say, Khorram-Shāhī or Fūlādvand, which can be perhaps described as less traditional, both render the phrase as "wisdom and knowledge", i.e. in a way that is similar to that of the usual English translations.

[5] *Tawḥīd* is usually translated as monotheism and is the general term that covers the Islamic conception of monotheism which posits not only that there is only one God ﷻ, but that He has providential lordship over all of His creation, including that of man's affairs; and that all of the orders of creation, from mineral to vegetable to animal and to man, are seamlessly integrated into God's ﷻ creation and innate will which, in the case of man who has been given limited free will, is exercised through God's ﷻ revealed sacred laws and His providential lordship. Man's *fetric* nature (his primordial or original disposition) is *tawḥīdic*; that is, it is in harmony with the ontic unicity or existential oneness of God ﷻ; it is monotheistic: it is naturally inclined toward and accepts God's ﷻ sovereignty over him and is innately inclined to serve only He who is his Maker.

community, he does so in accordance with an ideology that is based on a Divine Plan. The knowledge that has been bestowed on the prophet relates first and foremost to divine knowledge [having to do with this Plan]; i.e. it has to do with knowledge concerning man's self-understanding, concerning man's understanding of God 🕮 and man's duty of servitude toward Him, and man's understanding of his responsibilities concerning the administration of society and the establishment of a social order [based on] divine[ly-revealed tenets] whose purpose is [to provide the bases for mankind] to attain to [its individual and communal] perfection[s] – [in sum,] all of the knowledge that is required and essential for the establishment of Heaven on Earth, i.e. an Islamic society, and ultimately [to produce] a perfected bondsman and devotee of God 🕮. All of these ordinances (*ahkām*) have been bestowed on the prophet by the Lord of Providence and Nurturer [of the World] (*parvardegār*) without his having learned them from anyone else and without his being under the guidance and tutelage of anyone else.

When the source and leader of the prophetic insurrection [against the false order] and the ruler of the Islamic and prophetic (*nabawi*) society is [also] the source and wellspring of effluence of knowledge and discernment, it is only natural that the people of such a society will [also] be endowed with knowledge and discernment. The ignorance of a society's ruler will make the people of that society ignorant, and the knowledge, learning, and wisdom of a society's ruler will cause the people of that society to develop in an environment of sapiential knowledge and wisdom.

Thus, these are the three primary attributes: knowledge, wisdom, and moral purification. And this is why [when the prophets Abraham 🕮 and Ishmael 🕮 were raising the foundations of the House of God 🕮, they prayed for their progeny as follows:] [2:129] ... *and instruct them in scripture and wisdom and cause them to grow in purity.* [The prophets] purify their people [of moral impurities] because they themselves are morally pure; and they impart knowledge and wisdom to people, because they are learned and wise. There is a difference between wisdom and knowledge, as wisdom is higher than knowledge. [In this context,] having knowledge means being cognizant of the divine ordinances and teachings, whereas wisdom is that state of sapiential awareness that is cultivated in human beings [when they serve] under the aegis of servitude to God 🌸. It is that incisive and exacting vision which allows anyone who is endowed with it to understand the underlying spiritual realities of the world (*ālam*).[6] The people who see existence as being limited to this lower world (*dunyā*); those who consider the wealth of this world to be the highest value; those who chase after power and take pride in the power they have [over others]; and those people who relish the pleasures of the flesh and are unaware of the pleasures of the spirit – these are the people who are bereft of wisdom. Wisdom is being endowed with that incisive and exacting vision which enables a person to see the reality of the world as it truly is, which teaches one the meaning of life and of death.

These are the primary attributes of the prophets: that they are knowledgeable, wise, and pure; that they have been purified and are devoid of bad moral conduct; are bereft of selfishness and pride; do not desire anything for themselves; do not envy anyone; do not follow their lower urges and carnal desires; are not short-sighted; do not demean or humiliate the weak; and do not become enamored of those in positions of power and authority. These same three-fold primary qualities, which are present in prophets, make them into powerful men who are indomitable. Thus, this is the first characteristic: being knowledgeable, being wise, and having been morally purified.

Another attribute of the prophets which has been mentioned in the Quran as a refrain concerning certain prophets, and this is that prophets do not seek a reward for the work that they do: [42:23] *Say [O*

---

[6] In the Quranic usage, *ālam* is juxtaposed against the *dunyā* or lower world, and usually refers to the world to come once the veil of death is lifted, which is a world with a much higher level of reality or ontic amplitude. It can also refer to both worlds, the world of the present, as well as the world of the hereafter.

Prophet]: "No reward do I ask of you for this [message] other than [that you should] love [my] kinsfolk". The prophets have no expectation of any reward, despite all of the trials and hardships that they endure. And this is not limited to worldly or monetary compensations; they do not have any expectation even of being appreciated by their people or of their being remembered with good repute in the annals of history, such that if all of a given prophet's efforts were credited to someone else in history, this would not bother the prophet, and he would not express any dismay about this or say that his rights had been usurped. And this is the case not just about our prophet, but about all prophets.

I have jotted down two or three *āyas* (revelations) in the chapter entitled Yā Sīn: [36:20] *At that, a man came running from the farthest end of the city, [and] exclaimed: "O my people! Follow these message-bearers! [36:21] Obey those who ask no reward of you (for themselves), and who have themselves received Guidance."* These *āyas* are [evidence of] the attribute of the prophets whereby they do not seek any compensation from anyone. In the chapter of the Poets (*ash-Shu'arā*), the same concept is presented as follows in various places within the chapter in the words of the prophets Hūd, Sāleh, Noah, Shu'ayb, and Moses: *"And no reward whatever do I ask of you for it: my reward rests with none but the Rabb (Lord of Providence and Sustainer) of all the worlds."*[7]

Notice the importance [that the Quran places on] this subject: the thing that slackens one's spiritual will (*himma*), the thing that casts doubt in one's mind concerning the traversing of perilous journeys and undertakings, is for one to feel that his or her interests are endangered thereby. What is the thing that causes one not to speak one's mind explicitly before a group of people who disagree with one's thoughts and beliefs, and to dissimulate the truth and that which is right and which should be expressed openly in a shroud of false expedience? It is the same thing that the prophets are devoid of. But do you see, in today's world,

---

[7] 26:109, 127, 148, 164, and 180.

leaders who are willing to tell their people the truth about what is really going on in the world and in their respective societies? They would surely do so if they were unfettered [by their own interests] and were instead disinterested and impartial [leaders]. Everyone who appears before their people with [the] pretense [to leadership] but fails to give voice to [the concerns] which are in their hearts to avoid having to face uncomfortable situations – all of these people are afflicted with an illness which the prophets are immune to, because they are not after a wage for their efforts, they do not desire any recompense [save God's ❀ good pleasure]. Now compensation can be monetary, but it can also take non-monetary forms such as prestige and honor and standing within society. But the prophets do not want any of these from the people [to whom they have been commissioned, either]. This attribute is perfectly manifested in the [true] Islamic ruler.

When we say 'the Islamic ruler', to whom are we referring? Are we referring to one person, or rather, to the entirety of the Islamic governmental apparatus, each of whose members is duty-bound to conform their actions as much as possible to the attributes which are postulated for the Islamic ruler? Everyone who is involved in the business of statesmanship and rule over the community of Muslims must conform their actions to this characteristic of not expecting any reward for their actions other than with God ❀ alone, in accordance with this *āya*: *"And no reward whatever do I ask of you for it: my reward rests with none but the Rabb (the Lord of Providence and Sustainer) of all the worlds."* And the truth is that if one succeeds in performing one's duty before God ❀, this accomplishment and the reward which God ❀ will bestow on a given person for the performance of his or her duty before Him is the greatest of rewards.

This is one of the attributes of the prophets: that they are not after attaining their own desires and satisfying their own urges; they do not expect any recompense for all of their efforts. And this is true for all of the prophets who appeared prior to the formation of an Islamic form of government [at the hands of the Prophet ﷺ Muhammad] who passed away or were martyred [in this cause] but in any event were unsuccessful in accomplishing this task; and it obtains as well for the Most Noble Prophet ﷺ who was able to establish an Islamic governmental order, and did not slacken for a single day [in his efforts to strengthen its roots and to fortify and improve it] in the ten years of his reign over that community [in Medina]. Ten years of fighting a war with the enemies of Islam for its survival and very existence, and all of the trials and turmoil that goes with it – such is the nature of this characteristic.

Another attribute that can be seen in the lives of the prophets and which is extraordinarily important is that prophets begin their ministry from the midst of the underprivileged and disadvantaged classes of society, and these are the classes that have comprised the vast majority of the population of different societies within the course of history. Thus, another attribute is that the prophets had an affinity and empathy for the underprivileged and disadvantaged classes of society: they were not affiliated with the haughty and arrogant elements of society, but instead stood with the neglected masses.

The Commander of the Faithful has a sermon in the *Nahj al-Balāgha* called the *Qāse'a* sermon, which is a highly important sermon which is dazzling in its density of meaning and signification, one of whose themes is the condemnation and deprecation of arrogance and conceit. There are a few sentences concerning the prophets which I will recite for you. وَ لَكِنَّهُ سُبْحانَهُ كَرَّهَ اِلَيْهِمُ التَّكابُرَ And God ﷻ the Sublimely exalted caused arrogance and conceit to be reprehensible and disliked among the prophets. وَ رَضِىَ لَهُمُ التَّواضُعَ And caused humbleness and modesty to be appropriate to them, and was pleased that they should be humble and modest. It is also possible to read it as follows: وَ لَكِنَّهُ سُبْحَانَهُ كَرَهَ اليهِمُ التَّكَابُرَ might be a more suitable reading with وَ رَضِى لَهُمُ التَّوَاضُعَ, but the edition which I have has it as كَرَهَ اليهِمُ التَّكَابُرَ.

[Imam Ali continues:] فَأَلْصَقُوا بِالأَرْضِ خُدُودَهُم The prophets were so humble that they placed their faces {= foreheads} on the earth [in prostrations borne of humility], وَ عَفَّرُوا فِى التُّرَابِ وُجُوهَهُم and sullied their foreheads with the dust of the earth. Imam Ali then states: وَ خَفَضُوا أَجنحَتَهُم لِلمُؤْمِنِينَ وَ كانوا قَوماً مُستَضعفين And they would lower their wings for the true believers. The expression "the lowering of their wings" refers to an act which is the height of humility and humbleness. This is how the prophets treated the true believers. And that is why the true believers would always gather around the prophets, وَ كانوا قَوماً مُستَضعفين while they were weak and powerless. And this interpretation will convey our intended meaning either way: whether we interpret this as meaning that the prophets were weak and powerless, or the people to whom the prophets had been sent were weak and powerless, and the prophets showed such humility and humbleness to such a people. In any event, this is why some people found fault with the prophets in that وَ اتَّبَعَكَ الأَرذَلُونَ it was the lower classes of society which gathered around them [and heeded their calls].

Well, the point is that when a ruler is from the people and is a part of the people, he understands their problems and concerns. When the disadvantaged classes of society and the masses of the people have such a connection with the ruler of their society, such that the ruler pays heed to their concerns and so that they can explain their problems in detail to him, then it naturally follows that such a ruler will become intimately familiar with the problems and concerns of his people; and if he is a person of good will, the possibility will arise for him to help them [in a way that is effective] so that he will be able to resolve the knots which fetter their welfare. But the *tāghūts* or illegitimate powers and rulers of the world have not had such a relationship with the people over whom they hold sway. The *tāghūts* lack empathy and therefore do not understand the problems faced by the people. They do not undergo the hardships suffered by the people. They do not know what it means to be hungry, and the good things that the masses of people are deprived of mean nothing to them. Even in systems in which wealth is ostensibly held in common, everything must be doled out to the people by the government, and the people are equal to some extent in their shared social constraints, while members of the ruling class, those who occupy the positions of authority within society, are oblivious to their conditions.

Islamic society and the Islamic governmental order is not like this. The Commander of the Faithful states: "Should I content myself that I am referred to as 'The Commander of the Faithful' and then not share with them the hardships and hunger and privations which they suffer??" The lifestyle of the Commander of the Faithful is equal to that of the lowest class of the society of his day in terms of his food, clothing, and housing. And this is an attribute that is exclusive to the Commander of the Faithful. Uthmān b. Ḥanīf has stated: أَلَا وَ إِنَّكُم لا تَقْدِرُونَ عَلَى ذَلِكَ "This is something that is beyond your abilities; it is [exclusively] an Ālid art. Such powers of the Commander of the Faithful do not reside in the Uthmān b. Ḥanīfs of the world, وَ لَكِن أَعِينُونِى بِوَرَعٍ وَ اجْتِهَاد but strive to keep yourselves pure with [constant] striving." This is the secret to and an indication of a movement whose perfect examples are the prophets [who have been commissioned by God ﷻ and who arise] out of the midst of the people.

The Islamic ruler must "feel the pain" of the people and must be aware of what their problems and needs are, so that they can pursue solutions to their problems and see to their needs. In the continuation to the above sentences, the Commander of the Faithful states that وَ لَكِنَّ اللهَ سُبْحَانَهُ جَعَلَ رُسُلَهُ أُولِى قُوَّةٍ فِى عَزَائِمِهِم God ﷻ the Sublimely Exalted endowed His prophets with a firm and powerful will. وَ ضَعَفاً فِيما تَرَى الأَعْيُنُ مِن حَالاتِهِم And although their will is firm and powerful, their external appearance is humble and weak-seeming in an inverse proportion to that inner strength and is free of the usual signs and indications of power and strength and arrogance. Yet, on the other hand, how many arrogant and powerful

26

leaders the world has seen in whose hearts not a single iota of will for the betterment of humanity can be found! These are weak people: weak in the face of the corruption that power entails, weak in their ability to resist their carnal lusts and desires, and weak in the face of the great world powers. But before their own people, before the weak and powerless and disenfranchised and oppressed, they are haughty and arrogant and burly and tough. The prophets are the opposite of this: before the weak they are humble, but are strong as steel in the face of the enemies of God ﷻ and before the major obstacles [to His will being done].

مَعَ قَنَاعَـٰ تَمَلأُ القُلوبَ وَ العُيونَ غِنى There is a sense of contentment which fills the eyes and hearts. The eye is no longer hungry constantly to go in search of the goods and pleasures which the world has on offer, so that it can accumulate such goods wherever it encounters them. وَ خَصاصَـٰ تَمَلأُ الأَبصارُ وَ الأَسماعَ أذًى They demand and exact such high standards from themselves that the eye is distressed from such sights and the ears are distraught at hearing such things. The manservant of the Commander of the Faithful reports that he said to the Commander of the Faithful: "O the Commander of the Faithful! You have reached old age, and so this dry bread that you break on your knee and slowly take in {= moisten with your saliva} is no longer suitable for you. Pray allow me to go and procure some soft fresh wheat bread so that you can chew it [comfortably and without such arduous preliminaries]." [The report continues,] "The Commander of the Faithful did not give me his permission, but I went and bought some wheat flour and mixed the dough with some oil and placed the bread within reach of the Commander of the Faithful so that perchance he might partake of it and enjoy it. But when the Commander of the Faithful understood what I had done, he called me and asked me why I had done what I did. He then took the bundle of dry oat bread that he had and knotted it and sealed it to make sure that I could not be able to add anything to it. Afterwards I said to myself, يَأكُلُ هُوَ المُهَنَّأ وَ عَلَىَّ الوِزرُ why should I insist on this? If I persist in taking good food to the Commander of the Faithful without his knowledge and consent and if he eats that food, the sin [of what he considers inappropriate to a ruler] will fall on my neck and I will have to answer for it, because [Imam] Ali would not have approved of it. I therefore desisted." This was the way in which the Commander of the Faithful transacted his life. These are very clear and important characteristics: not being arrogant and haughty, being humble before your subjects, and respecting them and considering their concerns.[8]

1.2 Ruling in accordance with Divinely-Revealed Criteria and Tenets
God ﷻ the All-Knowing and All-Wise has stated in His Sacred Writ:

وَإِذِ ابْتَلَىٰ إِبْرَاهِيمَ رَبُّهُ بِكَلِمَاتٍ فَأَتَمَّهُنَّ ۖ قَالَ إِنِّي جَاعِلُكَ لِلنَّاسِ إِمَامًا ۖ قَالَ وَمِن ذُرِّيَّتِي ۖ قَالَ لَا يَنَالُ عَهْدِي الظَّالِمِينَ ﴿١٢٤﴾

[2:124] And [remember this:] when his Lord and Sustainer tried Abraham ﷺ by [His] commandments and the latter fulfilled them, He said: "Behold, I shall make thee the Imam of mankind." Abraham ﷺ asked: "And [wilt Thou make leaders] of my offspring as well?" [God ﷻ] answered: "My covenant does not embrace the unjust."

What is of primary, if not exclusive, importance in Islam are its values.[9] From the vantage of Islam, the person in whom Islam's values are more [instilled and manifested] is [endowed with a higher spiritual rank and therefore] given a higher priority. And this is the case irrespective of the generation, race, lineage or social stratum one might hail from. In the Quranic verse which I just recited, when the Prophet Abraham ﷺ is vested by God ﷻ in the office of the imamate (or comprehensive leadership of the community of the faithful), he asks God ﷻ the Sublimely Exalted, قَالَ وَمِن ذُرِّيَّتِي *"And [wilt Thou make leaders] of my offspring as well?"* In response to Abraham's ﷺ query, God ﷻ answers in the negative rather than the

---

[8] 1362/8/6.

[9] Reading *arzeshhā* for *me'yārhā* here *et passim*.

28

positive, saying, لَا يَنالُ عَهدِى الظَّالِمِينَ "*My covenant does not embrace the unjust.*" The criterion is not whether or not [he who is to be vested in the office of the imamate] is of one's progeny or "seed"; the issue as to who is to attain to the office of the imamate does not revolve around the question of whether or not one is or is not one of Abraham's ﷺ progeny. Rather, what is at issue is that the person who is vested in this office and who thus takes the helm of [interpreting and implementing] God's ﷻ command cannot and must not be iniquitous and oppressive. What is at issue here are values, not one's lineage or [familial] ties.

In another verse of the Quran, in the story of Tālūt and Jālūt[10], when the prophet of the Children of Israel appoints Tālūt [as their governor], some people protested that Tālūt is not wealthy [and is thus not worthy to be their leader]. وَلَمْ يُؤْتَ سَعَةً مِّنَ الْمَالِ [2:247] *And their prophet said unto those elders: "Behold, now God ﷻ has raised up Saul to be your king."* *They said: "How can he have dominion over us when we have a better claim to dominion than he, and he has not [even] been endowed with abundant wealth?"* Here we can see that it was the wealthy among the Children of Israel who lodged the protest. In response, [2:247] … *[The prophet] replied: "Behold, God ﷻ has chosen him over you, and endowed him abundantly with knowledge and bodily perfection. And God ﷻ bestows His dominion upon whom He wills: for God ﷻ is infinite, all-knowing."* What is at issue is not how much wealth one possesses or one's lineage or familial ties; [it is a question of God's ﷻ decision]: *God ﷻ has chosen him over you.* And God's ﷻ decision is based on values, for God ﷻ has familial ties with no one.

Now, if the people whom God ﷻ chooses stray [in their behavior] from the values [which have been stipulated by God ﷻ in His holy writ], then their fate will be no different than that which was in store for the

---

[10] Tālūt is considered to be the Quranic name for Saul, as he was the Malik of Israel, or Gideon, with the reasoning that the Quran references the same incident of the drinking from the river as that found in the Book of Judges, as well as other factors associated with the latter. The name Jālūt is associated with Goliath.

Children of Israel. At one time, Almighty God ﷻ chose and exalted the Children of Israel over all of the nations and peoples of the world, and this preeminence was on account of the fact that the other nations of the world were not endowed with as high a culture and civility which the Children of Israel enjoyed [as a result of] the ministry [of their prophets]. But this same Tribe of Israel carried on in such a way [that was contrary to the divine values and revealed law] that they were vanquished by other nations, as a consequence of which they became weak and suffered grievously, such that the Quran describes them in the following terms:

وَضُرِبَتْ عَلَيْهِمُ الذِّلَّةُ وَالْمَسْكَنَةُ وَبَاءُوا بِغَضَبٍ مِّنَ اللَّهِۚ ذَٰلِكَ بِأَنَّهُمْ كَانُوا يَكْفُرُونَ بِآيَاتِ اللَّهِ وَيَقْتُلُونَ النَّبِيِّينَ بِغَيْرِ الْحَقِّۚ ذَٰلِكَ بِمَا عَصَوا وَّكَانُوا يَعْتَدُونَ ﴿٦١﴾

[2:61] … And so, ignominy and humiliation overshadowed them, and they earned the burden of God's ﷻ condemnation: all this, because they persisted in denying the truth of God's ﷻ messages and in slaying the prophets against all right: all this, because they rebelled [against God ﷻ], and persisted in transgressing the bounds of what is right.

Almighty God ﷻ drove them down from the high position which He had given them. Thus, in Islam and in the logic of the Quran and of the culture [that is intimately attuned to and intent on implementing the will] of the Divine, all social positions and spiritual ranks (including [being vested in the] governance [of a nation], which is indeed a [high] spiritual rank) – all these are based on [the conformity of those vested in them to divine] values [and the tenets and ordinances of the revealed law].[11] There are certain values and criteria which exist [in the fabric of creation, and] God ﷻ chooses and appoints people [to the position of the leadership of the

---

[11] See the sub-section below: "The Criteria for determining the Legitimacy of the Islamic Leader".

community of those who have attained to faith in Him and His Way] based on those values and criteria. Obviously, there are instances where these values and criteria obtain in specific persons who are specifically designated [for such purposes] by Almighty God ﷻ; and these are the prophets and their rightful successors (*awsīā*).[12] And there are other occasions where such designations are not made specifically and by name. Rather, the person who is chosen by God ﷻ is identified by way of his attributes. In other words, such a person's specific characteristics and attributes are indicated by God ﷻ the Sublimely Exalted and by [the tenets and values of] the Islamic [magisterium and] culture to the people, who then follow the lead of such persons who are endowed with such characteristics. This is how the Islamic ruler is [designated and selected] in Islam [while the period of the occultation[13] lasts, i.e. in the absence of a specifically designated Imam who is immaculate or inerrant as well as

---

[12] See footnote 135.

[13] The Occultation (*al-ghayba*) is the event whereat the Twelfth Imam disappeared from the physical plane (in the year 260 HQ/ 874 CE) at God's ﷻ behest in order to protect him from being murdered by the Abbāsid authorities. The Shi'a believe that he will return to the physical plane at a time appointed by God ﷻ to fill the earth with equity and justice, where it had hitherto been filled with iniquity and oppression. The Minor Occultation (*ghaybat as-sughrā*) refers to the period when the Imam still maintained contact with his followers via deputies (*an-nuwwāb al-arba'a*). During this period, from 874-941, the deputies represented him and acted as agents between him and the faithful of the community. The Major Occultation denotes the second, longer portion of the Occultation, which continues to the present day, in which no specific deputy was designated by the Twelfth Imam to represent him, but in which the general class of persons, namely the magisters of sacred jurisprudence (the *fuqahā* or *ulamā*) are named by him to act in a leadership and guidance capacity while the occultation lasts.

sinless]. And of course, we have truly seen the miracle of Islam in this regard with our own eyes.[14]

In a political order that is erected on specific tenets and values, it is not a major issue if mistakes are made on occasion here and there. It is [even] not of the greatest consequence if one who is not endowed with the specific tenets and values [enshrined in its constitution] be thought of [temporarily] as being so endowed. This is not what is of the highest importance. What is of the highest importance is that the general direction and general policies of a given society and social order are such that people who are endowed with [the correct] tenets and values are appointed to positions of high authority and responsibility, and that positions of authority are not allocated on the basis of one's lineage or familial ties; and this is the great miracle of the our revolution.[15] Of course, at the outset of the revolution, these Islamic concepts [and values] had not yet taken their

---

[14] The reference is unclear. It would seem that it is a reference to the person of Imam Khomeini, or possibly to the triumph of the revolution which he led.

[15] This claim might seem somewhat farcical to those who are somewhat familiar with the current state of affairs in the Islamic Republic and who consequently know the extent to which it is suffering from nepotism, cronyism, and the like. But on March 21st, 1984, almost 35 years ago when this series of lectures were delivered, this was not the case, and the improvement in this respect compared to the situation which obtained during the Pahlavi regime was indeed miraculous. A couple of days ago from the time of this writing (February 2019), on the occasion of the 40th anniversary of the Islamic Revolution, Ayatollah Khāmeneī gave a speech in which he made it perfectly clear that he was aware of the gap that has arisen since then between the values of the revolution and the realities on the ground, and emphasized the need to work to close this gap. Of course in other important areas, huge improvements have been made which are indeed miraculous, such as Iran's rank on the United Nations' Human Development Index, Iran's rank as the nation with the greatest rate of increase in scientific knowledge, literacy, life expectancy, and dozens of other indicators in major indices.

rightful place in society; the value of faith in the revolution and revolutionary piety had not yet been [rightly] understood; and the glitzy values and glamorous governing criteria of the *ancient regime* were still on everyone's minds. And so some elements were able to take advantage of this and to take up positions in the executive branch [of the new order]; elements which can in fact be characterized as outsiders who were intent on the infiltration of the order. But the health of a given order depends on [its ability] to rid itself of such extraneous and infiltration elements and [to reform itself by] eliminating unhealthy cells and replacing them with healthy ones. And the factor that can prevent the infiltration of such elements and of those who tend to draw the values of the order back down from the heavenly values to the desires and urges of the lower self is paying due attention and ensuring that those who are entrusted with positions of responsibility in the new order are truly endowed with and committed to the attributes of our Islamic tenets and values.[16]

1.3 The Criteria for determining the Legitimacy of the Islamic Leader

There are certain values which all candidates for positions of high authority within the governmental system must embody, without which investiture it is not possible for anyone to qualify for candidature for elections to such positions; [in other words, there are] values [and qualities which are enshrined in the constitution of the republic as] mandatory prerequisites [for consideration of candidature to such positions].Thus, it is not the case that any Tom, Dick or Harry who is of base character or who is morally corrupt and who only follows the dictates of his carnal and lower lusts and desires has a right to a position of high authority and leadership within our social order merely because he is able to attract the votes of a bunch of people by way of the shenanigans that his wealth or charisma makes available to him; our constitutional order does not provide such persons with its seal of legitimacy. The opinion and vote of the people

[16] 1363/1/1 (March 21st, 1984).

is determinative, to be sure; but [this determination is operative] within [the circle of] those who are [properly] endowed with the necessary [qualifying attributes and] values. [Conversely,] if such values and attributes are not present in such a person, then they cannot be instilled in him by virtue of the election process. [The presence of] these characteristics and attributes must be [definitively] determined [prior to the acceptance of a given person's formal candidature]. Characteristics such as *taqwā*;[17] [a commitment to the tenets and ordinances of God's ﷻ] religion, i.e. Islam; soundness of moral character and equity in conduct (*ʿadl*),[18] and a familiarity with the teachings of Islam. He who is desirous of guiding Islamic society to Islam must himself be familiar with Islam.

أَفَمَن يَهْدِي إِلَى الْحَقِّ أَحَقُّ أَن يُتَّبَعَ أَمَّن لَا يَهِدِّي إِلَّا أَن يُهْدَى قُلْ هَلْ مِن شُرَكَائِكُم مَّن يَهْدِي إِلَى الْحَقِّ ۚ قُلِ اللَّهُ يَهْدِي لِلْحَقِّ ۗ أَفَمَن يَهْدِي إِلَى الْحَقِّ أَحَقُّ أَن يُتَّبَعَ أَمَّن لَّا يَهِدِّي إِلَّا أَن يُهْدَىٰ ۖ فَمَا لَكُمْ كَيْفَ تَحْكُمُونَ ﴿٣٥﴾

[10:35] Say: "It is God ﷻ [alone] who guides unto the truth. Which, then, is more worthy to be followed – He who guides unto the truth, or he who cannot find the right way unless he is guided? What, then, is amiss with you and your judgment?"

Such a person must know the Way and must be knowledgeable [about its pitfalls and its peaks and valleys]. He must be a doctor of religion, in other words. It is only once it has been established that a given candidate is

---

[17] *Taqwā*: a righteousness of character which is informed by a fear of appearing before God ﷻ on the Day of Judgement and of the everlasting consequences in the hereafter as a result of the possibility of a failure to perform well in this ultimate fateful Judgement.

[18] Professor Hāmid Algar has defined ʿadl as follows: The "quality of justice" (ʿadl; ādil) that is demanded of a religious scholar includes not only the practice of equity in all social dealings, but also complete abstention from major sins, the consistent performance of all devotional duties, and the avoidance of conduct incompatible with decorum.

endowed with these characteristics, with God-fearing righteousness (*taqwā*), with the ability to control his carnality and lower urges, with the prerequisite minimum of piety and religiosity (i.e. complete abstention from major sins, the consistent performance of all devotional duties, etc.) and religious learning and knowledge – only then does the opinion and vote of the people [take on jurisdiction and have any purchase, and it is only then that this second determinative criterion is allowed to engage the teeth of the electoral mechanism and to turn its wheel]. And even then, if the people do not vote for such a candidate [after his passing the vetting process which determines that he is sufficiently qualified in terms of his knowledge and character to run for high office], then he will still not have legitimacy [in the eyes of the constitutional order and laws of the Islamic Republic]. There is no such thing in Islam as lording it over the people by brute force. Rather, the origin and source of legitimate rule are the attributes and values that we have mentioned, and these have been determined, in their turn, by Almighty God 🕸; thus, in the Islamic order, God's 🕸 reign is intermingled with the will of the people.[19] Wherever there is talk or a claim to "Islamic governance", one's eyes must search for these [divinely-determined] attributes and values to see if they are present. And a governmental order approximates an Islamic order to the extent that such attributes and values are present [in its leaders and to the extent that they have been actualized in the body politic]. The Islamic form of government, i.e. the polities throughout the world of Islam, must be in harmony with all of the other tenets and values and social objectives of Islam, including [the tenet derived from the following two revelations]:

---

[19] اراده (will) for the second حکومت خدا در نظام اسلامی با حکومت مردم آمیخته است; reading instance of (reign) حکومت .

الَّذِينَ يَتَرَبَّصُونَ بِكُمْ فَإِن كَانَ لَكُمْ فَتْحٌ مِّنَ اللَّهِ قَالُوا أَلَمْ نَكُن مَّعَكُمْ وَإِن كَانَ لِلْكَافِرِينَ
نَصِيبٌ قَالُوا أَلَمْ نَسْتَحْوِذْ عَلَيْكُمْ وَنَمْنَعْكُم مِّنَ الْمُؤْمِنِينَ ۚ فَاللَّهُ يَحْكُمُ بَيْنَكُمْ يَوْمَ الْقِيَامَةِ ۗ
وَلَن يَجْعَلَ اللَّهُ لِلْكَافِرِينَ عَلَى الْمُؤْمِنِينَ سَبِيلًا ﴿١٤١﴾

[4:141] But God ۞ will judge between you all on the Day of Resurrection; and never will God ۞ allow those who deny the truth to harm the believers;

وَأَعِدُّوا لَهُم مَّا اسْتَطَعْتُم مِّن قُوَّةٍ وَمِن رِّبَاطِ الْخَيْلِ تُرْهِبُونَ بِهِ عَدُوَّ اللَّهِ وَعَدُوَّكُمْ وَآخَرِينَ
مِن دُونِهِمْ لَا تَعْلَمُونَهُمُ اللَّهُ يَعْلَمُهُمْ ۚ وَمَا تُنفِقُوا مِن شَيْءٍ فِي سَبِيلِ اللَّهِ يُوَفَّ إِلَيْكُمْ
وَأَنتُمْ لَا تُظْلَمُونَ ﴿٦٠﴾

[8:60] Hence, make ready against them whatever force and war mounts you are able to muster, so that you might deter thereby the enemies of God ۞, who are your enemies as well, and others besides them of whom you may be unaware, [but] of whom God ۞ is aware; and whatever you may expend in God's ۞ cause shall be repaid to you in full, and you shall not be wronged.

Policies based on tenets derived from the above revelations must be operational in order for us to be able to affirm that the governmental order which prevails over society is an Islamic one.[20]

1.4 Specific Attributes of the Islamic Ruler
God ۞ the All-Knowing and All-Wise has stated in His Sacred Writ:

يَا دَاوُودُ إِنَّا جَعَلْنَاكَ خَلِيفَةً فِي الْأَرْضِ فَاحْكُم بَيْنَ النَّاسِ بِالْحَقِّ وَلَا تَتَّبِعِ الْهَوَىٰ
فَيُضِلَّكَ عَن سَبِيلِ اللَّهِ ۚ إِنَّ الَّذِينَ يَضِلُّونَ عَن سَبِيلِ اللَّهِ لَهُمْ عَذَابٌ شَدِيدٌ بِمَا نَسُوا
يَوْمَ الْحِسَابِ ﴿٢٦﴾

---

[20] 1363/11/9

[38:26] [And We said:] "O David! Behold, We have made thee a [prophet and, thus, Our] vicegerent on earth: rule, then, between men with justice, and do not follow lower desire, lest they lead thee astray from the path of God ﷻ."

In the 131rd sermon of the *Nahj al-Balāgha*, the Commander of the Faithful states, "We did not shoulder this responsibility (i.e. that of the leadership of the community) for the sake of [the goods of] the world and for worldly gains, but accepted [the onus of] governance for God's ﷻ [good pleasure]." The Imam continues: "The person who is responsible and the one who holds authority over the affairs of the people; and who holds sway over the *nawāmīs*[21] of the people; and on whether the people's blood will or will not be shed; and who is responsible for the collective achievements of the nation; and who is responsible for [the maintenance and implementation of] the ordinances and sacred laws within the community of those who have attained to faith in Islam – it is not fitting for the person who is the leader of the Muslims to have the following characteristics:"

البَخيل فَتَكون فى أموالِهِم نَهمَتُهُ Firstly, that he should not be stingy (*bakhīl*), for if he is stingy, he will covet the property of his wards. What is meant here by "the property of his wards or people" is the public purse or treasury whose ways and means of expenditure is at the disposal of the state. In other words, if the ruler is stingy or miserly, even the wealth of the public which is gathered in the treasury will not reach the people as the leader will abuse his authority with respect to it.

وَ لَا الجاهِلُ فَيُضَلَّهُم بِجَهلِه Secondly, the Islamic ruler cannot be ignorant [of the teachings of Islam and the requirements of its implementation], so that he does not lead others astray due to his ignorance.[22]

---

[21] *nawāmīs*, singular: *nāmūs:* the order, honor, self-respect and dignity of one's self and one's wards and household; in this context, of the nation as a whole.

[22] Feqhicity as a Necessary Precondition for the Islamic Ruler. Feqhicity or *feqāhat* can be characterized as the Shī'a magisterium or as the body of authoritative

وَ لَا الجافي فَيَقطَعَهُم بِجَفائِه Thirdly, he should not be iniquitous or an oppressor; he should not be hard-hearted and ornery and aggressive, so that he does not repel the people because of these characteristics.

وَ لَا الحائِفُ لِلدُّوَلِ فَيَتَّخِذَ قَوماً دونَ قَومِ Fourthly, he should not waste public funds or show favoritism in the way they are expended; he should not show bias in administering the wealth of the people and should not consider this wealth to be his [to do with it as he pleases].

وَ لَا المُرتَشى فِى الحُكمِ فَيَذهَبَ بِالحُقوقِ وَ يَقِفَ بِها دونَ المَقاطِعِ Fifthly, the Islamic ruler must not be susceptible to bribery, nor should he extort money from

---

ethico-legal and doctrinal religious teachings for which there is consensus or near-consensus within Shī'a Islam, together with the body of the clerisy who have the authority (based on their knowledge and learning) to expound upon and elucidate these religious truths. In a speech dated 1359/12/15, Ayatollah elaborates on feqhicity as a necessary precondition for the Islamic ruler as follows: "Another condition which is necessary for the Islamic ruler is that he is aware of [the tenets and teachings of] Islam; that he should be a *faqīh* (or a doctor of sacred jurisprudence cum theologian), and to be [intimately] familiar with Islam. The Quran states: [2:247] [*The prophet] replied: "Behold, God ﷻ has exalted him above you, and endowed him abundantly with knowledge and bodily perfection."* In the story of Tālūt, when the powerful and wealthy [among the tribe of Israel] were surprised as to why their prophet appointed Tālūt as their governor, the prophet replied that *God ﷻ has endowed him abundantly with knowledge and bodily perfection.* The Commander of the Faithful similarly states in this regard: "The most worthy person for the position of leadership of the community of Muslims is one who has the ability to carry out such a responsibility, and who is more familiar with anyone else with respect to the ordinances and sacred laws of Islam." In other words, he must be a *faqīh* or doctor of sacred jurisprudence and must be familiar with what God ﷻ expects of His creatures, for if he does not know these things, he will be misled. Another thing that is necessary for the Islamic ruler is that he should depend on the love and respect of the people rather than on brute force; he must be beloved of his people so that he can carry out his duties and responsibilities with reliance on the people's support rather than with the use of coercion and force.

the people in order to implement that which is already their right as it is; for if this were the case, the divine ordinances will lie fallow and the ruler will have exited himself from the bounds of the sacred law of Islam.

وَ لَا الْمُعَطِّلُ لِلسُّنَّا فَيُهْلِكَ الْأُمَّا And finally, the Islamic ruler must not suspend the divine ordinances and sacred law of Islam, for by so doing, he will lead the people of the community to perdition.

Briefly speaking, this *hadīth* report tells us that in addition to the conditions which have been predetermined – without which conditions one cannot be vested in the office of the leadership of the community – there are a series of attributes which must also be present in the character of the Islamic ruler, and a series of attributes which must not be present. And what is more, if these conditions and requirements are not abided by, then certainly, the Islamic society which the Muslims intend to bring about for themselves will not obtain.

But two [other necessary] attributes concerning the Islamic ruler, which I will mention briefly, are, firstly, his having command over his lower carnal desires; and secondly, courage. Of course, these two characteristics are interrelated; I will discuss the relationship shortly. Concerning the first attribute, what we can say is that it is imperative that the Islamic ruler not give the reins of his soul and of his behavior and actions to his lower urges and desires. What I mean by this is that while it is true that it is incumbent on all people and all Muslims within an Islamic society to control their unlawful carnal desires, but the burden of this incumbency is heavier when it comes to the Islamic ruler himself. Human beings are an aggregation of such instincts, urges, and desires, which push and pull each person in different directions. Any person who desires to take on the burden of a trust as weighty as the governance of Islamic society must make the struggle against his lower desires one of his first priorities. It is not at all acceptable for someone who rules over society to pay heed to and follow his carnal desires and to act in accordance with such desires [in this capacity]; and this is particularly so in the case of Islamic society, whose whole basis is ethics and moral behavior based on divinely revealed tenets. I do not, of course, want to enumerate the various lower desires that exist; [but what I am referring to are] the desires having to do with the carnal and animal aspects of the soul, as well as those, also, which are of a higher stage than that of animality and the lower stages of human existence. [For example, the Islamic leader] does not have the right to waste his time [on frivolities]; nor does he have the right to expend his energies and powers in endeavors which run counter to the interests of the Muslim nation.

The perfect exemplary model of a life lead with total control over the lower urges and desires of the soul is provided to us in the person of the Commander of the Faithful and the life that he lead. And of course neither I nor any of the leaders of the Islamic community have ever laid claim to have been able to live life as did the Commander of the Faithful. Even Imam Sajjād 🕮, [the fourth Shi'a Imam] who was Imam Ali's 🕮 grandson and a student of his school and who is himself considered to be a divinely-inspired model of righteous behavior for people and was known for the long hours he spent in daily devotions to God 🕮, did not consider himself on a par with his grandfather when it came to such things. We know this because there are *hadith* reports in which Imam Sajjād 🕮 was asked why he discomfited himself to such an extent with all of his ritual devotions and hours spent in prayer and prostration. In response, the Imam compared himself to the Commander of the Faithful, saying that his devotions to God 🕮 are as nothing when compared to the devotions and piety of the Commander of the Faithful. Thus, it is not our intention to say that the Islamic ruler can and should act like the Commander of the Faithful; but to borrow a metaphor from the late Allāmah Tabātabāī, the Commander of the Faithful is positioned at the summit of a great mountain, and we must move on the outskirts of that mountain in the direction of that lofty peak. We must gather all of our spiritual will and head toward that exalted spiritual station, even though we know that it is not in our capacity to attain it. We must become like the Commander of the Faithful and struggle to overcome our lower desires; and this is a constant and never-ending battle which the Islamic ruler must wage during the entire length of his tenure as the person responsible before Almighty God ﷻ. This is the first and foremost requirement for success in the effort to bring about an Islamic society.

If the Islamic ruler is able successfully to go up against and conquer his lower desires and urges, then he will have succeeded in vanquishing all of the perils that a ruler faces, including the desire for status and honor for its own sake, the desire for money and power, the temptation to lie and to hide the truth from the people, acting against the interest of the people, and shrinking from making unpleasant decisions and undertaking perilous but necessary tasks. The key to all of these problems, which have been a blight on the lives of leaders and statesmen, is that they have been in bondage to their lower desires and diabolical urges in some form or another.

So much for the first characteristic, now the second characteristic is courage, which I want to focus on in particular. If this attribute is absent in the leaders of the Islamic society, it will assuredly proceed in a regressive direction, the revolution will not be able to attain its objectives, and Islam will not be properly implemented within such a society. If we are to be successful in the implementation of Islam in our society, we must have leaders who are courageous and bold, and who do not fear aught but God ﷻ in the field of battle, which is the proper administration of society. These are the kinds of leaders we need and must elect to positions of authority and responsibility.

Of course, bravery and courage come in all shapes and forms. The first kind of courage is courage in the face of and against one's own lower self. And this is the nexus which I mentioned earlier, where the two characteristics are interrelated. اَشْجَعُ النّاسِ مَن غَلَبَ هَواهُ The most courageous of people is he who conquers his lower urges and desires. The Islamic ruler is frequently confronted with a situation where his moral and religious obligation (*taklīf*) dictates that he take one path, and his lower self beckons him in various forms to another; and it is his courage that enables him to take the higher path and to conquer his lower desires, and to act out his duty as the administrator of the Islamic society.

Another form that courage takes is courage in confronting the enemies [of Islam]. And if this form of courage is absent [in an Islamic leader], then right will never be able to prevail, and no train will be set in motion toward higher goals and transcendent ideals. The Islamic ruler must know that the calling which he displays and [the nature of] the regency of God 🌼 of which he wants to be a manifestation of is diametrically opposed to the urges and desires which are the normal fare of all of the [so-called] great leaders and powers of the world. What the Islamic ruler stands in need of is courage in the face of the enemy; this is one of the greatest aspects of courage [as an attribute and requirement] of the Islamic ruler.

The Islamic ruler must have courage before friends as well as foe. Firstly, [there is the case of] friends who harbor the expectation that the ruler should do something to further their interests rather than the interests of the community as a whole. When there is something to be done in the interest of the people, then the ruler must certainly act on it out of a sense of duty. But if there is something that runs counter to the interest of the people but which a certain person or persons request, then it is the duty of the Islamic ruler to stand against it.

Secondly, there is the matter of courage to resist pressure groups and vested interests who lobby for the ruler and various leaders within government to further their own interests. One of the greatest challenges for the ruler and people in positions of authority is for them to stand on ceremony [in favor of pressure from such groups and to give in to demands] which run counter to the general interest. This can be seen to happen: where a group of people want to accomplish a certain goal, and they agitate for it and create an atmosphere that is in favor of it in the public discourse and in the minds of the public, and the ruler or responsible party decides in their favor against his better judgement and against the requirements of the sacred law. This is one of the greatest difficulties in society.

[As a society,] we are in possession of the first species of courage [which stands against external enemies], but we have yet to attain this second kind of courage. The Commander of the Faithful said, لا تَستَوحِشوا فى طَريقِ الهُدَى لِقِلَّةِ أهلِه; and this means, "Never let yourselves be overcome by fear in the Way of God ﷻ, in taking right decisions, in the way that leads to that which is just and to correct objectives; for you are few in number; for you are alone [in this undertaking]".[23]

1.5 The Safeguarding of Principles during the Reign of the Commander of the Faithful

The Commander of the Faithful stated:

وَ اللهِ لَأَن أَبيتَ عَلى حَسَكِ السَّعدانِ مُسَهَّداً أَو أُجَرَّ فِي الأَغلالِ مُصَفَّداً أَحَبُّ إِلَيَّ مِن أَن اَلقَى اللهَ وَ رَسولَهُ يَومَ القِيامَةِ ظالِماً لِبَعضِ العِبادِ وَ غاصِباً لِشَيءٍ مِنَ الحُطام

[I swear upon my oath] to God ﷻ that I would prefer to spend all night over a bed of sa'dān[24] thorns and to be dragged in chains over the earth than to encounter Allāh and His Apostle [Muhammad] on the Day of Resurrection while having transgressed the rights of any of God's ﷻ servants and devotees, or while having usurped for my own something from the worthless things of this lower world (the *dunyā*) [which did not belong to me].

---

[23] 1363/9/9
[24] A prickly desert shrub favored by camels.

This great Imam never wavered in [his adherence and commitment to] a single Islamic principle or value in any of the phases of his [blessed] life. Today, as followers of the Commander of the Faithful, we must raise this [fact] as a standard and banner before us. One of our greatest and most important slogans must be adherence and commitment to the principles and fundamental values of Islam. The Commander of the Faithful demonstrated his commitment to these principles from the very beginning in his words and deeds. And this is the case whether one looks at how he handled the disbursement of public funds or at executive matters and the appointment of righteous individuals to sensitive positions of authority. [At the beginning of the Commander of the Faithful's reign as caliph] he was advised that he should not be hasty in replacing powerful and influential people [from positions of high authority] as it was just the beginning of the road and such actions are not expedient for the [long-term] interests of his caliphate. The Commander of the Faithful responded أَ تَأْمُرُونِّي أَن أَطْلُبَ النَّصرَ بِالجَورِ فِيمَن وُلِّيتُ عَلَيه ; "Do you expect Ali to attain to victory by way of iniquity and oppression (*dhulm*) toward those for whose welfare he is responsible?" [The Commander of the Faithful continued,] وَ اللهِ لا أَطورُ بِهِ ما سَمَرَ سَميرُ وَ ما أَمَّ نَجمُ فِى السَّماءِ نَجماً "As long as the world exists in its current form, as long as day is day and night is night, Ali b. Abī-Ṭāleb ﷺ will never do such a thing. {Ayatollah Khāmeneī continues his interpretive translation and commentary:} Do they say that Ali has been defeated so that he should act against the principles and values of Islam on this account? This I will not do. I will never oppress my own people as a means of attaining to victory."

During the early days of his reign as caliph, the Commander of the Faithful was questioned concerning the monies and properties and disbursement which were divvied out [by the earlier caliphs] in the period before his tenure. To these questions, the Commander of the Faithful responded: "I will take back any property which was distributed unjustly from those to whom such property was given and restore them to their rightful owners". The way we would put it nowadays, the Commander of the Faithful said that he would "take it out of their gullets" even if they had used such property as a bride price[25] [for their daughters], or [as property or wealth on the credit of which] wives were wedded, or if such wealth was used for the purchase of slave-girls. The Commander of the Faithful announced this kind of resolve at the beginning of his tenure as caliph, and it was a resolve which he certainly acted on as well; by no means was it the case that the Commander of the Faithful would give voice to such sentiments, and then not follow through on his words with appropriate deeds. And the trials and hardships which the Commander of the Faithful faced during the almost five years of his tenure as caliph were on account of these and similar such commitments and resolve.

Of course, this is indeed the nature of commitment [to one's principles]. Now it is entirely possible that [such a] commitment might lead one to failure in a given incident or occasion; or to prevent one from attaining to one's goals or ideals at a given time or within a certain timeframe. But the upshot [of taking such a stand on principle] in the long run is that throughout history, all of the nations of the world and all of the people who are aggrieved by iniquity and who hunger and pine for justice will look to Ali b. Abī-Tālib ﷺ as an exemplary model and paragon of justice in the history of humanity, and as an unforgettable lesson [in what it means to be a human being at its best]. This is the great achievement of Ali b. Abī-Tālib ﷺ.

Allow me to mention two or three examples of taking a stance on principle from the deeds of Ali b. Abī-Tālib ﷺ to this gathering of those who are true believers in the faith of Islam and devotees of the Commander of the Faithful. Take a look and see how much we are in need

---

[25] *Mahriya* - The bride price or marriage portion. The price a man would have to pay his bride as a condition of being granted her hand in marriage; it is the opposite of a dowry, which refers to money or property brought by a bride to her husband at marriage.

of following this approach. It is imperative to preserve our principles with every iota of our resolve.

One of the instances where the Commander of the Faithful stood on principle and maintained it can be seen in the issue of the division of the wealth of the treasury among the Muslims. The story of 'Aqīl, the Commander of the Faithful's brother, has always been told as an illustration of Imam Ali's ﷺ acting with equity and justice, [no matter what the occasion might be]. After the Commander of the Faithful was martyred, 'Aqīl went to Mu'āwiya.[26] Mu'āwiya said, "Won't you tell me the tale of the red-hot poker, O 'Aqīl?" The story is that 'Aqīl had fallen on hard times, and poverty was clutching at his throat. What income he had did not suffice to cover his expenses. His eyesight was failing or had failed, and he also had several children for whom he was responsible. One day, he came to the Commander of the Faithful with the indications of poverty all over his body and clothing. The story is related by the Commander of the Faithful himself, with words that are moving.

Let me read these sentences of the Commander of the Faithful for you. وَ اللهِ لَقَد رَأَيتُ عَقِيلاً وَ قَد أَملَقَ حَتَّى استَماحَنِي مِن بُرِّكُم صاعاً He says, "I saw 'Aqīl at a time when he was in the throes of poverty and indigence, to the point that he was in need of a single Sā'[27] of your {= the public's} wheat flour, which he requested of me." 'Aqīl had come to the Commander of the Faithful and was not asking for an exorbitant amount of money or a large amount of capital. He wanted [nothing more than] three kilos of wheat [flour]. وَ رَأَيتُ صِبيانَهُ شُعثَ الشُّعورِ غُبرَ الأَلوانِ مِن فَقرِهِم We see here that he had brought his children along with him also. The Commander of the Faithful

---

[26] The governor of the Levant who had rebelled against the caliph Ali, thereby bringing about a civil war with catastrophic and lasting consequences for the Islamic community.

[27] The Sā' is an ancient measurement of volume. The Arabic word Sā' translates to "small container" and is related to the Quranic word ṣuwā'. It is roughly equivalent to 2.8 kilograms of flour.

says, "I saw his kids, with their hair all disheveled and the signs of poverty visible in the lackluster faces", كَأَنَّما سُوِّدَتْ وُجوهُهُم بِالعِظلِمِ "as if they had painted their faces with soot." وَ عاوَدَنى مُؤَكِّداً وَ كَرَّرَ عَلَىَّ القَوْلَ مُرَدِّداً "These poor children's faces had turned dark from the force of poverty". وَ عاوَدَنى مُؤَكِّداً وَ كَرَّرَ عَلَىَّ القَوْلَ مُرَدِّداً "My brother 'Aqīl came to see me on several other occasions, asking for my help." فَأَصْغَيْتُ اِلَيْهِ سَمْعى "When he came to me and repeatedly asked for my help, I heard him out," فَظَنَّ أَنّى أَبيعُهُ دينى وَ أَتَّبِعُ قيادَهُ مُفارِقاً طَريقَتى "and because I had turned quiet and was hearing him out, he thought that I had acquiesced to his pleas, and thought that I would sacrifice my religion and sell myself out on account of his need." فَأَحمَيْتُ لَهُ حَديداً The Commander of the Faithful responded to 'Aqīl by way of an action. "I placed a piece of iron in the furnace so that it would become hot and pliable. I then brought it close to 'Aqīl's body, such that he could feel it's heat." فَضَجَّ ضَجيجَ ذى دَنَفٍ مِن آلَمِها "Suddenly he let out a cry, believing that I wanted to brand him with this red hot poker." وَ كادَ أَن يَحتَرِقَ مِن ميسَمِها "The heat of the iron almost scorched him." At this point, this stout and steely will says, "I said to my brother 'Aqīl, 'O 'Aqīl, would that grieving mothers sit in grief for you {=at your passing}." أَ تَئِنُّ مِن حَديدَةٍ أَحماها اِنسانُها لِلَعِبِه وَ تَجُرُّنى اِلى نارٍ سَجَرَها جَبّارُها لِغَضَبِه You flinch away from a hot poker which I threatened to scald you with in jest, not having any intention of tormenting you with it; yet, you expect Ali not to shy away from the fire and brimstone which the Almighty, the One who subdues wrong and restores right, has prepared in His wrath for the iniquitous oppressors?'" أَ تَئِنُّ مِنَ الأَذى وَ لا أَئِنُّ مِن لَظى "You cried out on account of a small inconvenience, yet you expect me not to be concerned about the fire of Hell?"

This is the very lesson that has withstood the test of time and made its mark on history. This is the very hope that will have a place in the hearts and minds of every disadvantaged and disenfranchised man and woman who has a rudimentary familiarity with the personality of Imam Ali, irrespective of his or her religion or denominational affiliation. This is why those who have faith in the God ﷻ which Ali believed in, [also] have faith in Ali's lesson concerning justice. And it is for this reason that

47

Imam Ali's ﷺ sense of social justice is worthy of acting as a guiding light for all of the nations of the world and for all of the governments who are desirous of working in the interest of their people. This is what it means to be committed to and to take a stance in defense of one's principles and core beliefs.[28]

---

[28] Ali's sense of commitment: In a speech delivered on 1370/1/26, Ayatollah Khāmeneī has stated, "The Commander of the Faithful has a wonderful sentence (which appears in Hadīth Report No. 40): أَيُّهَا النَّاسُ اِنْ اَحَقَّ النَّاسِ بِهذَا الاَمْرِ اَقْواهُمْ عَلَيهِ وَ اَعلَمُهُمْ بِأَمْرِ اللهِ فِيهِ فَاِن شَغَبَ شَاغِبٌ اسْتُعْتِبَ "If anyone rises up in rebellion or sedition against this correct path that I am on, I will advise him against taking such a course of action; but if he refuses to listen, I will draw my sword on him". فَاِن آبَى قُوتِلَ "If anyone transgresses this path, he will come face to face with Ali's sword." In this same sermon, Imam Ali ﷺ states, اَلَا وَ اِنِّى اُقاتِلُ رَجُلَينِ رَجُلًا "I will fight two types of people." ادَّعَى ما لَيسَ لَهُ وَ آخَرَ مَنَعَ الَّذى عَلَيهِ The first is one who takes something – some property, a public office, or a right – which does not belong to him and wants to make it his own; and the second is one who has a duty to fulfill a responsibility but does not do so. For example, one who is duty-bound to engage in *jihād* in defense of the realm of Islam, but does not do so; or has a debt to pay but refuses to pay his debt; or is obligated to participate in some social cause but does not do so. Imam Ali ﷺ states this matter very categorically. وَ قَد فُتِحَ بابُ الحَربِ بَينَكُم وَ بَينَ اَهلِ القِبلَـک وَ لا يَحمِلُ هذَا العَلَمَ اِلّا اَهلُ البَصَرِ وَ الصَّبرِ "The gate to going to battle against those who have the same direction of prayer (*qibla*) has been opened onto you." When was there such an occasion during the time of the Prophet?"

[The reference is to the three civil wars that ensued in succession immediately upon Imam Ali ﷺ's accession to the caliphate: The Battle of the Camel, led by Ā'isha, Talha and Zubayr; the Battle of Nahrawān against the Khārejites; and the Battle of Seffīn, which the accursed Mu'āwiya waged against the rightly elected caliph of the Muslims and his army. Incidentally, it is precisely because of such "newly arising situations" as these that did not exist during the time of the prophet that the Shī'a maintain that it is incumbent on the grace (*lutf*) of Almighty God ﷻ to continue His divine guidance by way of immaculate (i.e. inerrant as well as sinless) guides after the passing of the Prophet from the material plane, which He

In one of his sentences, the Commander of the Faithful states, "If the wealth of the treasury that is at my disposal were mine to do as I pleased, I would have divided it up evenly among the people; let alone the wealth of the treasury [as a whole]! That wealth does not belong to me, but to the people themselves. This is the way in which resoluteness in safeguarding the principles upon which social justice is based is supposed to operate in the Islamic social order.[29] This was just one example which, as I stated at the outset, brought tears to the eyes of Mu'āwiya, who was Ali's enemy and who had waged battle against him; an example which made him admit to the grandeur of Imam Ali's ﷺ character.

We see this same decisiveness in another instance which has to do with the important matter of the administration or captaincy of the ship of state. 'Aqīl does not make an appearance in this story as a high official of state, but Abdullāh Ibn-Abbās does. Now Ibn-Abbās was Imam Ali's ﷺ paternal cousin, as well as being one of his most devoted students and one who was very close to the Imam; possibly he was someone who Imam Ali considered to be closer to him than anyone else. Ibn-Abbās was also the governor of the important city of Basra in the Iraq – a position to which he had been appointed by Imam Ali. Of course, while it is true that this incident has been related as part of the life of Ibn-Abbās, the letter in question makes its appearance in the *Nahj al-Balāgha* as well; but Ibn-Abbās is one of the persons who was a [devoted] student of Imam Ali's ﷺ and who remained loyal to him throughout the entirety of his life. And this is despite the severity of the action the Imam took against him – which

---

did indeed send to an ungrateful humanity. This is one of the main proofs for the necessity and reality of the continuation of immaculate guidance after the passing of the prophet, which is the main difference between the majoritarian conception of the leadership of the community (the caliphate) and that of the Shi'a one, which is the imamate.]

[29] See the sub-section below: "Justice in the Government of the Commander of the Faithful".

I will explain shortly – but again, this was because Ibn-Abbās knew that
the Imam's actions were motivated by a true believer's desire to act in
accordance with that which God 🕮 had ordained and that which would be
pleasing to God 🕮; a knowledge which caused Ibn-Abbās not only not to
be offended by his treatment at the hands of the Imam and to turn away
from him, but rather, caused him to be one who constantly sang Imam
Ali's 🕮 praises and never tired of publicizing and promoting the love for
the Imam.

It had been reported to the Commander of the Faithful that Ibn-
Abbās had availed himself illicitly of a certain amount of funds which
belonged to the public purse but which were at his disposal. His Eminence
Imam Ali wrote a letter to Ibn-Abbās saying that such a report had been
given to him, and asking Ibn-Abbās to provide him with a full accounting
of his expenditures. The fact that Ibn-Abbās was the cousin of the
Commander of the Faithful did not enter into the latter's thoughts or
calculus, nor did the concern that Ibn-Abbās might resent the fact that
Imam Ali did not trust him despite their close familial ties. He did not
think that this request of his would be taken as an insult by Ibn-Abbās.
[And this is because] when it is well known that anyone is liable to human
error, both in one's private affairs as well as in public affairs and even where
high levels of responsibility are at stake, then such considerations do not
and should not arise. It might well be the case that such actions might go
against someone's expectations and that such a person will then take
offense. Well, in that case, let him! So be it. Because monitoring the
activity and performance of high officials and holding them to account is
a mandatory obligation and duty of the one who has overall charge of the
affairs of the people.

This is why the Commander of the Faithful wrote to Ibn-Abbās
asking him to provide him with an accounting of his activities. But Ibn-
Abbās took offense and in response wrote something to the effect that his
right to withdraw funds from the public purse is greater than the paltry
sum that is at his disposal. There is this sense [of entitlement] in some

people on account of some service that they have rendered or the extent of a seniority that they might have [in their service to the state], or because of some service that they provided in times past to the cause of the revolution or to the people, that they are therefore entitled to a large share of the funds of the public treasury, and that subsequently, if some wastage occurs under their watch or in funds for which they have formal responsibility, then there is no problem as they are personally entitled to much more than the amount in question. This honorable man – Ibn-Abbās – suffered from this same mistaken view; and he wrote words to this effect to the Commander of the Faithful, possibly adding that such a request was unexpected, etc. At this point, the Commander of the Faithful responded to Ibn-Abbās with a harsh missive, which is the letter I had mentioned earlier which has also made its way into the noble compilation we know as the *Nahj al-Balāgha*.[30] The reproachful words to Ibn-Abbās in the Imam's letter are so surprising in their severity and even harshness as to be truly astonishing; it is to the point that had it not been for the fact that Ibn-Abbās was a man of true faith and a devotee of Imam Ali's ﷺ, he would have turned his back on the Imam and turn to Mu'āwiya's camp for solace and to exit from allegiance to Imam's Ali's regency and guardianship. But he was a greater man than that, and later, whenever Ibn-Abbās remembered the Commander of the Faithful, he would make mention of his great master and Imam's name with tears of adoration and longing in his eyes.

It is only natural that when the Commander of the Faithful's words and deeds are for the sake of God ﷻ, that their effect will be deeply felt and divine as well. This is an example of resolve in safeguarding the principles and values of Islam. The Commander of the Faithful disregarded the fact that Ibn-Abbās was his cousin and that he was his student and devotee; nor did Ibn-Abbās's long seniority and history of

---

[30] A compilation of Imam Ali ﷺ's sermons, sayings, and hadith reports concerning his words and deeds which the Shī'a faithful consider to be highly authoritative.

service to the cause of Islam detract the Commander of the Faithful from his resolve. Ibn-Abbās was one of the disciples of the Commander of the Faithful; someone who rose to the Imam's defense and confronted the latter's enemies most gallantly and eloquently. But when a report reaches the Imam accusing such a person of financial malfeasance, then malfeasance is malfeasance and it makes no difference who the accused party is: it must be properly investigated, even if the subject of the investigation or query is someone as honorable and august as Ibn-Abbās.

Another example of the resolve of the Commander of the Faithful when it comes to the safeguarding of the principles of Islam concerns the matter of the appointment to and dismissal from office of official appointees. There are specific values and attributes which enable someone to be appointed to a position of social responsibility. Not everyone is suited to every task. People who are appointed to a position of social responsibility must be endowed with certain competences and capacities. And if someone does not have such competences and capacities, this does not mean that he is a bad person; it simply means that he is not suited for a given job and must seek other employment. This consideration was adhered to in the administration of the Commander of the Faithful. An instance of this consideration which caught my attention relates to the time when Egypt was attacked by forces from Shām or the Levant. The Commander of the Faithful felt that he needed to remove Egypt's governor, Muhammad b. Abī-Bakr, who was another one of the Imam's disciples and students and devotees, and replace him with one who is more experienced in matters of warfare, who was Mālik Ashtar. Of course, the enemies of Islam plotted against Mālik Ashtar and took his life before he had a chance to reach Egypt, martyring him as he made his way there. But be that as it may, the fact that the Commander of the Faithful decided to remove Muhammad b. Abī-Bakr and replace him with Mālik Ashtar displeased Muhammad b. Abī-Bakr. He was human, after all... Thus, we see that the Commander of the Faithful removed Muhammad b. Abī-Bakr and replaced him with Mālik Ashtar despite the fact that the former was one of the Imam's greatest companions and was thought of as a son by the Imam who had great affection for him when the Imam saw that the situation had changed and that Mālik Ashtar was a more suitable candidate under the changed conditions. For his part, Muhammad b. Abī-Bakr became upset and wrote a letter of complaint to the Imam. The Imam, in turn, wrote back that he had not lost his confidence in Muhammad b. Abī-Bakr and does not consider him unworthy, but that the changed conditions make Mālik Ashtar the more suitable person to carry out the duties of governor at this time; or something close to this effect.

This is what we mean by commitment and resolve to safeguarding the principles of Islam. The collectivity of these actions and commitments on the part of the Commander of the Faithful to these principles is what has made him an honorable and unforgettable character in world history, and a legendary and luminous figure in the minds of the Muslim peoples, and even in the minds of the non-Muslims who get to know him.[31]

1.6 Justice in the Government of the Commander of the Faithful

Another point which can be gleaned from the event of Ghadīr Khumm[32] is the fact that the Commander of the Faithful demonstrated in the few years in which he was vested in the office of the caliphate that his priorities

---

[31] 1363/1/24

[32] Reference to the appointment of Ali b. Abī-Tālib to the succession to the Prophet's ministry at the Sermon of Ghadīr Khumm on the way back from Mecca to Madina in his final pilgrimage

were the establishment of the divine and Islamic vision of social justice, i.e. bringing about the objective that has been stated in the Quran as the reason for which prophets were commissioned and for which divine writs and sacred laws were revealed: the establishment of equity and justice.

لَقَدْ أَرْسَلْنَا رُسُلَنَا بِالْبَيِّنَاتِ وَأَنْزَلْنَا مَعَهُمُ الْكِتَابَ وَالْمِيزَانَ لِيَقُومَ النَّاسُ بِالْقِسْطِ ۖ وَأَنْزَلْنَا الْحَدِيدَ فِيهِ بَأْسٌ شَدِيدٌ وَمَنَافِعُ لِلنَّاسِ وَلِيَعْلَمَ اللَّهُ مَنْ يَنْصُرُهُ وَرُسُلَهُ بِالْغَيْبِ ۚ إِنَّ اللَّهَ قَوِيٌّ عَزِيزٌ ﴿٢٥﴾

[57:25] Indeed, [even aforetime] did We send forth Our apostles with all evidence of [this] truth; and through them We bestowed revelation from on high, and [thus gave you] a balance [wherewith to weigh right and wrong], *so that men might behave with equity* toward one another.

The establishment of equity as envisioned by the tenets and ordinances of the Quran is the best way to guarantee social justice. This was the Commander of the Faithful's foremost priority. It is with equity and justice that Islamic societies are sustained and become formidable, and can act as exemplary models and bringers of glad tiding to the other nations of the world. Such a thing is not possible without social justice being duly established, irrespective of whether or not all of the other material and superficial worldly values are provided; if justice is not established, in reality, nothing has been accomplished. When the Most Noble Prophet ﷺ appointed such an element[33] to have regency over the Muslim faithful and to lead them in the new political order he established, what he was actually doing was annunciating the importance of social justice. The Prophet ﷺ knew how the Commander of the Faithful thought and thus in what direction he would be taking the community. The Commander of the Faithful was raised by the Prophet ﷺ personally and furthermore, was

---

[33] Reference to the Sermon of Ghadīr Khumm.

his best student, and was devoted to following the command and the teachings of the Prophet ﷺ to the letter. By appointing the Commander of the Faithful, the Prophet ﷺ gave priority to social justice in Islamic society. And for his part, in the four years and nine or ten months in which the Commander of the Faithful was vested with the leadership of the community [as the fourth caliph], his highest priority was the establishment of equity and justice in society. His Eminence Imam Ali considered social justice to be the lifeblood of Islam and the spirit of what it means to be a Muslim and how to live within Islamic society. And this is exactly that which all nations stand in need of and all human societies in bygone eras have been deprived of to a greater or lesser extent, just as they were at the time of the ministry of the Prophet ﷺ of Islam. And if we look at the way in which the superpowers act on the world stage today and the way in which they govern the world based on material and this-worldly considerations, we see that the problem is still the same. The problem of humanity, in effect, is the absence of social justice, Islam {=submission to the will of God}, and rulership in accordance with the model provided by [the Prophet ﷺ and] the Commander of the Faithful.

The Commander of the Faithful opened the floodgates of social justice and let its waters flow among the Muslim faithful and within Islamic society, and prevented the unjust distribution and wasteful consumption of the wealth of the public treasury. He prevented specific interests from being able to use the highest offices of the community to further their own personal and group interests at the expense of the public interest at large, and prevented the wealth of the public purse from being pilfered and squandered by way of iniquitous and unjust disbursements.[34]

---

[34] 1371/3/30

1.7 The Importance of Economic Regulation, Monitoring and Oversight in Islam

During the time {= caliphate} of the Commander of the Faithful, "*qadhis*" or judges existed, to whom people referred their problems for resolution. If a crime such as a murder, theft or any other crime took place, it was the qadhi who would prosecute those who transgressed the law. But at the same time, during his reign, we see – according to this *hadith* report which has been reported in various sources (كانَ يَخرُجُ إلَى السّوق وَ مَعَهُ الدِّرَّخ) Hadith No. 47) – that the Commander of the Faithful would personally enter upon the marketplace armed with a whip. And needless to say, he did not come with whip in hand in order to caress people. The Commander of the Faithful would not refer someone who had broken the law to the law courts and ask them to punish him; rather, he would administer the punishment himself in order to prevent iniquity and any transgression of the law.

This matter has been reported in more detail in another *hadith* report:

كانَ عَلىُّ عليه‌الصلاة والسلام كُلَّ بُكرَتٍ يَطوفُ فى أَسواقِ الكوفَتِ سوقاً سوقاً وَ مَعَهُ الدِّرَّتُ عَلى عاتِقه

What this means is that the Commander of the Faithful used to do this on a daily basis. It was not an *ad hoc* or one off occurrence but a continual practice of the Commander of the Faithful, whose habit it was to frequent all marketplaces and places of business مَعَهُ الدِّرَّتُ عَلَى عاتِقه with whip in hand or draped over his shoulder, i.e. ready for business! So that if he happened to come across someone who was breaking the law, he would administer the punishment required by law right there and then.

The Commander of the Faithful stipulates to Mālek Ashtar, his governor [appointee] for Egypt, فَمَن قارَفَ حُكرَتٌ بَعدَ نَهيِكَ إيّاه فَنَكِّل به that once you have enjoined the people against hoarding goods which the people need, in the event that anyone commits this crime, فَنَكِّل به deal with him severely; and take your revenge. Of course, he follows his advice with the following: فَنَكِّل بِهِ وَ عاقِبهُ فى غَيرِ إسراف but do not exceed bounds: this is the main principle [to bear in mind]. Those who are in charge of the administration of justice and for ensuring that the bounds of the law are adhered to in the affairs of the Muslim community must always guard against exceeding the bounds [of the law in their administration of justice]. As the Commander of the Faithful has stated, they must let God-fearing righteousness (*taqwā*) guide their actions and must not allow their actions to be the cause of the squandering of the public purse; because such wastefulness and prodigality is itself a form of corruption, similar to the corruption of that corrupt hoarder who hoards goods [at a time of need] – it makes no difference. In point of fact, he might well be worse than such a person, because he is acting on behalf of the government.

Nor should it be imagined that when the Commander of the Faithful frequented the bazaars of Kūfa,[35] that he was not acting in his capacity as the ruler [of the community and state], and that his actions were being carried out, say, as part of the religious obligation of enjoining the doing of that which is right, and forbidding the doing of that which is wrong (*amr bi ma'rūf wa nahy min al-munkar*); because if it was indeed [an instance of] "forbidding the doing of that which is wrong", then such an act should logically have occurred throughout all of His Eminence's life in Medina [as well]. If the Commander of the Faithful carried out this activity [of the administration of justice] in Kūfa, then [it follows] that it was part and parcel of carrying out the duties of his office as the leader of the community and as the executor of the judicial branch of the Islamic government of the time. [Nor] should it be imagined that the Commander of the Faithful administered justice in this way on account of the fact that he was immaculate (*ma'sūm*); [this allocation is also false, because] the immaculates (*ma'sūmīn*)[36] never entered the marketplace [with such intentions or for such purposes], in order to carry out such punishments

---

[35] A garrison town in the south of present day Iraq and the caliphal capital during the caliphate of Imam Ali ﷺ.

[36] The other eleven immaculate Imams ﷺ.

which they were entitled to do on account of their immaculacy and inerrancy. Thus, it is abundantly clear that the Commander of the Faithful administered justice in this fashion in his capacity as the ruler of the Islamic community and as the head of the Islamic state.[37]

1.8 The Necessity of Self-Development for the Islamic Ruler

God ☙ the All-Knowing and All-Wise has stated in His Sacred Writ:

أُذِنَ لِلَّذِينَ يُقَاتَلُونَ بِأَنَّهُمْ ظُلِمُوا ۚ وَإِنَّ اللَّهَ عَلَىٰ نَصْرِهِمْ لَقَدِيرٌ ﴿٣٩﴾ الَّذِينَ أُخْرِجُوا مِن دِيَارِهِم بِغَيْرِ حَقٍّ إِلَّا أَن يَقُولُوا رَبُّنَا اللَّهُ ۗ وَلَوْلَا دَفْعُ اللَّهِ النَّاسَ بَعْضَهُم بِبَعْضٍ لَّهُدِّمَتْ صَوَامِعُ وَبِيَعٌ وَصَلَوَاتٌ وَمَسَاجِدُ يُذْكَرُ فِيهَا اسْمُ اللَّهِ كَثِيرًا ۗ وَلَيَنصُرَنَّ اللَّهُ مَن يَنصُرُهُ ۗ إِنَّ اللَّهَ لَقَوِيٌّ عَزِيزٌ ﴿٤٠﴾ الَّذِينَ إِن مَّكَّنَّاهُمْ فِي الْأَرْضِ أَقَامُوا الصَّلَاةَ وَآتَوُا الزَّكَاةَ وَأَمَرُوا بِالْمَعْرُوفِ وَنَهَوْا عَنِ الْمُنكَرِ ۗ وَلِلَّهِ عَاقِبَةُ الْأُمُورِ ﴿٤١﴾

[22:40] And God ☙ will most certainly succor him who succors His cause: for, verily, God ☙ is most powerful, almighty, [22:40] [well aware of] those who, [even] if We firmly establish them on earth, remain constant in prayer, and give in charity, and enjoin the doing of what is right and forbid the doing of what is wrong; but with God ☙ rests the final outcome of all events.

In truth, there are three dimensions to the character of the Just Ruler in Islam. One of these dimensions, whose importance is not less than the other two, relates to his moral traits and practice. As for the other two dimensions, one has to do with knowledge and correct thought: thinking aright; and the second is the ability to use the power and authority which has been vested in him to properly administer and manage the task [of governance] which has been entrusted to him. If these last two attributes exist [in the personality of the Islamic ruler] but such a person lacks the

---

[37] 1366/11/1

requisite moral traits and does not have full command of his behavior and is not on the path of self-development and improvement, then not only will those other two attributes not serve any beneficial purpose for the society in question, but they will be detrimental as well. If a ruler is powerful and intelligent but is selfish and proud and untrustworthy and does not have mastery over his lower urges and desires and thus wants all of the amenities which society has to offer to be his own personal property, then the more powerful and intelligent such a person is, the greater his danger to society. Therefore, good morals in the character of the Islamic ruler are what turn his intellectual and practical capacities into positive traits.

During the early years of the establishment of the Islamic community and in the first and second centuries [of the Islamic calendar], Islamic society experienced a difficult and formative period [in its developmental history]. The reason Islamic society degenerated and lost its moral anchor and humane character and also lost its historically morally superior position was not due to the incompetence or ineptitude of the Umayyad and Abbāsid caliphs; there were many competent administrators and statesmen among the Umayyad and Abbāsid caliphs. These same people who have made names for themselves and are well known in history; if one scrutinizes the entirety of the lives and actions of these same people, one will not find a single bright spot or anything that they can be proud of – many of them were powerful and capable people who were endowed with great military and political strength, as well as social skills and administrative competence. But all of these physical and intellectual skills were used in the service of themselves. The norm of the practice of a caliph who reigned over hundreds of millions of people in those days, that is, from the western-most reaches of northern Africa and its Atlantic coast to the coasts of the Indian ocean up to Transoxiana [in central Asia] – from the point of view of such caliphs and rulers, the wealth of the public treasury was his personal property to do with as his wished.

And so, if these kinds of characteristics and behavior patterns are manifested in a given Islamic ruler, then these will produce the same results that ensued in those early days. Take a look at what resulted in those days: the blessings of the presence of the Prophet ﷺ and of the Quran and of the freshness of Islam whose effects could still be felt and seen on the fabric and soul of that society completely dissipated from society as a result of the evil presence of those malevolent and unworthy successors. Whereas الاسلام يَعلو وَ لا يُعلى عَلَيه Islamic society is [intrinsically] superior. The ultimate result of such behavior was that Islamic society became abject and miserable and humiliated before other powers; that is what happened. On the surface, these unworthy successors expanded the [physical] dominion and realm of Islam, but in actuality, nothing of the values of Islam could be seen in those societies.

The sentence of Imam Ali's ﷺ that we find in the hadith report which is reported in the *Nahj ul-Balāgha* مَن نَصَبَ نَفسَهُ للنّاسِ اِماماً فَليَبدَأ بِتَعليمِ نَفسِه قَبلَ تَعليمِ غَيرِه, is about us. The Commander of the Faithful says: 'He who positions himself as the ruler of the people should begin by training and controlling [the urges and desires of] his own lower self before he manages others'. It is not possible to expect a people who see, for example, the highway patrol themselves carrying out violations of the traffic code, to then expect the people to follow those same codes. It is not possible to expect a people who see their rulers and leaders not living frugally and squandering the public wealth, to live frugally and not be wasteful in their expenditures. One cannot expect a people who are witness to the fact that there is no courage in the leadership of their country in terms of how they deal with the country's problems, that there is no moral courage, and no taking of stances on matters of principle; it makes no sense to then turn around and expect such a people to demonstrate moral courage in their behavior, and to show boldness and courage in the way they deal with matters in their day to day lives. Rather, if we want the people to behave in ways which the authorities require of them, then it is up to the leadership to first see to themselves and to rectify their own behavior and to conform their actions with those standards and criteria which they call upon others to abide by. This is a fundamental principle for [the correct administration of] Islamic society.

In these words, فَلْيَبْدَأْ بِتَعْلِيمِ نَفْسِهِ قَبْلَ تَعْلِيمِ غَيْرِهِ the Commander of the Faithful teaches us the following: وَلْيَكُنْ تَأْدِيبُهُ بِسِيرَتِهِ قَبْلَ تَأْدِيبِهِ بِلِسَانِهِ. A leader of Islamic society who wants to engage his people in a dialogue and to urge them to behave in ways that are righteous, and to urge them to be present and participate in the front lines and arduous tasks of life, must do so by way of setting his own example; simply talking about it is not enough. If one talks about the benefits and merits of doing something but such a person does not perform that which he urges on others, then this is a very ineffective way of leadership.

وَ مُعَلِّمُ نَفْسِهِ وَ مُؤَدِّبُهَا أَحَقُّ بِالْإِجْلَالِ مِنْ مُعَلِّمِ النَّاسِ وَ مُؤَدِّبِهِمْ He who disciplines and trains himself is more worthy of respect and praise compared to one who wants to teach people but who has failed to work on himself and, what is more, has no intention of realizing the teaching in himself. Servitude to God &, righteous moral conduct, humbleness, self-sacrifice, purity of intention, kindness towards all, meager expectations and copious hard work in the service of the people and God & – these are all parts of the moral duties of one who holds a position of authority in an Islamic society. Of course, this burden is heavier for those who are closest to the center of this circle [of authority and responsibility], and these authorities are duty-bound to effect these attributes [more fully] in their lives. We must be humble. We must not expect a higher social standing for ourselves than we afford the people.

[At one time], the Commander of the Faithful delivered a sermon concerning the mutual rights of the leader and of the people. When the Imam finished delivering the sermon, one of his Companions stood up and, addressing the Commander of the Faithful, started to sing the Imam's praises in an exaggerated and undue manner. Perhaps it was his intention to state that he believed the Imam to be higher than a ruler whose rights the people were duty-bound to maintain. When the gentleman's oratory came to an end, the Commander of the Faithful – whose sermon had to all appearances been drawn to a conclusion – started speaking again to that person with words to the effect that he should not say things or act in a way that might give the impression that he, the Imam, is pleased with the praise that is doted on him. The worst condition for a leader in the mind of intelligent observers is for him to take pleasure in being praised by the people and to want the people to praise him in public, to such an extent that a sense of pride and arrogance overtakes them and consider themselves to be of a higher social rank and station than others, as this would be the greatest misfortune. And this is a calamity which unfortunately all of our leaders have constantly been afflicted with in the history of the various Muslim nations, whose leaders had no inkling about what Islam is truly about. There are so many bad teachings in the words and books of our poets and literati and [one can say] sages (*hukamā*) and ethicists even, to the effect that the leaders of the community are in a class of their own [and are not subject to the same moral standards which apply to everyone else]. But the truth of the matter is that the sacred ordinances of Islam and the rights and responsibilities which people enjoy under its sacred law apply to everyone equally, irrespective of whether one is or is not the ruler of a given society. [The only difference is that] the ruler has shouldered a greater burden of responsibility and is therefore duty-bound to carry out that burden [while he is subject to the same laws as everyone else].

One of the greatest responsibilities of the Islamic ruler is self-development and self-correction in the path of his personal progress [as a pilgrim headed back towards God ﷻ]. Such a person must reform and rectify his personal conduct, must not allow himself to be driven by carnality and his lower urges, and must not allow the affection which the people show toward him to be converted into hatred and enmity. He must show kindness [equally] to all, like a loving father – even towards the sinner. The Islamic leader is the successor to the Prophet ﷺ – a Prophet ﷺ who prayed God ﷻ for [grace] and guidance for the unbelievers of his tribe: اللهُمَّ اهدِ قَومى فَإنَّهُم لا يَعلَمون as has been related concerning the words and

62

deeds of the Most Noble Prophet. Thus, the Islamic leader must have love and affection even for sinners and criminals. Of course, there is no contradiction between having such kindness and affection on one hand, and the administration of justice on the other. One who commits a crime in society must certainly face punishment. But this punishment should never be on account of a personal revenge on the part of the ruler.

The leader of a society and those in positions of high authority must strive to cover all elements within their society under their wings; they must act with loving kindness towards all members of society. They must act with love and affection towards all people of goodwill and with pure hearts, and towards everyone who lives under their aegis – everyone who stands in need of the love and attention and guidance of the leaders of society. This is one of the greatest responsibilities of the Islamic ruler.[38]

1.9 The Islamic Ruler as the Ruler of the Servants of God

God ۞ the All-Knowing and All-Wise has stated in His Sacred Writ:

إِنَّ اللَّهَ يَأْمُرُكُمْ أَن تُؤَدُّوا الْأَمَانَاتِ إِلَىٰ أَهْلِهَا وَإِذَا حَكَمْتُم بَيْنَ النَّاسِ أَن تَحْكُمُوا بِالْعَدْلِ ۚ إِنَّ اللَّهَ نِعِمَّا يَعِظُكُم بِهِ ۗ إِنَّ اللَّهَ كَانَ سَمِيعًا بَصِيرًا ﴿٥٨﴾

[4:58] Behold, God ۞ bids you to deliver all that you have been entrusted with unto those who are entitled thereto, and whenever you judge between people, to judge with justice. Verily, most excellent is what God ۞ exhorts you to do: verily, God ۞ is all-hearing and all-seeing!

The Islamic political order is the continuation of God's ۞ governance, the continuation of the sovereignty (*wilāya*) and cosmic and constitutional providential lordship[39] of God ۞ [on Earth]. In other words, God ۞ the

---

[38] 1363/8/11

[39] *Solte-ye takwīnī va rububīat-e parvardegār.*

Sublimely Exalted created the world, created human beings, commissioned the prophets [to their ministries], الَّذى أَعطَى كُلّ شَىءٍ خَلقَهُ ثُمَّ هَدَى and placed the right path before all of His creatures, to which He guided them. A vast, continuous, and endless movement which encompasses all has come into being throughout creation at the will, behest, and contrivance of God's ﷻ providential lordship, which leads in the direction of transcendence and perfection. In other words, when one pays [close attention], one sees that the entirety of creation is a single procession; a unitary march consisting of humans and other beings who are traversing the same path in order to attain to the same goal and *telos* and objective. Of course, humanity is the central pole (*mehvar*) of this caravan, and the primary movement, the one which moves in accordance with reason and logic and which is volitional, belongs to mankind, for it is human beings who have a will and who will their [own] motion.

God ﷻ the Sublimely Exalted has created this world, humanity, and all of the other beings and blessings in the world in accordance with a specific principle and law and for a particular *telos*[40] and purpose. He has vested the prophets with the responsibility to place everything in the world in its true and proper place, and to teach human being how they are to put the various potentialities which are latent in the body of nature to proper use, including how to treat other creatures and how to put the natural resources [of the planet] to [proper] use; how to put all of the laws [of nature] to [beneficial] use, and how to reach one's own perfection as well as that of one's environment.

The next step [in this process] is divine and Islamic governance. The Just or Islamic Ruler or the Divine Guide (*ḥākim-e ilāhī*) is in fact God's ﷻ vice-regents on Earth [who is present] among the people, and who is in fact the continuation of the same Path which God ﷻ the Sublimely Exalted has devised and established for human beings. يا داوُدُ اِنّا جَعَلناكَ خَليفَةً فِى الاَرضِ Addressing the prophet David, the Lord says to him:

---

[40] The ultimate purpose or end of a goal-oriented process.

"O David! Behold, We have made thee a [prophet and, thus, Our] vicegerent on earth." In other words, [We have made thee] the successor to Our Providential Will (*erāde-ye parvardegār*), i.e. [We have made thee] the Manager (*edāre-konande*) and Guide of Men [and their affairs, guiding them] to the *telos* and ultimate objective of perfection which We have in mind for them, to which end-goal they can attain by way of [submission and conformance to] various principles and [moral and physical] laws [which We have devised for them and embedded in the fabric of creation]. Islamic governance and government [is the implementation of the constitutional order which] is responsible for [enabling the members of the community who have attained to faith in Islam, i.e. who have self-surrendered to the various principles and moral and physical laws which God 🕮 has ordained for mankind,] to traverse along this Path in a given period of time and within a certain sector of creation.

Therefore, based on the above understanding, the Islamic governmental order acts in accordance with the will of God 🕮, and enables people and the community of the faithful as a whole to traverse along this same Path with the same objectives, and moves society in the same direction which Almighty God 🕮 has willed. And this is why the duties and responsibilities of the Just Ruler of Islamic society are the self-same duties and responsibilities of God 🕮, only in miniature. In other words, the Just Ruler must act towards the citizens of the Islamic society [of which he is the Guardian-Regent] no differently than the way in which God 🕮 acts towards all of the creatures of His creation, except that this encounter must of course be at the level of the capacities which God 🕮 has instilled in him and at the level which is therefore expected of him, given these limitations. And this is why we assume the following spirit to be operative in an Islamic governmental order which is truly worthy of its name: it must be imbued with a spirit of kindness and caring, it should be paternal, and it should be geared to encourage reform and self-improvement.

The Islamic governmental order and Islamic government does not stand in opposition to those who are under its jurisdiction and aegis, nor does it compete with any of its subjects or have any enmity towards them. It does not participate in a race with them as to who can accumulate the greatest personal wealth, as its [interests] are not in conflict with theirs. It is possible, at times, for the Islamic order to be strict with one or more of its wards, but this strictness is like the austerity which a strict but loving and insightful father imposes on a favorite child; like the severity of a doctor and nurse with their patient. It is just as a doctor would not allow a child who is ill to partake of some food that is not suitable for his well-being and recovery. And in the same way that [a loving father] would prevent a child within a home in a given society from transgressing the rights of other members of the household, from eating more than his or her share of food, from sleeping in someone else's bed or room, or playing with someone else's toys. And in the same way that [a loving father] would quarantine a child who has an infectious illness and prevent him from mixing in company until he has recovered from his illness. Islamic government similarly should act with a fatherly concern toward society, as well as with the concern of a physician for a patient; with kindness and affection towards all of the members of society, which will occasionally require some austerity as well.

All of the responsibilities of Islamic government must be carried out within this framework, i.e. with kindness and respect to all, including malefactors. The way in which Islamic government deals with its malefactors and criminals and sinners is a fatherly one and one which encourages reform and self-improvement through understanding and kindness; it is not out for retributions or reprisal. Rather, retribution and hostility are reserved for those who attack this holy sanctuary from outside of its borders; for those who attack the servants of God ﷻ with violence and who want to disturb their peace and security and progress. But in the divinely ordained social order, رُحَمَاءُ بَيْنَهُم, they are full of mercy towards one another, even with the sinners.[41] Therefore, the nature of the Islamic administration of justice, the nature of Islamic correctional institutions, the nature of Islamic punishments and the nature of the austerities of Islamic government and the limitations they impose – all of this is done with a spirit of love, caring and guidance pursuant to [the demands of] God's ❀ Providential Lordship.

The second issue is the heavy burden of responsibility which the Islamic political order and its executives have with respect to self-development. Not everyone is fit to carry this burden of responsibility; the only people who can bear the heft of this load are those in whom the prerequisites of endurance, strength and self-development exercises are manifested in abundance. Those who do not work to profit themselves; and who look upon the servants of God ❀ and even upon sinners and criminals with loving eyes; and who are able to maintain fidelity to the colossal amounts of public wealth which have been entrusted to them and not to look at their trust with treacherous intent; and those who have the self-restraint to expend the entirety of their abilities and their very beings in the interest of the nation and in the interests of others; and to work to maintain the welfare, prosperity and peace of mind of those who have elected them [to office], that is, the general public – these people should be endowed with a very high moral character; not anyone can qualify [for such an onerous and demanding task]. Thus, the Islamic ruler must possess a number of other attributes and characteristics in addition to the main features and principles of which we have already spoken in delineating the Islamic ruler's general responsibilities.

---

[41] [48:29] *Muhammad is God's ❀ Apostle; and those who are [truly] with him are firm and unyielding towards all deniers of the truth, [yet] full of mercy towards one another.*

The Commander of the Faithful said of two notables of his day: 'If they didn't have so much lust for power, I would perhaps have done something for them. But these are people whose hearts crave the governorship of such and such a province.' From the perspective of the Commander of the Faithful, a person who lusts for power and political position to such an extent is not worthy of being entrusted with high office in Islamic society. Pay attention to the subtlety here: in today's world, expressing a desire for public office is not considered a demerit or as a negative value; but this is not the case in Islam. This is why the Islamic social order must necessarily take into account factors such as self-development and improvement and the moral character of its potential leaders.[42]

1.10 More Comments on the Meaning of Wilāyat[43]

A government which is based on coercion; a government which has attained to power by way of a coup d'état; a government whose ruler does not accept the will of the people and does not take the thoughts and feelings of its people into account; and a government which is based on the conventional norms of the people, like [many of] today's polities, but in which its leaders nevertheless have access to special facilities and privileges and to special places where they can enjoy the blessings of the world [to the exclusion of the people whom they supposedly represent on a "democratic" basis] – none of these forms of government reflect what we mean by *wilāyat*. *Wilāyat* refers to a political order in which the relationship between the ruler and the people is one in which there is a creedal, intellectual, and emotional bond [of commonality] and [mutual respect and] affection; in which the people are connected and bonded to their leader; in which the people have affection and love for their leader,

---

[42] 1363/6/9

[43] See Chapter 3 for the definition of this key word.

who is the source of the entirety of the political order, considers all of his duties [as originating] from God ☼, and thinks of himself as God's ☼ servant and devotee. There is no trace of arrogance and haughtiness in such a governmental order. The governmental order which is presented by Islam is more democratic than the democracies which are current in the world today. It has a relationship with the hearts, thoughts, emotions, and beliefs of the people as well as with their intellectual needs, and serves the interests of the people.[44]

1.11 Duties of the Islamic Ruler

God ☼ the All-Knowing and All-Wise has stated in His Sacred Writ:

إِنَّ اللَّهَ يَأْمُرُكُمْ أَن تُؤَدُّوا الْأَمَانَاتِ إِلَىٰ أَهْلِهَا وَإِذَا حَكَمْتُم بَيْنَ النَّاسِ أَن تَحْكُمُوا بِالْعَدْلِ ۚ إِنَّ اللَّهَ نِعِمَّا يَعِظُكُم بِهِ ۗ إِنَّ اللَّهَ كَانَ سَمِيعًا بَصِيرًا ﴿٥٨﴾

[4:58] Behold, God ☼ bids you to deliver all that you have been entrusted with unto those who are entitled thereto, and whenever you judge between people, to judge with justice. Verily, most excellent is what God ☼ exhorts you to do: verily, God ☼ is all-hearing and all-seeing!

Generally speaking, the duties of the Islamic Ruler can be divided into several headings.[45] One of these headings has to do with the ruler's duty

---

[44] 1379/10/6

[45] Four duties of the Islamic ruler: In a speech delivered on 1363/8/11, Ayatollah Khāmeneī has stated, "The duties of the Islamic political order are of four kinds. The first relates to the duties of the leadership relative to their own persons and ensuring the continuation of their personal moral wayfaring and self-purification; and the importance of this duty is on a par with that of their social responsibilities, the establishment of social justice, providing security, and the regulation of the social interaction of the citizenry. Another duty relates to the spiritual aspect of

of self-development and wayfaring on the path to the improvement of his moral character. While it is true that all Muslims within the nation of Islam have a religious duty to conform their conduct to the Islamic code of moral conduct (*moqarrarāt-e akhlāqī*), and that it goes without saying that each person will only attain to his or her individual perfection once he or she incorporates and assimilates all of the virtues of the Islamic code of moral conduct in their personality; but at the same time, the question of the perfection of one's character and mode of moral conduct takes on a higher significance when it comes to the person of the ruler of the Islamic state, as well as to that of persons who hold positions of high social

---

people's lives, such as [providing the necessary conditions for] their spiritual and moral growth and improvement, [providing the necessary conditions for] allowing people's aptitudes to flourish, seeing to the education and training of the people, and these kinds of matters. The third duty relates to responsibilities having to do with the administration of people's affairs, such as the establishment of social justice; ensuring security for the public at large; the establishment and proper administration of the institutions of state which are necessary for providing public services; increasing the standard of living of the people, the quality of life, the gross national product, and the like. And the fourth duty relates to the relations of the Islamic community with that of the nations of the rest of the world; i.e. setting foreign policy, decisions concerning the waging of war and peace, establishing healthy international relations, and the maintenance of the power and position and honor of the Islamic social order and of the nation of Islam throughout the world, be this in terms of the relationship with states or with individual people, corporations and non-governmental organizations.

"These are the four main headings of the duties of the Islamic political order. Needless to say, Islam has much to say concerning each of these headings. The primary sources of Islam and books which contain the teachings of Islam contain numerous tenets and ordinances concerning each of these subjects. And all of these matters must become perfectly clear for us and we have no choice but to master these matters and implement them properly if we are to be able to establish a perfect Islamic governmental order and to become an exemplary model for other states and nations."

responsibility within its government. And this is because an individual's wayfaring and quest for the perfection of his moral character affects the limited ambit of his private life, and covers a small social compass; whereas this compass expands greatly when it comes to the effects of the moral character of the Islamic ruler. If the Islamic ruler is humble, his humbleness and humility does not affect a limited circle, but rather has an effect on the whole nation and on the minds and thoughts and acts and progress of each and every citizen. And this is why one of the duties of the political order is to ensure that the criteria which have been established in the code of Islamic moral conduct are duly followed. Of course, when we talk of the Islamic ruler, we do not necessarily mean to limit our intention to a specific individual or even to a specific public office. Rather, these criteria and duties pertain to any and all persons who hold public office in the Islamic political order and are influential in some way; and those who are closer to the center of the circle [of authority] have a heavier burden of responsibility.

Thus, this is one heading, which can itself be divided into numerous sub-headings if we look at the *Nahj ul-Balāgha*, to [other authoritative books in] the hadīth report corpus, and to the Quran itself. For example, some of the moral attributes of the Islamic ruler consist of forbearance (*hilm*), broadmindedness (*sharh-e sadr*), having patience and perseverance in the face of hardships, distortions and intemperance of character; being able to withstand provocations, large and small; and being content with moderate means in one's personal life, such as being content with moderate means in terms of food, clothing, housing, means of transportation, and other such personal considerations – being content with the bare minimum in these things. The lives of the Most Noble Prophet ﷺ and of the Commander of the Faithful of course provide us with a plethora of colorful and memorable examples of these attributes.

Another example [which can be gleaned from our sources] is holding oneself to account and being faithful to the performance of one's duties. And again, while it is true that this is a responsibility which applies to everyone, special attention must be paid to it by the Islamic ruler and by those in positions of high social responsibility within the political order. Another example which is necessary for the Islamic ruler is mastering and taking control of any ambition he might have for autocratic rule. These are some of the sub-headings of the duties and responsibilities which must be adhered to by the Islamic ruler and by those in positions of high social responsibility within the political order if that order is to be in accordance with the tenets and teachings of the Quran and of Islam.

Another set of duties and responsibilities for the Islamic ruler concerns the ideals of society, which are primary in importance. These include seeing to the education and training of the individuals whose sum total comprises the community, seeing to their moral education, rectification and perfection, and developing their individual capacities and aptitudes. It also includes the full utilization of all available means and facilities to bring out the treasures which God 🕸 the Sublimely Exalted has secreted in the hearts of each of His creatures, such as the individual talents, creative and innovative powers, virtuous and righteous behavior, and all of the other beautiful virtues that are hidden as potentials within the being of each and every individual within society. This is the responsibility of the Islamic social order.

If people's moral conduct is wanting within a given society; if corruption is rampant among the people; if the people are not receptive to the educational and moral training regimen; if literacy is at a low ebb; if the level of political consciousness of the people was at an unacceptably low level – if these things exist in society, one cannot blame the people for it. Rather, it is the political order of society which is to blame. It is the rulers whose hands pull the stings on which the material and ideal riches of society are dependent who must be held to account and blamed and punished. And today, this is the situation to which we are witnesses. And this is the case whether we are talking about those who are endowed with political acumen and consciousness but are bereft of spirituality and morality; or among those who have not been afforded the chance to acquire political acumen and to become politically conscious, and have not been allowed to think and understand [what is going on in the world] – in all of these cases, we do not blame the peoples and nations and do not consider them to be responsible for the tragic state of affairs that exist; *these* are not our interlocutors. It is not the people who are the decision makers; it is the governments and the leaders [of the people who are ultimately to blame].

The spiritual ideals of a society such as political growth and awareness, the development of analytical abilities and skills, the power to comprehend and understand [current] events, or [greater] awareness within the branches of knowledge and scientific and technological progress as well as progress in the administrative wherewithal of a nation's ability to educate and train its populace – the provisioning of these kinds of attributes and facilities is one of the primary duties of the Islamic ruler.

There is another group of duties which are incumbent on the Islamic ruler which are necessary for the administration of the material [and spiritual] affairs of life within society whose neglect will preclude a secure environment from obtaining in which people can make cultural, educational and spiritual progress with peace of mind. An example is the provisioning of social justice. The burden of establishing and maintaining social justice falls on the shoulders of the various branches of government. One cannot reproach the people for not having abided by the demands of social justice. It is the governmental apparatus which is responsible for putting in motion and implementing the laws and regulations which give rise to social justice and for tapping the fecund fountainhead of social justice and setting its headwaters in motion and to bring about a situation that guarantees social justice in society.

It is for this reason that the powers and latitude which are afforded the Just Ruler in Islam are vast and wide-ranging: so that he can establish social justice within society. Or so that he can establish security: a secure environment for work and enterprise; a secure environment in which the rule of law prevails and the administration of justice is carried out in accordance with these laws; a secure environment for the basic infrastructures of life such as housing and roads, urban and rural security, and secure borders. The creation of these secure environments is one of the most important duties which the Islamic political order and the Islamic ruler are duty-bound to provide.

And alongside security, there is the matter of the welfare and prosperity (*rifāh*) of the people. These two attributes are two of the most important factors in human society, irrespective of whether that society is Islamic or non-Islamic. It is decidedly not the case that on one hand we say that it is incumbent on the Islamic political order to provide the means for its people to make moral, intellectual and scientific progress and to improve their level of political consciousness, but that it is not necessary for it to ensure that material welfare and prosperity of the people, and for it not to have any [onus of] consideration for the public's housing and for job creation, and for it not to have any concern for ensuring that the people can live a life of comfort where they do not have to be concerned about the basic standards of a prosperous life. No, this is assuredly not the case. Rather, Abraham's 🕮 supplication is رَبِّ اجعَل هذا بَلَداً آمِناً وَ ارزُق اَهلَهُ مِنَ الثَّمَراتِ مَن آمَنَ مِنهُم بِاللهِ وَ اليَومِ الآخِرِ [2:126] *And, lo, Abraham 🕮 prayed: "O my Sustainer! Make this a land secure, and grant its people fruitful sustenance - such of them as believe in God 🕮 and the Last Day;"* which His Eminence the prophet Abraham 🕮 supplicated to his Lord on the day in which he built the Ka'ba and founded the holy city [of Mecca]: the supplication which he made for his people was one in which he prayed God 🕮 to provide them with peace, security and prosperity. What this means is that security and peace of mind are real needs that people have, and the Islamic political order is duty-bound to ensure these conditions [are established].

We are not, of course, talking about the welfare and prosperity of a particular class or segment of the population, or about the welfare and prosperity of, say, the city dwellers [at the expense of the rural population], or of some parts of the country and not of other parts. No; what we mean is the welfare and prosperity of the *whole* population; of each and every citizen, regardless of his or her social stratum, vocation, or geographical location. And naturally, the Islamic government must first see to and provide for those citizens who have the greatest needs. These sorts of things are part and parcel of the important duties and responsibilities of the government as well. Or another example is ensuring the health of the people and human services and the like. Ensuring the proper administration of the private and social and material lives of the people is an [important] duty for which the Islamic governmental order is responsible.

Another part of the duties of the Islamic government is the administration of the Islamic society's policies with respect to international relations and world affairs. It makes no sense for us to imagine a society and a state living comfortably within its borders and for that state not to have a strong presence in the global scene and not to be active and innovative within the ambit of international relations. This falls outside the realm of possibility. And this is not only the case today, where the whole world is interconnected. Civilization, culture and morality and matters of right and wrong, and problems and their solutions range from one end of the world to the other and take in all nations [in their wake]; in the past it was like this also; [this interconnectivity] has [to some extent] always been like this. It is not possible for us to imagine a successful society and a successful government, without also assuming a strong diplomatic corps and international relations for such a society. So this is one of the duties of the government too. Thus, Islamic government does not favor isolationism, does not favor separation from other nations and governments and isolating itself from international issues. Rather, it is in favor of having a pro-active presence on the global scene and being a player in international affairs and having a decisive impact on regional and global issues. And so, this is yet another group of responsibilities. Of course, each of these multiple tasks which we have enumerated stand in need of facilities, institutions, rules and regulations, and administrative and executive apparatus; and it is the responsibility of the Islamic political order to bring these about in order to be able properly to carry out its responsibilities.

What is important is that the government is only acceptable when it admits these responsibilities and is committed to carrying them out. From the vantage of Islam, a government and a ruler who does not accept these responsibilities as its own is unacceptable. And this is why [again, from the point of view of an Islamic metaphysics and political science], if [the institution of] government is [used] for the satisfaction of one's [personal] ambitions and for the satisfaction of one's own selfish lusts and carnal desires, and at all events is not used as an instrument for the implementation of social responsibility, it is [nothing but] a heavy encumbrance on the shoulder of the ruler and naught but a burden of troubles. But if the government is used to carry out these duties and for the sake of these services, not only is it not a heap of trouble, it is, rather, a [form of] worship, a sacred duty in the service of God ﷻ, and a righteous deed.

A hadith report is related from the Most Noble Prophet ﷺ in which a man who was in the service of the Prophet ﷺ said, "O Prophet ﷺ of Allāh, بِئسَ الشَّىءُ الامَارَتُ what a base thing governance is!" This is a sentence which expresses the sentiments of an ascetic or one who has cut all ties with the world; in any event, it was a sentiment that this fellow expressed before His Eminence the Prophet ﷺ of Islam, may God's ﷻ peace be unto him and unto the purified and immaculate members of his Household. The Prophet ﷺ responded: نِعمَ الشَّىءُ الامَارَتُ لِمَن أَخَذَها بِحِلِّها وَ حَقِّها government is an excellent thing, on two conditions: the first condition is that the person who takes the reins of power in his hands should have the right to do so, and should not be a usurper of the office of rulership, and should have attained to this office in accordance with criteria which are divine in their origin. And secondly, that he should perform in accordance with that which is religiously incumbent upon him; and to perform the duties that his investiture in that office encumbers him with. And this is why the

76

The Islamic Ruler

question of governance is at the forefront of issues within [the teachings of] Islam.

There is also the hadith report reported about the Eighth Imam, [Imam Ridā,] in which he spoke concerning the issue of the leadership of the Islamic community or concerning the imamate in the city of Marv. In his explication of the issue, the Imam focuses on the imamate as the central axis [around which] all issue [revolve]. And this is why the concepts of *wilāyat* and *imāmat* are the subject matter of so many of the hadith in our hadith report corpus: because the spiritual and material concerns of the people; their progress and the question of the possibility of their felicity in the hereafter and whether they will enter into Heaven, are all in the hands of the governmental order. If this order is a capable and effective and suitable one, and one that is based on the tenets of Islam and is concerned for the well-being of its citizens, it will guide all of its people to Heaven. It will assure (*ta'mīn*) Heaven and [felicity in] the hereafter for the people. But if, God 🕮 forbid, the leadership is incompetent, or are not committed to their responsibilities or are not properly informed about them or are not concerned for the well-being of their citizens, then Hell and perdition will await not only the leadership in general and the supreme leader in particular, but will also await all of the people who live under the aegis of such a governmental order. Thus, the issue of the responsibilities of government is one which raises the stakes and value of the governmental order to such a high extent.[46]

1.12 The Mutual Rights of the People and the Government

Within the Islamic political order, the laws and ordinances which ruling apparatus impose on the people are just and deserving [of obedience], and [this is why] compliance with them is compulsory. People must conform their actions to these laws. That having been said, we have of course come across [the writings and opinions] of some of the great magisters and

---

[46] 1363/6/23

doctors of sacred jurisprudence who made a distinction between immutable laws and laws which are subject to change, and who then went on to say that mutable laws in the *sharī'a* or sacred law of Islam are those which are legislated by Islamic governments and imposed on the people. There is much that can be said about this issue, but it is not the topic that I want to address presently. What needs to be addressed is the question of whether laws which are legislated by an Islamic governmental order should or should not be considered to have the same sacred status as the other laws of the *sharī'a* which we hold to be sacred, such as the ordinances concerning the daily ritual devotions (*namāz*; Arabic: *salā'*) and the purifying dues (*zakā'*).

The line of reasoning which I would like to focus on is that if we grant that a governmental order is established in a given society, and that governmental order is righteous and just (*haqq ast*) and is in accordance with the *sharī'a* or sacred law of Islam; then, if the laws and regulations of such a government are not religiously incumbent (*wājib al-etā'e*) on the people living under the jurisdiction of that order, then this would defeat the purpose (*naqz-e qaraz*) [of wanting to establish such an order].

A government must be able to forge laws and regulations and follow through with their implementation in order to be able to administer society and the state. If we proceed on the assumption that the people are not duty bound by the sacred law to abide by these laws and regulations, and that no incumbency arises onto the people to be cognizant of the laws that are being forged and to know what it is that the Islamic governmental order requires of them so as to conform their actions to these requirement, then this [hypothetical situation] would be self-stultifying, and the establishment of such a government would be a useless act. A governmental order in which the people do not pay heed to its laws and do not obey its commands and do not consider its laws as binding on them will either degenerate into chaos and anarchy – and of a certainty anarchy is against the position of Islam – or, it will not be able to sustain itself and will give way to a different order, which is unjust and iniquitous and oppressive.

When is it possible for the Islamic governmental order perfectly to administer society? When it forges laws and regulations with precision and due diligence in ensuring that they fall within the framework of the *sharī'a* or sacred law of Islam, and implements these laws, and when the people, in their turn, submit to its laws and act in accordance with them.

There is a sermon in the noble book, the *Nahj ul-Balāgha*, which enlightens us completely concerning this issue. In the 34th sermon, the Imam says, أَيُّهَا النَّاسُ إِنَّ لِى عَلَيكُم حَقّاً وَ لَكُم عَلَىّ حَقٌّ O people! I have a right over you, and you have a right over me. Rights are mutual in Islam; it is not the case where the government has a right over the people, but the people have no right over the government. Nor is it the case that the people have a right over the government, but the government does not have a right over the people. Rather, both parties have rights over each other, and it is necessary to understand these rights, and for each to respect the right of the other.

The Commander of the Faithful stated the right which the people enjoy over the government earlier in the sermon. He says, أَمَا حَقُّكُم عَلَىّ And as to the right which you have over Ali b. Abī-Tāleb ﷺ. فَالنَّصِيحَـةُ لَكُم [My acting with] benevolence and goodwill [toward you] and acting in your interest [is your right]; وَ تَوفِيرُ فَيئِكُم عَلَيكُم providing the copious material benefits of life to you [is your right]; وَ تَعلِيمُكُم كَيلا تَجهَلوا providing you with education in order that you do not remain in a state of ignorance [is your right]; وَ تَأدِيبُكُم كَيما تَعلَموا as [it is your right] to be trained and disciplined so that you become aware. These four sentences are highly portentous and pregnant with meaning.[47]

---

[47] Elsewhere, in a speech delivered on 1363/10/7, Ayatollah Khāmeneī provides additional commentary on these four sentences: فَالنَّصِيحَـةُ لَكُم Where the interest of the people differs from the interest of the ruler, the ruler must not hesitate for a moment to relinquish his personal interest in favor of the interest of the people. وَ

[The Commander of the Faithful] continues: وَ أَمّا حَقّی عَلَیکُم But as to my right over you. فَالوَفاءُ بالبَیعَـة Firstly, that you remain faithful to your pledge of allegiance; i.e. that you do not go against the promise that you gave me to obey me as your ruler. وَ النّصیحَـةُ فی المَشهَدِ وَ المَغیبِ Act with good will towards me and want that which is best for me both in my presence and when my back is turned. In other words, want me to succeed both when you are among yourselves; but also, provide me with wise counsel and constructive criticism when I am among you. If you see a fault in me, do not keep it from me. Ali b. Abī-Ṭālib ﷺ is not after flattery and adulation; he wants the truth from his people. وَ الاجابَـکَ حینَ أَدعوکُم When I call on you, respond to my call: for the defense of the realm, for [other socially necessary] activities, for [your presence in] the Friday congregational devotions, and for other activities; Respond to Ali b. Abī-Ṭālib ﷺ's summons when he calls upon you, and be present. And the last sentence: وَ الطّاعَـاُ حینَ أَمُرُکُم When I command you to do something, obey my command.

This last sentence refers to those laws and regulations which we were talking about earlier. There can be no doubt that one cannot take the position that the necessity of obeying the commands of the ruler here stated by Imam Ali is due to the fact that Ali b. Abī-Ṭālib ﷺ is an Immaculate Imam; because if it had to do with [the period of] the immaculate [*de jure*] imamate of Ali b. Abī-Ṭālib ﷺ, it would not be limited to the period wherein he was vested [by the people] in the office of the caliphate and leadership of the community. Here, Ali b. Abī-Ṭālib ﷺ is speaking as a ruler, not as an immaculate Imam whose commands must be obeyed by all Muslims, whether they accept him as their Imam or not; and whether he is vested in the highest office of the land, or not. He

---

تَوفیرُ فَیئکُم It is my duty as your ruler to maximize your material circumstances; to ensure that poverty has no place in your lives, and that you have no [unmet] material needs, including the need to be free from insecurity, prejudice and biased or unfair treatment [at the hands of the government].

is speaking as an Islamic ruler. This is one of the attributes of the Islamic ruler: when the Islamic ruler demands something from the people, when he commands the people to something, the people must obey his command. This is one of the attributes of the Islamic governmental order.[48]

1.13 The Ruler's Taqwā[49] as the Guarantor of the Sacrality of the Governmental Order

God ﷻ the All-Knowing and All-Wise has stated in His Sacred Writ:

يَا دَاوُودُ إِنَّا جَعَلْنَاكَ خَلِيفَةً فِي الْأَرْضِ فَاحْكُم بَيْنَ النَّاسِ بِالْحَقِّ وَلَا تَتَّبِعِ الْهَوَىٰ فَيُضِلَّكَ عَن سَبِيلِ اللَّهِ ۚ إِنَّ الَّذِينَ يَضِلُّونَ عَن سَبِيلِ اللَّهِ لَهُمْ عَذَابٌ شَدِيدٌ بِمَا نَسُوا يَوْمَ الْحِسَابِ ﴿٢٦﴾

[38:26] [And We said:] "O David! Behold, We have made thee a [prophet and, thus, Our] vicegerent on earth: rule, then, between men with justice, and do not follow lower desire, lest they lead thee astray from the path of God ﷻ.

It is said that if despotism is to be eradicated from society, then the rule of law must prevail in society; because law is the basis of the policies and procedures upon which the movement of society is determined and regulated. When law prevails, urges and desires, friendships and enmities, false judgments and unsubstantiated opinions, all lose their purchase. The hands of the tyrant in effect become bound by the rule of law; thus, in our country, when they wanted to confront the dark dictatorial regimes of the past, the first step that was attempted was the introduction of a

---

[48] 1362/6/11

[49] *Taqwā*: a righteousness of character which is informed by a fear of appearing before God ﷻ on the Day of Judgement and of the everlasting consequences in the hereafter as a result of a failure to perform well in this ultimate fateful Judgement

constitutional form of government, which consists of the rule of law. Of course, the tyrants opposed the constitutionalist wave of the people for a long time and refused to give way to it, but in the end the pressure of public opinion, in which the great religious scholars and politically conscious religious authorities and sources of emulation played a leading role, was able to break that dam and establish a legislature and constitution government in the country. Thus the rule of law is the first line of defense against tyranny. But this antidote, which is the first thing that occurs to the minds of reformers and political activists in the early stages of combatting tyranny is not sufficient in itself. And the reason for this insufficiency is that when a tyrant is intent on acting in accordance with his own wishes, he will do so irrespective of whether or not the society is [nominally] governed by the rule of law.

The dictator has no respect for the law, violates the law, disregards the decisions of the representatives of the people, and takes the proceedings of the legislature as for naught. Of course, sometimes some of the world's despots make a pretense of obeying the law while breaking it, but when rebellion [against God's ﷻ order and against the will of the people] passes all bounds, they will act openly and disregard the law patently. We saw an example of this ourselves in our own country during the period of the moral, political, and economic degeneration and collapse of the disgraceful regime of the past. At first they put up a pretense of respect for the law, but towards the end [of their tenure], they could not be bothered by such pretenses, and did not even bother to comply with the constitution law of the constitutional revolution (1905 – 1911), and this was especially the case with its constitutional amendment, which was completely ignored and disregarded.

The same thing is happening in the world today. In many countries where the people are not present on the political scene and where their existence is completely ignored by hegemons and despots who have total authority [over their affairs], the rule of law ostensibly exists; but where can one find a ruler in such countries who abides by the law? The powerful do not pay any heed to the law.

And this is where there must be an additional remedy alongside the prevalence of the rule of law. And again, political thinkers and reformers and those who have thought about social issues in the past, have come up with the solution. What these pundits said was that in order for the law not to be disregarded and violated, there must be two other elements in addition to the rule of law: the first is providing the people and their representatives the right to monitor and supervise [compliance with the law]; and the second is an independent and powerful judiciary which can use its powers to ensure compliance with the law irrespective of who violates it. Thus, public supervision on the part of the people and a powerful, intelligent and active judiciary are two institutions which act to prevent lawlessness. As such, Islam takes into account the enforcement of law, by violent means if necessary, as well as the principle of the rule of law itself.

The Quranic verse which I recited [at the beginning of this session] is one of several verses which is used to point to the Quran's attention to this matter. يا داوُدُ إِنَّا جَعَلناكَ خَلِيفَـةً فِى الأَرضِ *"O David! Behold, We have made thee a [prophet and, thus, Our] vicegerent on earth."* What is meant by vicegerent here is God's ﷻ successor for the purposes of organizing and administering people's affairs. فَاحكُم بَينَ النّاسِ بِالحَقِّ وَ لا تَتَّبِعِ الهَوَى *"Rule, then, between men, with justice."* In other words, rule in accordance with the *lex aeterna*[50] in which justice is embodies. Justice is meaningless absent law, nor is it possible without law; because if justice is not embodied in a system of laws, it can never be corroborated and validated, as each person will claim as just that which he desires [for himself]. *"Rule, then, between men, with justice."* وَ لا تَتَّبِعِ الهَوَى *"and do not follow lower desire."* There other verses in the Quran to this affect also.

---

[50] The eternal law of God ﷻ; the moral law; the law of nature; the law which is woven into the very fabric of creation.

And it is the same in the case of public supervision. One of the ordinances which has been ordained in Islam as religiously obligatory for people is the obligation of النَصيحَـاُ لِاَئِمَّـا المُسلمين. What this means is that it is a religiously obligatory duty for Muslims to provide good counsel to their leaders, to guide them, to tell them the truth, and where necessary, to question them, hold them responsible, and to point out the error of their ways. In the early days of Islam, this spirit was strengthened among the people and was not suppressed. During the reign of the second caliph, the caliph went to the pulpit and said to the people, "If I go astray, correct me." Guide me, in other words, tell me where I have erred. A Bedouin stood up, unsheathed his sword, and said, "If you go astray, I will rebuke you with my sword!" This incident speaks to the extent of the latitude which was afforded the people with respect to how forthrightly they were allowed to address their leaders. Of course, the obligation to provide counsel does not just mean providing leaders with rebukes and reprimands; it also entails constructive criticism and friendly reminders. A criticism which is not well-intentioned but is tinged with malice or is made more as a pretext for subversion or sedition is not Islamic in its nature. In order for a criticism to be Islamic, it must be well-intentioned and constructive; it must be offered with the intention of seeking out the solution to a problem; it must be offered in the spirit of guidance.

Therefore, these two factors, that is, the element of public oversight and the role of an independent judiciary, can be effective. Of course, in Islam, the issue of an independent and powerful judiciary is extremely important. If one looks to the early years of Islam, one will see how much emphasis was paid to the importance of independent judges and courts. The act of judgement was considered to be one of the most sensitive of functions, which is why judges must be independent of political groupings and interest groups and not allow such forces to influence their judgements.

A judge must not be the subject of pressures or threats. If the judiciary is weak or corrupted, it is tantamount to the breakdown of a preservative salt whose absence will bring about the decomposition and putrefaction of the whole of society. The people must be able to have a reliable refuge for the restitution of their rights; a place that they can take their grievances to, knowing that their rights will be respected and restored. An institution which will act to prevent the transgression of law – and that is the judiciary. This is the reason why judges enjoy a position of respect in Islam.

The Commander of the Faithful was walking in a street one day when he came across a Jew who was carrying the Imam's body armor which had been missing for some time. His Eminence drew near to the Jew and said, "This armor belongs to me!" But the Jew denied this. And even though this incident happened during the tenure of the Commander of the Faithful as caliph, His Eminence called on the Jew to appear before a judge so that they could resolve the matter [in accordance with the due process provided by the law], and the Jew accepted this request. When they appeared before the judge and were seated, the Commander of the Faithful put forward his case that the armor was his, and that the Jew had taken possession of what does not belong to him. The judge turned to the Jew, who denied that the armor was not his. The judge asked the Commander of the Faithful, "Do you have any evidence or any witnesses who can support your claim?" The Commander of the Faithful gave this question some thought and then said, "No, I have no witnesses." The judge then said that as you have no evidence or witnesses, I rule against you; I cannot make a ruling for this armor to be given to you. The Commander of the Faithful was silent and was persuaded and did not say anything more. The Jew picked up the armor and left the court, as the Commander of the Faithful kept staring at him as he left with his armor in hand, with the full support of the ruling of the judge. He did not utter a word of complaint, nor could he have done so [legally if he were so inclined]. After the Jew had gone some distance, he stood, turned back and came to the Commander of the Faithful, and said, "But I testify that there is no God ❁ other than Allāh, and that your religion is true, and that you have spoken the truth. A social order in which a judge dares to issue a ruling against the Commander of the Faithful, and a community in which the Commander of the Faithful cannot force a non-Muslim person who he sees is in possession of his armor to part with it without reason and witnesses, this is a social order and a religion that is true (*al-haqq*),[51] and I have attained to faith in it. This armor is yours." He returned the armor to the Commander of the Faithful and entered into Islam.

This is the measure of the independence of the judiciary in Islam. But I [go further and] say that even the existence of a strong and independent judiciary and the existence of powerful public oversight institutions with all of their institutional powers and reach are not sufficient to preclude the rise of dictatorships and despots and cannot in themselves uproot tyranny from society. The tyrants who are entrenched on the thrones of absolute power will not be moved by strong and independent judiciaries and institutions that provide public oversight. They will strive to weaken the judiciary and to infiltrate it, and will weaken the people's oversight and nullify it with the force of propaganda and lies. Despotism will of course be curtailed to some degree with the prevalence of the rule of law, with public oversight, and with a strong judicial apparatus, but it will not be eradicated.

That which is capable of eradicating despotism is something else altogether which can only be seen in the Islamic social order and in the

---

[51] *Al-haqq* is a key Quranic term which simultaneously carries the meanings of ultimate reality, truth and justice. It is also one of the Quranic Names of God ﷻ and is often used interchangeably with the word 'God'. William C. Chittick adds concerning this key word: "The sense of appropriateness and rightness in haqq is very strong, and the words "real" or "truth" simply do not express it in English. To say that everything has a haqq is to say that everything has a right and appropriate mode of being and that, in addition, it is our duty before God ﷻ, the Real, to recognize it and to act accordingly... Each thing has a right upon us, and hence each is our "responsibility" (another word that can translate *haqq*)."

person of the Just Ruler in Islam, and is something which has only been identified by the teachings of Islam. No other school of thought or political ideology has been able to recognize this solution or to provide any warrant [for its implementation]. And this element is *taqwā*; the piety and righteousness of the character of the ruler, and his commitment to the servitude of God ﷻ and of His order. This is why Islam stipulates that the ruler of society should be a person who is righteous and who has attained to a high level in the Islamic code of moral conduct, and thus is someone who does not sin and who is not driven by his lower urges and carnal desires but is in full control of them. He must be a person who has submitted his will to that of God's ﷻ and does not give preference to his own opinions over those which God ﷻ has ordained for humanity. His primary concern should be to determine what God ﷻ has ordained for a particular situation, and to find the best way of implementing such ordinances.

The only thing that can guarantee the rule of law which is necessary over and above a strong and independent judiciary and powerful public oversight institutions is the *taqwā* of the leader of a given society, i.e. his fear of God ﷻ (*taqwā*) [and the subsequent self-control and self-discipline required meticulously to abide by His ordinances]. Because when *taqwā* is present in a leader, when he is endowed with righteousness as an integral and inseparable part of his moral character, these are the bridles which prevent the steed of concupiscence and carnality from breaking loose and running wild; and thus *taqwā* acts as a restraint which ensures that each person, nation and humanity as a whole are guided on the Straight path. Thus, the most the most important issue for the Islamic ruler is servitude and devotion to God ﷻ through *taqwā:* the righteousness of character which is informed by a fear of appearing before God ﷻ on the Day of Judgement and of the everlasting consequences in the hereafter as a result of the possibility of a failure to perform well in this ultimate fateful Judgement.

Therefore, against the tyranny that rulers in illegitimate social order have, the Islamic community has a ruler who strictly refrains from carnal desires and lower and selfish urges, who is meticulous in terms of his obeying the law, and not just any law or one that is agreed upon by convention, but the sacred law, the divine law, the *lex aeterna*. Therefore, the Islamic ruler honors and respects a judiciary that is fee and strong and its independent judgments, and welcomes [and encourages] the presence of people on the political scene and the involvement of the people in their fate and their involvement in the decision-making processes and in the determination of policies which will determine the future of their country. He is a leader who is God-fearing and endowed with an upright code of moral conduct, who is positioned at the head of society in order to guide it towards justice.

The tyrant who is positioned at the head of the community turns all human beings into mini-tyrants. The culture of tyranny seeps down from the top to the bottom, everyone becomes a mini-despot, everyone begins to disregard the opinions of others, everyone becomes self-centred and out to satisfy their own lusts and sensual desires. But the pious and God-fearing ruler, who is endowed with a sound moral character (is *ādel*) and who is who is possessed of moral rectitude (*adālat*) will turn society into one that is righteous and God-fearing. He will have an effect on people such that more and more people will [be moved to] offer their obligatory daily ritual devotions (*namāz*); they will be more generous and magnanimous of character; they will be more charitable; and will be more committed to performing the ordinances having to do with the moral stewardship of the community (*ahkām-e nezāratī*) such as *al-amr bi'l-ma'rūf wa an-nahy min al-munkar* which is a pillar of the religion and which refers to the imperative to enjoin the doing of that which is right and to forbid the doing of that which is wrong. In short, the Just Ruler will make for a pious, righteous and God-fearing (*bā-taqwā*) society. This is the effect that righteous and God-fearing leaders and dignitaries and people in positions of high office will have on society at large.[52]

---

[52] 1362/10/16

2 Ayatollah Khāmeneī's Commentary on *Imam Ali's Epistle to Mālik Ashtar*

Editor's Note:

Each year, during the holy month of Ramadan, a delegation from the esteemed government [of the day] meet with the Supreme Leader. In addition to this beneficent meeting being an opportunity for learning and renewal and becoming revitalized for another year of service to the social order of the Islamic Republic, it also takes the form of a class in which the principles of Islamic governance are explicated by Ayatollah Khāmeneī. The text for this class has been the noble book of the *Nahj al-Balāgha*, a collection of sermons, addresses and epistles of Imam Ali b. Abī-Tālib 🕮 compiled by Seyyed Sharīf Rāzī in the fourth/ tenth century.

The 53rd epistle was written by the Commander of the Faithful, Imam Ali b. Abī-Tālib 🕮, for Mālek Ashtar, when he appointed the latter as Governor of Egypt. It is a lengthy letter, and Ayatollah Khāmeneī recites parts of it in the course of these classes and provides commentaries on them as part of his advice to the government officials present. As Ayatollah Khāmeneī states, the most important tasks that the authorities face are enumerated in this Epistle, which must be studied carefully.

In this chapter, the commentary and exegesis of Ayatollah Khāmeneī on *Imam Ali's* 🕮 *Epistle to Mālik Ashtar* are collated and presented as one continuous presentation in the order of the text as it appears in *Imam Ali's* 🕮 *Epistle to Mālik Ashtar*. Therefore, all subdivisions and section and sub-section heading titles have been deliberately omitted in conformance with the requirements of the nature of such a compilation, whose objective is to create a text and presentation which is a virtual simulation of a single seamless session in which we read Ayatollah Khāmeneī presenting his commentary on *Imam Ali's* 🕮 *Epistle to Mālik Ashtar* starting from its beginning and going all the way through to the end. In the totality of all of Ayatollah Khāmeneī's commentaries on *Imam Ali's* 🕮 *Epistle to Mālik Ashtar* which have been collated, approximately one quarter of the *Epistle* has been commented on.[53]

During the days of the month of Ramadan, we usually invite a delegation from the esteemed government in order to be at their service during the breaking of the fast. And it is our custom to read a few sentences from the *Nahj ul-Balāgha* or from some *hadith* reports so that our gathering will be endowed with a spiritual content and will also take on the form of a counseling session of sorts. In other words, the intent is to change the form of these sessions so that they are not in the format of the usual gathering of government officials, but rather, so that they will take on the form of

---

[53] The final compilation is based on 48 different lectures of various dates. The original text presents all of the dates of the lectures which the individual excerpts are taken from, but I have chosen not to include these as they are available in the original Persian for those who are interested, and I did not see a need to clutter the text with an additional 48 footnotes.

normal gatherings of the general public during the month of Ramadan in which various views are exchanged. Of course, all of those present are not in need of this advice, and, praise be to God 🕮, everyone is knowledgeable and well informed.

Perhaps, as in the previous occasions where some of you were also present, what we have to say will not be new to you. But the nature of advice is not in its being novel. Of course, one's information should be up to date. One learns lessons of general knowledge once only, and this suffices one for the rest of his or her life. If you have learned something once already and someone wants to teach it to you again, you would [rightly] say that you have already learned this lesson and already know about this matter. But advice is not a matter of already being knowledgeable about something or not being knowledgeable about it. Rather, advice falls in the category of being effective by way of remembrance and recollection. Thus, if there is a matter that we are already familiar with, to hear about it twice, three times or even five times as advice and by way of counsel and guidance is not too much. Most advice and many of the teachings of the Quran are in a similar vein.

It occurred to me to recite a few sentences from *Imam Ali's* 🕮 *Epistle to Mālik Ashtar*, which is the most expansive counsel and instructions of his eminence, Imam Ali 🕮.

These words are addressed to the noble [warrior and statesman] Mālik Ashtar, and as you will see, [that despite this,] the epistle includes words that are harsh and bitter and which almost verge on acrimony. His eminence's counsel is indeed bitter at times, and this harshness of tone is such that if someone gave each of us advice with such a harshness of tone, it would upset us. Mālik Ashtar is someone who his eminence Imam Ali 🕮 introduces in the following terms in another epistle: "He is someone who is fearless." (فَإِنَّهُ مِمَّن لا يُخافُ وَهنُهُ) And: "He is someone who will not fall short or fail in his duties." (وَ لا سَقَطَتُهُ) And: "No one can imagine him performing something slowly where alacrity and haste are required" (وَ لا بُطؤُهُ عَمَّا الإسراعُ إلَيهِ أحزَمُ). And its obverse: "No one can imagine him

93

performing something hastily where patience and thoroughness are required" (وَ لا إِسراعُهُ إلى ما البُطءُ عَنهُ أمثَلُ). In other words, he is someone who is aware of his surroundings and is also endowed with wisdom. That is, he does not do anything hastily where haste is not called for, nor does he slow down where alacrity and haste are required. This is how his eminence Imam Ali ﷺ introduces Mālik Ashtar to two of the commanders of his army at the Battle of Siffin.

It is said that this instruction (*ahd*) is the longest of Imam Ali's ﷺ letters and is the most complete from an aesthetic point of view, and that no other epistle measures up to this one in terms of the comprehensiveness of its rhetorical beauty as well as its spiritual content. I should also point out that one of the meanings of the word *ahd* is "instruction" or "command", like a governmental order or edict that is written for someone. Here *ahd* does not mean "covenant" or "treaty", where some people mistakenly call it the "covenant" or "treaty" of Mālik Ashtar. A "covenant" or "treaty" is a contract between two parties, but [the use of the word] *ahd* here does not connote such a thing at all. Rather, it is a case of Imam Ali ﷺ instructing Mālik Ashtar to go to Egypt and to act in accordance with the instructions that he has been given.

Unfortunately, Mālik Ashtar was martyred *en route* to Egypt and did not live to become her governor, but this historical document remained extant for us. Given the solid provenance titles (*asnād*) in terms of [the letter's] chains of transmission and custody, it can be said that its attribution to Imam Ali is well established and proven; and everyone quotes from it (*hame ān rā naql karde-and*).[54] That which appears as advice in *Imam Ali's* ﷺ *Epistle to Mālik Ashtar* are matters that are still relevant even today, although governmental institutions and the way in which governments are organized and structured today is very different than the

---

[54] The original allows for two interpretations of this phrase. I have chosen to render it as "everyone quotes from it" because it would make no sense to say that "everyone has transmitted it".

way they were structured at the time of Imam Ali ﷺ and Mālik Ashtar. For example, in those days there were scribes (*kuttāb*) and administrators (*ummāl*), whereas nowadays governmental institutions are highly complex and their organizational structure (*tashkīlāt*) is immense. But because his eminence does not discuss this aspect of governance, i.e. because the type of his advice and counsel does not pertain to the structure of a given institution but to its content and direction, it is equally valid today. It matters not whether the person who is at the head of a government is a governor of a province or is the president of Egypt, or whether he has some other official rank, be it Egyptian or non-Egyptian. Today, this letter is valid and has efficacy and applicability to the whole world of Islam and for those who believe in Islamic principles and values; all these can benefit from its principles and counsel.

After invoking the name of God ﷻ, Imam Ali ﷺ states: "This is that with which Ali, the servant of God ﷻ and Commander of the Faithful, charged Mālik ibn al-Harith al-Ashtar in his instructions to him when he appointed him governor of Egypt".

The Commander of the Faithful goes on to mention four points, and what is interesting is that when I examined these points in some detail, I saw that they are the four most important points that are expected of a government and which can be expected of us.

Other than the issue of diplomacy and international relations, the rest of the issues [pertaining to governance] can be found in the same four points of instruction, which are also arranged in their order of importance and priority. Let us suppose that when a ruler or an emir wants to carry out a project in a given country, the first thing that he needs is a budget; at all event, there are costs for any given project which must be met. The first of the four points is to collect the land tax from the people (جِبايَة خَراجِها); because you will need money to do whatever it is that you want to do. You will need money; that is the first step. Then you have to wage war against your enemies in order to eliminate any external or internal obstacles that exist (وَ جِهادَ عَدُوِّها). Waging *jihād* against the enemies of Egypt is a duty that is incumbent upon you. If an enemy attacks from without or rises up in rebellion from within, you must defend that country and its people against such elements. Both inner enemies as well as external ones undermine a country's security. Thus, ensuring that security is provided is one of the points that Mālik Ashtar is instructed to pay heed to. This is the second point.

Now let us assume that the required budget is available and that there are no enemies to have to deal with. Naturally, the country's development must be seen to. A part of development that is more important than the others concerns human development. Thus, His Eminence states: "and improve the condition of the people" (وَ اسِتِصلاحَ أهلِها) and guide them towards that which is right." What is meant by "that which is right" (*silāh*) is not limited to the intellectual and spiritual domains; it is inclusive of both material and spiritual domains. And what is meant by doing that which is right in the spiritual and intellectual domains is enjoining the doing of that which is right and for the best; it means acting in accordance with the tenets and precepts of the religion. In the Supplication (Du'a) of the *Makārim al-Akhlāq* we read: وَاستَصلِح بِقُدرَتِكَ ما فَسَدَ مِنِّى . And here *istislāh* means to drive one toward that which is right; to drive whatever action of mine that is capable of being reformed back on to the right path and toward that which is right. Thus, the first stage of development is the development of the human individual.

The fourth and final point is that His Eminence states: "and engender prosperity in the country's regions" (وَ عِمارَةَ بِلادِها). If Mālik Ashtar has been appointed the governor and ruler of Egypt, this does not mean that he is sent there in order to make a name for himself and to empower himself and to make personal profit from this appointment. Rather he has been sent there to do the following: To levy taxes from the people in order to pay for its administrative expenses; to wage war against the nation's enemies and to provide them with security against their enemies; to guide them towards the doing of that which is right in the wide sense that the concept appears in the *Nahj ul-Balāgha*; and to "engender prosperity in the country's regions". In sum: to develop the nation's human potential, develop the material infrastructure and superstructure of the nation, to raise the ethical and moral code of conduct of its people, and to utilize the people's capabilities and aptitudes in performing that which is their responsibility with respect to the ruling order.

So we see that there are four natural functions which must be performed for the administration of a state. First we must make the budget available by way of taxation. In addition to availing the government of its budget, this act of taxation also benefits those who fund the budget with their taxes in so far as the funding of the budget on the part of the people is a form of benefaction. The best form of benefaction is the money the people give to the government and their ruler so that he can see to their affairs. *Zakāt*[55] and *khums*[56] both fall into this same category. The first benefit of charity goes to the donor and the benefits to the recipient follow. The following verse concerns the benefit of giving in charity:

$$\text{فَاتَّقُوا اللَّهَ مَا اسْتَطَعْتُمْ وَاسْمَعُوا وَأَطِيعُوا وَأَنِفُقُوا خَيْرًا لِّأَنفُسِكُمْ ۚ وَمَن يُوقَ شُحَّ نَفْسِهِ فَأُولَٰئِكَ هُمُ الْمُفْلِحُونَ ﴿١٦﴾}$$

[64:16] ... And spend in charity for the good of your own selves: for, such as from their own covetousness are saved – it is they who shall attain to a happy state![57]

The mere act of reaching into our purses and withdrawing some money saves us from the miserliness and avarice that exist in our hearts. Of course,

---

[55] See footnote 17.

[56] Khums is the Arabic word for 'one-fifth'. In Shī'a law, one-fifth of certain items which a person acquires as wealth must be paid as a tax on a yearly basis to the Imam, or, in his absence, to a religious authority of one's choosing.

[57] See also verse 59:9.

once this money reaches its intended recipient and God 🕮 willing, it is also expended appropriately, a second benefit will also accrue for us.

Therefore, Imam Ali's 🕮 instructions to Mālik Ashtar begin with the collection of the land tax from the people (جِبايَةَ خَراجِها); which is then followed by waging war against the enemies of the state in order to eliminate any external or internal obstacles (وَ جِهادَ عَدُوِّها); this is followed by the need to "improve the condition of the people and guide them towards that which is right (وَ اسِتصلاحَ أهلِها); and finally, "engendering prosperity in the country's regions" (وَ عِمارَةَ بِلادِها). What this demonstrates to us is that as far as international affairs are concerned, they were not the responsibility of the governor of Egypt. In other words, the governor of Egypt – or Mālik Ashtar – was not the decision maker in this case, and the Commander of the Faithful would make any decisions that needed to be made in this regard.

All right. Now that Mālik Ashtar is journeying to Egypt to see to its administration, the question arises as to whether the first matters which his eminence Imam Ali 🕮 commends to him relate to the specific work at hand or not? The answer is negative. What Imam Ali 🕮 writes about does not relate to the specific work at hand but rather relates to the person of Mālik Ashtar himself. In fact, the crux of the matter is that Imam Ali 🕮 tells Mālik Ashtar that if we are to lay the groundwork for the development of the people and the nation [of Egypt] and if we are to develop that nation, then we must first work on improving and developing ourselves. The Commander of the Faithful does not tell Mālik Ashtar in the first instance, say, to deal with the people in a given way: to do this or not to do that. He teaches the techniques of the details of governance to him later. But he starts with Mālik Ashtar himself and says, "Now that I am sending you to Egypt to be its governor, I command you first and foremost to be righteous and god-fearing (i.e. to have *taqwā*)"[58] (اَمَرَهُ بِتَقوَى اللهِ). *Taqwā* means that you should [have piety and a righteousness of character which is informed by a] fear [of appearing before] God ﷻ [on the Day of Judgement and of the everlasting consequences in the hereafter as a result of a failure to perform well in this ultimate fateful Judgement], and to act accordingly. *Parvā* and *parhīz-kārī* are good words which have been used from olden times [and are the Persian equivalents of *taqwā*]… Beware of God ﷻ; be conscious of the fact that He exists. This is what is meant by *taqwā*. Whatever deed that one wants to do, or whatever deed one wants to desist from doing, one should be aware that God ﷻ is vigilant and is watching. [And this recalls] the very important point that Imam Khomeini made, that we should [always] see ourselves as being in the presence of God ﷻ. This is, in fact, another way of defining *taqwā:* that one should always be on guard and to say to oneself, "At this very moment, as I am speaking, God ﷻ is watching over me; so I should beware not to become the subject of His wrath". This is *taqwā*.

Taqwā is the [indispensable] substance of all of your and my endeavors. In other words, everything that we want to do and for which we are responsible, which are indeed difficult tasks and together make up a heavy burden of responsibility, cannot be realized without god-fearing piety and a fundamental righteousness of character (*taqwā*). And if we are indeed righteous and god-fearing in our behavior and outlook (i.e. if we have *taqwā*), then we can accomplish these tasks; and conversely, we cannot do so if we lack *taqwā*. And of course, it goes without saying that *taqwā* is a necessary but not sufficient condition for many of the technical

---

[58] *Taqwā*: a righteousness of character which is informed by a fear of appearing before God ﷻ on the Day of Judgement and of the everlasting consequences in the hereafter as a result of the possibility of a failure to perform well in this ultimate fateful Judgement..

and managerial tasks involved in administering a state. But irrespective of this truism, wherever *taqwā* is present, its positive effects will be felt, and wherever it is absent, the negative effects of its absence will also be felt. This is why the Commander of the Faithful tells Mālik Ashtar first and foremost to be righteous and god-fearing (i.e. to have *taqwā*); because without this, not a single branch of a tree will bear any fruit, just as this very metaphor makes its appearance in the *Nahj ul-Balāgha*, that is, nothing [of value in God's ﷻ eyes] will take place without *taqwā*.

Therefore, one must be godfearing and bear *taqwā* in mind when selecting one's personnel. Of course, when we say this, we do not mean to imply that one should not be meritocratic and not take other qualifications into account. No; that would be a highly illogical and meaningless position which nobody advocates. What is at issue is that when there are two candidates who have all of the other requisite qualifications [and are equally qualified in that respect,] and where one of them has *taqwā* whereas the other does not, then the one who does not have *taqwā* should be passed over in favor of the one who does. Because of course, if one does not have all of the other qualifications for the position, then he or she will not be able to perform well in that position. It is obvious that a physician who has *taqwā* is more beneficial than one who does not. But this does not mean that if someone was not qualified as a medical doctor but had *taqwā*, that we should allow such a person to tend to the sick; clearly, nobody would say such a thing.

In *Imam Ali's* ﷺ *Epistle to Mālik Ashtar*, his eminence provides some examples of *taqwā*. Preferring God's ﷻ obedience over obedience to people (وَ ايثارِ طاعَتِهِ); this brief aphorism is itself a lofty and exalted maxim concerning *taqwā*, that mankind should always prefer obedience to God ﷻ over obedience to His creatures and servants and to their various individual, familial, social and political and personal considerations and preferences.

"And to follow what He has directed in His Sacred Writ" (وَ اتَّباعِ ما آمَرَ بِهِ في كِتابِهِ) In other words, it should not be the case that something that has been made religiously obligatory (*wājib*) or is prohibited in God's ☙ sacred writ should be ignored for the sake of expedience or a supposed "greater good". No expedience has priority over things which have been made religiously obligatory (*wājibāt*). Of course, there are secondary ordinances which have their own place and are clear; but the basis [of our actions] should be governed by [the objective of] realizing the ordinances (*ahkām*) and personally incumbent obligations (*farā'id*).

God ☙ the Sublimely Exalted has stipulated in His Sacred Writ that none attains felicity but he who follows His directions, and none is overcome by wretchedness but he who denies them and lets them slip by (مِن فَرَائِضِهِ وَ سُنَنِهِ الَّتِي لايَسعَدُ أَحَدٌ إِلَّا بِاتِّباعِها وَ لايَشقَى إِلَّا مَعَ جُحودِها وَ إِضاعَتِها) If we were to analogize the pious fear of God ☙ (*taqwā*) to an ode, then one of its couplets would be giving preference to obedience to God ☙ over obedience to other.

"Of his ordinances (*farā'id*) and paradigmatic example (*sonnat*; arabic: *sunna*)"[59] (مِن فَرَائِضِهِ وَ سُنَنِهِ); this is one of the many subjects which has been inscribed in God's ☙ Sacred Writ (literally: "the Book of God"; *kitābullāh)* which has the same meaning as scripture or that which God ☙ has ordained (*mā katab allāh*), and is inclusive of both ordinances (*farā'id*) and paradigmatic examples (*sunan*; plural of *sunna*). *Sunan* is also a part of scripture or the Sacred Writ (*mā katab allāh*) in the sense that God ☙ has ordained us to follow the paradigmatic examples (*sunan*) [of the Fourteen Impeccables];[60] but it is not [a part of the divine dispensation] that is

---

[59] *Sunnat*: The paradigmatic and exemplary pattern of behavior and model of moral conduct revealed by God ☙ as embodied revelation in the person of the Prophet Muhammad ﷺ, and in Shi'a belief, in the person of his luminous and impeccable daughter, Lady Fāṭimaᵗ az-Zahrā ☙, and that of the Twelve Immaculate (inerrant as well as sinless) Imāms ☙, whose emulation is to be strived for by all who have attained to faith.

[60] A Shi'a expression: the Prophet Muhammad ﷺ, Lady Fāṭimaᵗ az-Zahrā ☙, and the Twelve Imāms ☙.

necessarily written down as text, as in the Quran. One should not imagine that we are free [to abide by or to ignore] the exemplary pattern of behavior and model of moral conduct revealed by God 🌼 as embodied revelation (*sunan*) or that we have [absolute] latitude concerning conduct that is recommended and laudatory but not mandatory (or the juridical category we refer to as *mustahabāt*) [61] or even concerning the supererogatory ritual devotions and supplications (*nawāfil*; singular: *nāfilah*). No; these are similar to the mandatory religious obligations (*wājibāt*), just as many of these were mandatory for the Prophet 🌼, as it appears in our *hadith* report corpus that the night supererogatory ritual devotions and supplications (*nawāfil*) were mandatory for the Prophet. Or where Almighty God 🌼, addressing the Prophet 🌼 in the chapter entitled *al-Muzammil*, states:

قُمِ اللَّيْلَ إِلَّا قَلِيلًا ﴿٢﴾ نِصْفَهُ أَوِ انْقُصْ مِنْهُ قَلِيلًا ﴿٣﴾ أَوْ زِدْ عَلَيْهِ وَرَتِّلِ الْقُرْآنَ تَرْتِيلًا ﴿٤﴾

[73:2] Keep awake [in prayer] at night, all but a small part [73:3] of one-half thereof - or make it a little less than that, [73:4] or add to it [at will]; and [during that time] recite the Quran calmly and distinctly, with thy mind attuned to its meaning.

After which He states: [73:5] *Behold, We shall bestow upon thee a weighty message.* In other words, it would appear that this "weighty message" is a phenomenon and event which entails such prerequisites and such capacities. [It is as if God 🌼 is saying,] "You must prepare yourself for that "weighty message" and the way to do so is to stay up for a portion of the night." Thus, the purport of these verses as they appear on their surface to the mind of this humble servant [of God's 🌼] refers to the same thing. But I do not know whether or not this interpretation also appears in our *hadith* report corpus.

---

[61] *Mustahabāt* are contrasted with mandatory religious obligations (*wājibāt*).

And none is overcome by wretchedness but he who denies them and lets them slip by (وَ لايَشقَى إلّا مَعَ جُحودِها وَ إِضاعَتِها). Their denial is on the part of the unbelievers and infidels, whereas those who let them slip by are the believers who believe in [following] the ordinances (*farā'id*) and paradigmatic examples (*sunan*) but who waste away [their opportunity to do that which is right]. And if this happens, then it will bring about wretchedness and misery.

Imam Ali also charged Mālek Ashtar "to help God ﷻ with his heart, his hand and his tongue (وَ أَن يَنصُرَ اللّٰهَ سُبحانَهُ بِقَلبِهِ وَ يَدِهِ وَ لِسانِهِ), and what this tells us is that aiding God ﷻ to victory is necessary even at the level of the heart. What does aiding God ﷻ to victory at the level of the heart mean? First of all, we must know that aiding God ﷻ to victory means aiding the religion of God ﷻ, aiding the Path of God ﷻ, and aiding the divine values. OK, so then if this is the case, how does man "help God ﷻ with his heart"? Who is the enemy here? Because *nusrat* means triumphing or prevailing over something. Prevailing over something with our hands and tongue is understood. But who is the enemy that we are to conquer with our hearts, which victory we can call "the triumph of the heart" (*nosrat-e qalbi*)? That enemy is, in fact, our own inner desires and urges and tendencies and the inner deviations which we are to overcome. This is the greatest of triumphs. If we fail to aid God['s Way] at this stage and He failed at this stage (using the metaphor of triumphing (*nusrat*), which, if triumphing is appropriate, then failure is appropriate also); if we fail to help God ﷻ at this stage, it is not possible to come to His aid at the stage of [using] our hands and tongues. We will be able to come to the aid of God['s Way] with our hands and tongues when we have come to His aid in our hearts [first], and to have created that firm [and correctly directed] resolve within our hearts. [So Imam Ali advises Mālik Ashtar to] be sure to do this whenever you feel that the front [which is fighting to establish and maintain] divine [values] and objectives stand in need of your help. First you must [purify] your heart to ensure that it is on the right path, after which you can put your hands and tongue to work.

In [ordinances having to do with the moral stewardship of the community such as] the imperative to enjoin the doing of that which is right [and to forbid the doing of that which is wrong], the stage prior to taking action is [the purification of] the heart. If one is intent on enjoin the doing of that which is right sincerely, he must himself be committed to the right which he enjoins others to; for otherwise it will not be sincere. It is the same here: if coming to the aid of God['s Way] is to be done only with one's tongue (and where one's heart does not really believe what the tongue is saying), that is not sufficient. If the heart is not committed, the act becomes an act of pretense which is empty of any true content and will not be accompanied by any divine blessings. Nor will it have any external effects. Thus, it is imperative to start with the heart, after which the hands and tongue can be put to work.

The Commander of the Faithful then says, "for verily, He – glory be unto His Name – has promised to help those who exalt Him" (فَإِنَّهُ جَلَّ اسمُهُ قَد تَكَفَّلَ بِنَصرِ مَن نَصَرَهُ وَ إِعزازِ مَن أَعَزَّهُ). Nor is anything more important for you than to be aided by God ﷻ, for who can want for a better helper than God? If God ﷻ comes to one's aid, then one will pass through one's difficulties. You will be able to break through the bottlenecks and the impediments in your path will be cleared for you.

Immediately following these two points, that is, following the do's and don't's of the Divinely-revealed Way and [the principle of] divine aid, Imam Ali charged Mālik Ashtar "to break the passions of his soul and restrain it in its recalcitrance" (وَ أَمَرَهُ أَن يَكسِرَ نَفسَهُ مِنَ الشَّهَواتِ) or to take control of his passions. One who has responsibility over a number of people cannot be captive to lust and to his lower desires, and he should be better anchored than ordinary people who sway back and forth with the waves and tides of their natural lower urges and desires. Thus, he must firmly anchor the ship of his concupiscence.

And Imam Ali goes on to further charge Mālek Ashtar "to restrain his soul in its recalcitrance, for the soul incites to evil, except inasmuch as God ﷻ has mercy" (فَإِنَّ النَّفسَ أَمَّارَةٌ بِالسّوءِ إِلّا ما رَحِمَ اللهُ). When the expression "the soul which incites to evil" (*an-nafs ammāra bi's-sū'*) is used, some people think that there are certain entities within man's being, one of which is, say, "the soul which incites to evil"; whereas that is not how it is. The word "*nafs*" means one's self. Your *nafs* means your self. And my *nafs* means my self. And this "self" is naturally comprised of a composite of attributes, drives and [other] realities. One such reality is the lower reality (*haqīqat-e suflā*) which draws human beings down (*be samt-e sufl*) and toward the material domain of existence which man's lower urges and instincts are desirous of, such as the sensuality of the soul, one's sexual desires, the desire for social status and recognition, the lust for money, and these sorts of things. Another reality which the soul is composed of is the higher reality (*haqīqat-e 'elawī*) which draws one toward God ﷻ which is referred to [in the Quran] as "the soul that has attained to inner peace" (*an-nafs al-mutma'inna*). In any event, these are all [parts] of one's [overall] self, and there is nothing [that exists in man] over and above one's self. We must secure and maintain ourselves. And when the expression "the soul which incites to evil" (*an-nafs ammāra bi's-sū'*) is used, the intention is to draw attention to the fact that this part of the self, the lower self, greatly incites to evil, "except inasmuch as God ﷻ has mercy" (إلَّا ما رَحِمَ اللّه).

<hr />

After having said all these by way of a preamble, Imam Ali ﷺ tells Mālik Ashtar that he is sending him to a land that has had rulers before him. Mālik Ashtar will not be the first person to rule over Egypt. There were others before him who ruled Egypt, either during the time of the Islamic conquests or during the times of the pharaohs. Imam Ali ﷺ tells Mālik Ashtar that he is sending him to Egypt, and that the people there will look upon the way in which he manages his affairs in the same way that he is

ثُمَّ اعلَم يا مالِكُ أَنِّي قَد [wont to look upon the affairs of the rulers before him
وَجَّهتُكَ إلى بِلادٍ قَد جَرَت عَلَيها دُوَلٌ قَبلَكَ مِن عَدلٍ وَ جَورٍ وَ أَنَّ النَّاسَ يَنظُرونَ مِن أُمورِكَ في
مِثلِ ما كُنتَ تَنظُرُ فيهِ مِن أُمورِ الوُلاةِ قَبلَكَ وَ يَقولونَ فيكَ ما كُنتَ تَقولُ فيهم].

We sit in judgement of those who ruled before us and examine their deeds under a microscope and criticize each and every one of their utterances and deeds. We say, for example, that it would have been better if he had not said such and such a thing, or that what he did was not right. You should know, [O honored delegation of the elected government of the day] that we are positioned in the same situation that Mālik Ashtar was situated in, where we are in the proverbial fishbowl, as it were, and all eyes are upon us, examining and judging our every move. Thus, O Mālek, you should be careful and beware that every word and deed that issues forth from you is subject to the public gaze of the people; the gaze of a people whose hearts [you must win and whose hearts] must be with you. In other words, those who are examining your actions are not outsiders and people who live in a land that is distant [from the seat of the Islamic caliphate]; they are people whose hearts and minds must be won by your words and deeds, thus, you must be very careful about how you behave and what it is that you say. And the righteous are only known by that which God ﷻ causes to pass concerning them on the tongues of His servants (وَ
إنَّما يُستَدَلُّ عَلَى الصَّالِحينَ بِما يُجري اللهُ لَهُم عَلَى ٱلسُنِ عِبادِهِ).

Imam Ali ﷺ then says, "So let the dearest of your treasuries be the treasury of righteous action" (فَليَكُن أَحَبُّ الذَّخائِرِ إلَيكَ ذَخيرَةُ العَمَلِ الصَّالِحِ). You should not think of this position which you have been appointed to as one that should be used for the purposes of accumulating wealth and property for yourself, telling yourself that these things will come in handy to you the day that you are no longer in such a position of authority. In places where our presence can be of some benefit, given our work experience [and qualifications], titles and responsibilities can be likened to these treasuries. Although I have heard that some officials in different countries of the world who have not yet been divested of their office enter into negotiations with various corporations and conglomerates in order to secure a position prior to the termination of their term as minister or president! And others take advantage of their terms in office to procure various college degrees which will serve their interests once they are no longer in office! This is something that I am against. All these are repositories that petty bureaucrats stockpile for themselves during their terms of responsibility. The Commander of the Faithful tells Mālik Ashtar not to stockpile such wares, for the greatest repository for you is the cache of your righteous deeds. Act in a way, he advises, that when your term of responsibility comes to an end, you will feel that you have accumulated a store of righteous deeds, for this accumulation of righteousness will be useful to you both in the eyes of God 🏵 and of His court of justice, as well as in the eyes of the people.

It is not the case that the people do not understand what we do and the effects of our work [on them]. And even if we assume that they will not understand what we do for a few mornings, yet they will eventually come to know. So it is not as if righteous deeds will be unappreciated and wasted; no: the truth will always find its own place eventually.

The empty rhetoric and propaganda that can be heard [issuing from the mouths of politicians and governmental officials] throughout the world, including in our country, are like naught but fleeting winds; they have no durable substance.

أَنزَلَ مِنَ السَّمَاءِ مَاءً فَسَالَتْ أَوْدِيَةٌ بِقَدَرِهَا فَاحْتَمَلَ السَّيْلُ زَبَدًا رَّابِيًا ۚ وَمِمَّا يُوقِدُونَ عَلَيْهِ فِي النَّارِ ابْتِغَاءَ حِلْيَةٍ أَوْ مَتَاعٍ زَبَدٌ مِّثْلُهُ ۚ كَذَٰلِكَ يَضْرِبُ اللَّهُ الْحَقَّ وَالْبَاطِلَ ۚ فَأَمَّا الزَّبَدُ فَيَذْهَبُ جُفَاءً ۖ وَأَمَّا مَا يَنفَعُ النَّاسَ فَيَمْكُثُ فِي الْأَرْضِ ۚ كَذَٰلِكَ يَضْرِبُ اللَّهُ الْأَمْثَالَ ﴿١٧﴾ لِلَّذِينَ اسْتَجَابُوا لِرَبِّهِمُ الْحُسْنَىٰ ۚ وَالَّذِينَ لَمْ يَسْتَجِيبُوا لَهُ لَوْ أَنَّ لَهُم مَّا فِي الْأَرْضِ جَمِيعًا وَمِثْلَهُ مَعَهُ لَافْتَدَوْا بِهِ ۚ أُولَٰئِكَ لَهُمْ سُوءُ الْحِسَابِ وَمَأْوَاهُمْ جَهَنَّمُ ۖ وَبِئْسَ الْمِهَادُ ﴿١٨﴾

[13:17] … and, likewise, from that [metal] which they smelt in the fire in order to make ornaments or utensils, [there rises] scum. In this way does God 🏵 set forth the parable of truth and falsehood: for, as far as the scum is concerned, it passes away as [does all] dross; but that which is of benefit to man abides on earth. In this way does God ۞ set forth the parables [13:18] of those who have responded to their Sustainer with a goodly response, and of those who did not respond to Him. (فَأَمَّا الزَّبَدُ فَيَذهَبُ جُفاءً وَ أَمّا ما يَنفَعُ النّاسَ فَيَمكُثُ فِي الأَرضِ)

The righteous deeds that you have done which are profitable [for others] will remain and will be recognized [for what they are]. If the Commander of the Faithful accepted being invested in the office of the caliphate and pursued the duties and responsibilities of that office in earnest and with a seriousness of purpose, it was because of this very reason.

He then says, "Control your desire and restrain your soul from what is not lawful to you, for restraint of the soul is for it to be equitable in what it likes and dislikes" (وَ شُحَّ بِنَفسِكَ عَمّا لا يَحِلُّ لَكَ فَامِلِك هَواكَ). *Shuh* means to be miserly; the Arabs have the word *bukhl* as well, but *shuh* is stronger. *Shuh* is when you don't want to give something to someone which object you are very fond of; this is what is referred to as *shuh*, which is an amalgam of stinginess (*bukhl*) and avidity or avarice (*hers*). In this Quranic verse [59:9] *for, such as from their own covetousness are saved*,[62] it is used in the same sense. His Eminence Imam Ali ۞ tells Mālik to be miserly or to have covetousness (*shuh*) with respect to his self (*nafs*). And what this means is that Mālik should guard his self [or soul] and his identity with covetousness and avarice. From what? "From what is not lawful to you" (عَمّا لا يَحِلُّ لَكَ); in other words, do not provide it with anything that is illicit. That is the meaning of being miserly or to guard one's self or soul (*nafs*) with covetousness and avidity (*shuh*).

"For being miserly or to guard your self or soul (*nafs*) with covetousness and avidity (*shuh*) is for it to be equitable both with respect

---

[62] See also [64:16], where it is translated similarly, as well as [4:128] where it is translated as "selfishness".

to that which it likes as well as with respect to that which it dislikes" (فَاِنَّ الشُّحَّ بِالنَّفسِ الإنصافُ مِنها فيما اَحَبَّت آو كَرِهَت). In other words, it should not be the case that one should provide the soul with that which it likes, and to keep whatever it is that it dislikes out of its reach. This is not being covetous and avaricious (*shuh*) with your self or soul (*nafs*); rather, one must treat it with equity and justice; i.e. to provide it with what it needs and what is in accord with all that is good and right for it, which is what God ﷻ the Sublimely Exalted has made licit for it in His wisdom; and to refrain from giving to it that which is bad and detrimental for it, which is what God ﷻ the Sublimely Exalted has made illicit for it. This is the meaning of guarding your soul with covetousness (*shoh be nafs*).

The explication of the meaning of this word also appears in our *hadith* report corpus, and it seems to me that there was a report to this effect which was narrated by His Eminence, Imam Sajjād ﷺ.[63] And then again there was another one which was narrated by the Commander of the Faithful, in which he states: "Is there not a freeman who will foreswear the good and desirous things of this world for the sake of his loved ones? Assuredly, the value of your existence is nothing less than [everlasting] Heaven; so do not sell it for anything less than that!" (الا حر يدع هذه اللماظة لاهلها؟ انه ليس لانفسكم ثمن الا الجنة فلاتبيعوها الا بها). Do not sell yourself for anything other than Heaven. The expression "selling one's soul" is sometimes used to mean humiliating oneself and accepting humility, that is, for something whose worth is less than that of Heaven. Of course, whatever exists [on Earth] is [necessarily] less than [what everlasting] Heaven [is worth]. Whatever desirable thing there might be, no matter how valuable and desirable, it will still not be worth demeaning oneself and disparaging one's character, which is why belittling and subjugating oneself is prohibited by the sacred law [of Islam]. It is a tenet that can be found throughout the *hadith* report corpus that one can do whatever he or she wants with his or her soul other than to demean and to disparage it.

---

[63] The Fourth of the Shi'a Imams ﷺ.

At times, [the danger which faces the soul] is of this nature, and at other times, it is of the type where one throws oneself into the clutches of sin and of the various vices that abound; and that is another form of selling one's soul and losing it.

Imam Alī ﷺ continues by saying that "[Infuse your heart with mercy, love and kindness for your subjects. Be not in face of them a voracious animal, counting them as easy prey, for] your subjects are of two kinds: either they are your brothers in faith or they are your equals in creation." (فَإِنَّهُم صِنفان اِمّا اَخٌ لَكَ في الدّينِ وَ اِمّا نَظيرٌ لَكَ في الخَلقِ) I.e., they are human beings like yourself. For the Commander of the Faithful, whether one is or is not a Muslim is irrelevant when it comes to the matter of defending the oppressed and ensuring that the rights of people are realized; Muslims and non-Muslims alike enjoy these same rights. Pay close attention here to the exalted logic and the distinctive standard which the Commander of the Faithful has unfurled in history! [But despite this,] we see some people bandying about the meme of "human rights". But this is pure pretense; nothing but a tissue of lies! Nowhere do these people have any respect for human rights, even in their own countries, let alone throughout the globe! The Commander of the Faithful defined human rights in its true sense as we saw here, and it was a tenet which he acted upon as well.

Imam Alī says, "Never say, 'I am invested with authority, I give orders and I am [to be] obeyed,'" (وَ لا تَقولَنَّ اِنّي مُؤَمَّرٌ آمُرُ فَأُطاعُ). *Lā taqulanna* is the emphatic form, so that we see Imam Alī emphasizing the fact that such a thought should not even enter your mind, let alone be uttered by your tongue. This is the spirit of thinking that 'people should follow my orders because I am in a position of authority', and this spirit will "surely corrupt your heart" (فَإِنَّ ذلِكَ اِدغالٌ في القَلبِ). *Wa manhakahud*-dīn (وَ مَنهَكَةٌ لِلدّينِ) which means that [this spirit will bring about] the enfeeblement of the religion and one's faith, and "bring about unwanted changes [in one's character and fortune] (وَ تَقَرُّبٌ مِنَ الغِيَرِ). Feeling proud and self-satisfied and believing that 'no one should contradict me because

I am in charge' are the things that bring about these undesirable changes; changes in fortune which one does not want. That is, [this posture] weakens one's authority and power and will and ability to take advantage of the opportunity to serve.

This [attitude] will bring the people's wrath closer to you. When you speak like this, the people will forever be dissatisfied with your selfishness and egocentricity and your failure to accept any responsibility [concerning the need to consider other people's views].

There is another sentence which reads, "See that justice is done towards God[64] and justice is done towards the people by yourself and by your family" (أَنصِفِ اللهَ وَ أَنصِفِ النَّاسَ مِن نَفسِكَ وَ مِن خاصَّةِ أَهلِكَ وَ مَن لَكَ فيهِ) (هَوًى مِن رَعِيَّتِكَ). There is an expression in Arabic which means 'Do not allow yourself to be condemned by the people'. Do not petition yourself in other people's favor. His Eminence explains here that the meaning of the sentence is to feel the full burden of responsibility before God ﷻ, and hold yourself fully to account concerning your responsibilities before Him. Let it not be the case that you [reprieve yourself easily and] feel that you have performed all of the burdens of responsibility which were on your shoulders completely and perfectly. No; instead, always consider yourself to be in [the] debt [of the rights that God ﷻ and the people have over you].

Then it says, "See that justice is done towards the people by yourself" (أَنصِفِ النَّاسَ مِن نَفسِكَ). What this means is always to hold the people as being in the right in your judgments and always to think of them as your creditors, and always to think of yourself as being in their debt. This does not of course mean that one should not insist on one's own rights when one's rights have been specifically violated; rather, that this should be the general consideration.

---

[64] I.e., Perform for Him the worship which He has made incumbent upon you and the requirements of intelligence and tradition" (Ibn Abi-l-Hadid's commentary, vol. I7, p. 35).

People have certain needs and demands and express these needs and sometimes raise their voices and even yell. Assume for a moment that a group of people have gathered in some government office and are giving vent to their demands. The first thing that comes to your mind should not be that someone has put these people up to this so that they should come and raise a ruckus against me, who is innocent of all blame! No; rather, the first thought should be that these people have a right to demand whatever it is that is on their minds, and I am responsible to getting to the bottom of what it is exactly that they are demanding.

Therefore, "See that justice is done towards the people by yourself", by your family (مِن خاصَّهِ أَهلِكَ), as well as "by those who are close to you among your subjects" (وَ مَن لَكَ فيهِ هَوًى مِن رَعِيَّتِكَ). If there is a group or class among the people who are subject to your special attention and protection, be sure to exact the rights of the people from them as well. As a ruler or governor or minister who is allied with a certain faction, you will necessarily favor that faction with certain prerogatives and that faction will thus enjoy a certain competence which will foster the grounds for their abusing their position with respect to the rights of the people. So be on your guard against this.

[Imam Ali continues: "For if you do not do so, you have acted wrongly]. And as for him who wrongs the servants of God ﷻ, God ﷻ is his adversary, not to speak of His servants. God ﷻ renders null and void the argument of whosoever contends with Him. Such a one will be God's ﷻ enemy until he desists or repents" (وَ مَن ظَلَمَ عِبادَ اللهِ كانَ اللهُ خَصمَهُ دونَ عِبادِهِ وَ مَن خاصَمَهُ اللهُ أدحَضَ حُجَّتَهُ وَ كانَ لِله حَرباً). While it is true that the Commander of the faithful has addressed this letter to his governors – Mālik Ashtar, Ash'ath b. Qays, Uthmān b. Hanīf, and others – but its [principles and lessons] applies equally to all levels of those who hold positions of responsibility [in the government].

"Let the dearest of your affairs be those which are middlemost in rightfulness, most inclusive in justice and most comprehensive in [establishing] the satisfaction of your subjects." (وَ لِيَكُن أَحَبُّ الأُمورِ إِلَيكَ أَوسَطُها)

(فِي الحَقِّ وَ أَعَمَّها فِي العَدلِ وَ أَجمَعَها لِرِضَى الرَّعِيَّةِ). Choose to do that which guarantees the satisfaction of the masses; the masses as opposed to the elite and the upper classes. Today, the world is suffering from this blight that in most countries there are distinct stratifications by class, and the upper echelons in this stratification are the ones who determine the policies by means of which the political destinies of the entire population are decided.

In rich countries, in the countries of the West and in the United States, it is in fact the large industrialists and the fantastically rich who in effect determine [the vast majority of] their social policies. Every law, every thought, every method and approach in those countries are considered and undertaken for their sake. And if it so happens that the people derive some benefit in this midst, it is from the leftovers at their table.[65]

Our own country was no different during the time of the former dependent regime. It was the rich, or the "thousand families" [who were attached to the Shah's court], as they were popularly known, for whose interests everything was determined. In a given country at a given historical period, it was this class [who predominated]; and throughout the history of Islam, there have been various other classes whose interests have prevailed over the interests of the majority of the population, be these the literati, or the scholars of religion (the *ulamā*), or some other group or class, whose vested interests the rest of the population was condemned to suffer. Thus, the people, the interests of the masses or the great majority of the people, were arrayed against the interests of a special class. And so the Commander of the Faithful warns Mālik Ashtar to beware that the decisions you make aims to satisfy the masses of the people rather than the elites of society.

Pursue policies which avoid both extremes and which promote social justice in a way that is most inclusive and widespread; i.e. the

---

[65] This inhuman social policy used to be referred to as "trickledown economics" during the era of Ronald Reagan and Margaret Thatcher. It was a policy which these two politicians espoused with pride.

promotion of social justice should be undertaken in such a way that its effects affect the lives of the greatest number of people and their interests, and which aims to attract the contentment and satisfaction of the masses and of the greatest possible number of people. Do not concern yourself with trying to please a select group of people, that is, of those who are rich and powerful. It is you and I who are the interlocutors of these words [of advice of the Commander of the Faithful's, O honored delegation of the present government]. If any of you is presently serving as a minister or as a representative of the people in the Majlis,[66] or if you are in a position of authority among the armed forces, are affiliated with the office of the Supreme Leader, or are an official within the judiciary – wherever you happen to be, you should beware that the work that you do should not be directed towards the satisfaction of the desires of the rich and powerful; which have been described in the instructions of the Commander of the Faithful as the "elite" (*khāssa*).

The list of things that one needs to do is a long one, and we will not have time to touch on them all. His Eminence says that the dearest of the things that you can do should be those which are "middlemost in rightfulness" (اوسَطُها فِي الحَقِّ); that is, the path between the two extremes and which is not biased in either direction. And this corresponds exactly with that which is right and just (*al-ḥaqq*): never to sway with any bias to either direction.

Secondly, it should be "the most inclusive in terms of its justice" (وَ آعَمُّها فِي العَدلِ). The justice that it disseminates should cover the widest possible number of people. It is possible, at times, for something to promote social justice; but that only a limited number of people benefit from its affects. And it could be that it is not an iniquitous or oppressive act, but that it is limited in its efficacy or scope. On the other hand, there could be other times where one envisages a wider scope for one's acts, in

---

[66] The Iranian equivalent of the House of Representatives or Senate (or Parliament, in Britain).

which case a large number of people become its beneficiaries. His Eminence Imam Ali instructs Mālek to make sure that this latter category of works is dearest to his heart. And of course what this means is that this latter course of action should always be given preference when confronted with a choice between the two. In other words, he advises us to abide by the very same priorities which we are always talking about. This is one of the criteria of determining our priorities.

"[And let the dearest of your affairs be those which are] the most comprehensive in [establishing] the satisfaction of your subjects" (وَ أجمَعُها لِرِضَى الرَّعيِهِ). *Ar-Ra'ia* refer to the people; that is, those whose rights must be respected. It does not have a negative connotation. Some people think that the word "*ra'iat*" is derogatory, whereas it refers to those whose rights must be observed. It means the masses. The expressions "*an-nās*" and "*ra'iat*" usually refer to the masses of the people, not to the elites. The focus of the Commander of the Faithful and of the Prophet ﷺ and of the Quran is on the masses of the people. It is the same group that we refer to as the multitudes or the vast majority of the people. It is the same group which the profligate elites oppose in political matters and in setting social policy, and which they refer to as 'populism'. To think that a specific group or class or party can be elected and invested in office, and for them to be the policy-makers and decision-makers and have control over the budget and, naturally, over all disbursements; and then to believe that when it comes to the apportioning of the profits, that they would recuse themselves like so many ascetics and insist that the masses of the people be the beneficiaries – such thoughts are very fanciful indeed, and we have seen and experienced that this is not the way things work. Nor are such thoughts in harmony with any logic.

And this is why the focus and emphasis of Imam Ali's ﷺ logic is on the masses. [According to this logic,] specific groups and elites are not credit worthy. Not in the sense that their rights should not be respected; but rather in the sense that their specific identity and character as a group should not be singled out for special treatment. And that is why Imam Ali advises Mālek that he should "let the dearest of [his] affairs be those which are the most comprehensive in [establishing] the satisfaction of [his] subjects" (وَ أَجمَعُها لِرِضَى الرَّعِيهِ).

"For the discontent of the common people invalidates the content of favorites, and the discontent of favorites is pardoned at (the achievement of) the content of the masses" (فَإِنَّ سُخطَ العامَّةِ يُجحِفُ بِرِضَى الخاصَّةِ). And it is for this reason that wherever the general population is dissatisfied with the performance of the ruling regime in any country, then the tenure of that regime will not last. This is an experience that has been realized in our country and in the Islamic Republic. Our people were unhappy with the performance of the previous regime, which strove to please the privileged classes: the rich, the great merchants, the big industrialists, the great landowners, and the numerous literati and artisans which were in their pay: from poets [and authors and journalists to] artists who accepted monies with which to glisten their whiskers. These were all well satisfied with the regime, but the masses of the people were dissatisfied; and we all saw how all that ended.

The criterion [by which] the work [of governance is to be evaluated] is the satisfaction or dissatisfaction of the general public. Why? Because if the general public is dissatisfied, the satisfaction of specific groups will be for naught and will be wasted. It could well be that a group of intellectuals and political elites support a ruler and his political order and that the people remain dissatisfied at the same time. This popular dissatisfaction will grow larger and larger, eventually destroying the satisfaction of the intellectual and political elite. Just as we saw that this is exactly what they did.

The converse of this also holds true: "whereas the discontent of elites and select groups is pardoned at [the achievement of] the satisfaction of the masses" (وَ إِنَّ سُخطَ الخاصَّهِ يُغتَفَرُ مَعَ رِضَى العامَّهِ). In other words, [such discontent] is not that important and does not have that great of an effect. Therefore, proceed along the policy of bringing about the satisfaction of the masses of the people. That is where His Eminence's outlook is most sagacious. And we have seen and felt [the wisdom of this policy] during the time of our tenure in office.

Note well the clarity of the guidelines which the Commander of the Faithful provides us when he tells us that if our policy of serving the general population upsets certain vested interests, that we should not let that bother us. This is the same clear policy guideline of the Islamic Republic which tells us never to barter away the satisfaction of the masses for the satisfaction of any given group of elites; and to let them remain dissatisfied. And the masses are comprised of the people; those who were present on the battlefields and on the front lines; those who were present at the Friday communal prayer service; and those who were and are present in all of the arenas of this revolution. Let *them* be satisfied with the performance of this governmental order. For it is they who are the ones which this order is duty-bound to support. Because that which brings a political order honor and pride is nothing other than its ability to satisfy the masses of its populace; and this is the policy of the Islamic social order and of the Islamic Republic [of Iran]: it is the same guideline that the Commander of the Faithful has given us.

[After all,] democracy is not just about electioneering and campaign promises and bringing a number of people to the voting booths and getting them to vote, and then to bid them farewell and have nothing to do with their interests after that! After this first half is realized, it is the turn of the second half: the turn of being answerable to the public.

"Moreover, none of the subjects is more burdensome upon the ruler in ease and less of a help to him in trials than his favorites. [None are] more averse to equity, more importunate in demands, less grateful upon bestowal, slower to pardon [the ruler upon his] withholding [favor] and more deficient in patience at the misfortunes of time than the favorites." (وَ لَيسَ اَحَدٌ مِنَ الرَّعِيَّةِ اَثقَلَ عَلَى الوالِي مَؤونَةً فِي الرَّخاءِ وَ اَقَلَّ مَعونَةً لَهُ فِي البَلاءِ وَ اَكرَهَ لِلإنصافِ وَ اسأَلَ بِالإلحافِ وَ اَقَلَّ شُكراً عِندَ الإعطاءِ وَ اَبطَاَ عُذراً عِندَ المَنعِ وَ اَضعَفَ صَبراً عِندَ مُلِمَّاتِ الدَّهرِ مِن اَهلِ الخاصَّةِ). Special interest groups are everywhere a burden [upon the government]. Firstly in times of peace and abundance,

117

their costs are greater to the government; their expectations are high; expecting all sorts of favors and opportunities. "And in times of difficulty, it is these same groups which pitch in the least" (وَ أَقَلَّ مَعُونَةً لَهُ فِي البَلاءِ). For example, if a war breaks out, or if there is a state of insecurity or if an enemy attacks, you will scarcely find any members of these groups volunteering in the field of battle.

"They are more averse to fairness and equity than anyone else" (وَ أكرَهَ لِلإنصافِ). They hate social justice and impartiality more than anyone else. "And they are more adamant in their demands than anyone else" (وَ آسأَلَ بالإلحافِ). Ordinary people write letters and request things too, of course. And sometimes, where the possibility exists, these requests will be granted, and sometimes they will not be; but that will be the end of it. But these special interest groups stick to you like leeches if there is something that they want. They will not let go until they succeed in tearing something away and taking it away with them.

"And when you give them something, they show the least gratitude" (وَ أَقَلَّ شُكراً عِندَ الإعطاءِ); [they act] as if it was a right of theirs that had to be fulfilled. They have no gratitude, unlike ordinary people. If you build a school in some far off corner of the country, for example, they pray for you, they show you kindness, and give thanks. The others, on the other hand, will not show any gratitude even if you provide them with the best facilities possible.

"And if one does not grant them anything, they will not accept one's reasons for not doing so, even if there is a perfectly good reason for it" (وَ أَبطَأَ عُذراً عِندَ المَنعِ). "And when the nation is experiencing difficult times, these people show the least amount of patience and forbearance" (وَ أضعَفَ صَبراً عِندَ مُلِمّاتِ الدَّهرِ). If the nation is struck by a natural disaster or some social plight, these people show the least amount of patience and complain the most. They show impatience and constantly stomp their feet on the ground in their impatience.

"Whereas the support base of the religion, and the solidarity of Muslims, and the preparedness of the community in the face of the enemy lie only with its common people (وَإِنَّما عَمادُ الدّينِ وَ جِماعُ المُسلِمينَ وَ العُدَّةُ لِلأَعداءِ

العامَّةُ مِنَ الأُمَّةِ). These are the words of Imam Ali; so if this is "populism", it is a populism of the Ālid variety; it is something that we respect and hold as sacred. "So let your inclination and affection be toward them" (فَليَكُن

صِغوُكَ لَهُم وَ مَيلُكَ مَعَهُم). The pillars of Islam in society and among the collectivity of the Muslim peoples and the preparedness to fight the enemies of Islam all lie with the great masses of the people, with the common folk. It is these people whose interests must be protected. This is a lesson that is handed down from the Commander of the Faithful, and this is how a peoples-oriented political order should be.

This [bifurcation into] special and popular interests is precisely the divide that we have been talking about in our time. Don't worry about the special interest groups; concern yourselves with the interest of the masses. This is Imam Ali's advice. That is not to say that we should not provide [due] support for the elite also. In the Islamic Republic, if a thief climbs the wall of an anti-revolutionary element, we have a duty to catch that thief and prevent him from continuing to steal, even if such a person's political stance runs counter to the security interests of the state; there can be no doubt about that.

But in general, our society is to be divided into two groups, one consisting of the vast majority of the people (the masses) whose hearts and minds and faith are always on the side of their religion and will fight to support it with all of their being; and another group which consists of the elite, whether these be the elites within the scientific community, or the technical elites, or some other vocation. We must be positioned on the side of the masses. This does not mean that we should be "populist" as the word is presently conceived. No; the masses does not mean the idiots and the fools; it does not mean the uninformed and the illiterate. It means the majority of the people. It means the vast majority of the people whose income bracket is usually below par. Whereas the elites are those elements within society who are "clever" and quick-witted and whose arms have a greater reach and can grab the ladle's handle faster and skim the cream, placing it in their own bowls. And what about the masses, who are they? They are those who did not reach the pot first and did not skim the cream and place it in their own bowls. They are the ones who will divide what is left of the pot among themselves once the cream has been skimmed from it. These are the masses, and we must be positioned alongside them in their frontlines. And so, take a look around you to see how it is possible to join them on their frontline. Sometimes we claim to be on the side of the people, which is something that we have done since the beginning of the revolution, thank God 🙰. But there are also other times where our support for the people is nothing but lip service. It is this second instance that is important and which we have to pay attention to, although the first instance is not a lie either. The Islamic Republic works in the interest of the people, praise be to God 🙰.

Another sentence which appears in this bountiful epistle is the following: "Then look into the affairs of your administrators" (ثُمَّ انْظُرْ فِي أُمُورِ عُمَّالِكَ). First comes the way in which the administrators are chosen: "Employ them [only after] having tested [them]" (فَاسْتَعْمِلْهُمُ اخْتِبَاراً); in other words, see who has more merit for each position. We talk about meritocracy often nowadays, but it must be implemented in the true sense of the word. The Commander of the Faithful commends us to it here in this *Epistle*. "And appoint them not with favoritism or arbitrariness, [for these two attributes embrace different kinds of oppression and treachery]" (وَ لَا تُوَلِّهِم مُحَابَاةً وَ أَثَرَةً); because if you do not appoint them with due consideration to [Islamic] values and ideals, and just on the basis of an acquaintanceship which you might have, [then you will have committed an act of oppression].

Then [Imam Ali proceeds to] describe the specific character traits of these candidates: "Among them look for people of experience and modesty from righteous families [who are] foremost in Islam, for they are nobler in moral qualities, more genuine in dignity and less concerned with ambitious designs, and they perceive more penetratingly the consequences of affairs." (ثُمَّ أَسْبِغْ عَلَيْهِمُ الْأَرْزَاقَ وَ تَوَخَّ مِنْهُمْ أَهْلَ التَّجْرِبَةِ وَ الْحَيَاءِ).

120

Then once you have chosen your administrators, provide for their livelihoods. I always tell the administrators to constantly monitor their subordinates; to monitor them constantly and not to forget the task of their supervision. You have seen how watchmen and security guards constantly scan their flashlights and aim them into all of the nooks and crannies; you should constantly monitor and control your affairs in a similar manner. And so to repeat: do not be neglectful of the task of supervising your administrators.

"Then investigate their actions" (ثُمَّ تَفَقَّد أَعمالَهُم). See if they are performing their tasks or not, and whether they are performing them properly, or whether there are problems in the performance of their jobs. "Dispatch truthful and loyal observers [to watch] over them, for your investigation of their affairs in secret will incite them to carry out their trust faithfully and to act kindly toward the subjects" (وَ ابعَثِ العُيونَ مِن آهلِ فَإِنَّ تَعاهُدَكَ في السِّرِّ لِأُمورِهِم حَدوَةٌ لَهُم عَلَى استِعمالِ الآمانَةِ وَ الرِّفقِ الصِّدقِ وَ الوَفاءِ عَلَيهِم بِالرَّعِيَّةِ). Investigate! This is the sum total of about twenty lines that tells us it is imperative that we monitor and investigate [the performance of our appointed administrators and managers]. We must never rest assured that all is well, even if the person who is in charge of a given portfolio is competent and has our trust; because it is entirely possible that he is himself trustworthy but that those who work under him are not. For you are not aware of the personalities of those who work for him. Or contrarily, he might himself be trustworthy, but does this mean that he also does not make mistakes? Or that his choices and decisions are ideal? Thus, you must monitor even those in whom you have trust.

"Be heedful of aides. If one of them should extend his hand in a treacherous act, concerning which the intelligence received against him from your observers concurs," (فَإِن أَحَدٌ مِنهُم بَسَطَ يَدَهُ إِلَى خِيانَةٍ اجتَمَعَت بِها عَلَيهِ); "and if you are satisfied with that as a witness, subject him to corporeal punishment and seize him for what befell from his action. Then install him in a position of degradation, brand him with treachery and gird him with the shame of accusation." (إِكتَفَيتَ بِذلِكَ شاهِداً فَبَسَطتَ عَلَيهِ)

(العُقوبَةً في بَدَنِهِ وَ آخَذتَهُ بِما آصابَ مِن عَمَلِهِ). In such an eventuality, he must be punished. Punishment can take on all sorts of shapes and forms, of course; and each infringement calls for a punishment that is commensurate with the crime; and that is how we should proceed.

Imam Ali continues: "[Let your care for the prosperity of the earth be deeper than your care for the collecting of land tax, for it will not be gathered except in prosperity.] Whoever exacts land tax without prosperity has desolated the land and destroyed the servants [of God ﷻ]. [His affairs will remain in order but briefly]." (وَ إِنَّما يُؤتَى خَرابُ الأرضِ مِن إعوازٍ آهلِها). The desolation of the land results from the indigence of the people. His Eminence mentions this as a tenet and a reality. And he uses the word 'land' (*ard*) in the sense of the 'country' of Egypt, to which Mālik Ashtar has been appointed as its governor. And of course other 'lands' such as the Levant, Iraq, Iran, Medina, and any other place which has a governor is comparable to Egypt. What the Imam is saying is that the land to which you are travelling will prosper if you are successful in making its people prosper; but that if you make or keep the people poor, then the land will be similarly lacking in prosperity and will be desolate. It is the people who must make the land prosper with their energies and motivations. It is the people's innovations and hard work that brings prosperity throughout the land.

Imam Ali then says, "Truly the destruction of the earth only results from the destitution of its inhabitants, and its inhabitants become destitute only when rulers concern themselves with amassing and hoarding [wealth]" (وَ إِنَّما يُعوِزُ آهلُها ... لِاشرافِ آنفُسِ الوُلاةِ عَلَى الجَمعِ عَلَى الجَمعِ). It is the action of the rulers that causes the indigence of the people, because they want to amass for themselves whatever wealth is produced by the toil of the people. This is what causes the people's poverty. "The rulers want to amass wealth because they have misgivings about the endurance [of their own rule] and when they profit little from warning examples" (لِاشرافِ آنفُسٍ). (الوُلاةِ عَلَى الجَمعِ عَلَى الجَمعِ وَ سوءٍ ظَنِّهم بِالبَقاءِ). And they enter into this hoarding mentality because they mistakenly feel insecure about the future. One should not have a negative outlook. One should be optimistic with respect to God ۝ the Sublimely Exalted and with respect to oneself. And finally, he says that rulers and administrators hoard wealth because they have a negative outlook concerning their own future, and because "they profit little from warning examples" (وَ قِلَّةِ انتِفاعِهِم بِالعِبَر).

If rulers and Islamic authorities are to perform these duties properly, they stand in need of another attribute which is sincerity and the desire to perform their work [solely] for seeking God's ۝ good pleasure, and for the sake of maintaining their good relationship with God ۝. The responsible authorities in the Islamic political order must not only be answerable to the people, they must also answer to God ۝; for if they are not answerable to God ۝, the work they do for the people, i.e. that which is their main preoccupation, will flounder. The factor which provides the main support for their mission and for all of the responsibilities which they are tasked with is thier relationship with God ۝. And this is why the Commander of the Faithful continues in his epistle to Mālek Ashtar as follows.

"Set aside for yourself in what is between you and God ۝ the most excellent of these hours and the fullest of these portions" (وَ اجعَل لِنَفسِكَ فيما بَينَكَ وَ بَينَ اللهِ أفضَلَ تِلكَ المَواقيتِ). In other words, do not establish your connection to the Lord and do not offer your ritual devotions to him and do not supplicate Him when you are tired and worn out after a long day's work. He goes on to add, "Even though all of these hours belong to God ۝ if in them your intention is correct and because of them the subjects remain secure" (وَ إِن كانَت كُلُّها لله). When you are in a position of authority in the Islamic social order, all of your time and work belongs to God ۝, as long as your intention is pure and as long as you do not do anything that aggrieves the people. But at the same time, set aside a time among all of these activities – all of which are a form of worship – set aside a time to seclude yourself with God ۝. This is the image of those who are in a position of authority in the Islamic social order as we find them in the instructions of Imam Ali.

"Then surely the ruler has favorites and intimates" (ثُمَّ إِنَّ لِلوالي خاصَّةً وَ بِطانَةً). This will occur no matter what, and it cannot be avoided. *Khāssa* means special; ones friends and closer acquaintances. *Batāna* means those who are allowed into one's inner circle: close friends and family. When all is said and done, one will have familial bonds, and one will have sons and sons in law, brothers, and close friends. And every administrator and person in authority will ineluctably have these also. His Eminence Imam Ali stipulates three attributes for these. One of these is *ist'thār*, meaning the quality of wanting everything for oneself. *Ist'thār* is the opposite of selflessness and self-sacrifice (*īthār*), which means separating something from oneself and entrusting it to someone else; whereas *ist'thār* means separating something from someone else and joining it to oneself. And *tatāwul* means the arrogance of encroachment and the transgressing of bounds in this respect, as in: "I am so and so's son!" Or, "I am so and so's brother, or daughter, or bridegroom, or bride!" *Tatāwul* usually connotes a sense of arrogance having to do with the failure to respect the bounds of others; it is an act of over-reaching.

Another characteristic which can normally be seen in these is their lack of fairness in business transactions (وَ قِلَّةُ إِنصافٍ في مُعامَلَةٍ), which is why they don't play fair at times in their business dealings. But it should be noted that the Imam is not saying that everyone who is close to those in positions of authority are endowed with all three of these characteristics without exception. Rather, what the grammatical form connotes is that there are a certain number of people within that given group who display such attributes. Thus, not everyone in those circles is necessarily characterized in this way. And it is only natural that decent and reasonable people should be among the people in these circles too. But the point is that we are not immune from such people being within the ranks of those who are close to us.

OK, so what are we to do with these types of people? His Eminence provides us with instructions as to what we are to do: "Remove the substance of these [qualities] by cutting off the means of obtaining these situations" (فَاحسِم مادَّةَ اولئِكَ بِقَطعِ آسبابِ تِلكَ الآحوالِ). Cut off that which engenders these three qualities. And what causes these qualities? What is the main cause? His Eminence instructs us to find the main causes and to cut them off at their roots. Let us assume for the sake of the argument that one such person feels that he is immune from prosecution, because he believes that he has the backing of such and such a ruler or high official. Another cause of such difficulties is that these kinds of people tend to grab up and monopolize all of the important positions in the administration. In other words, they become in charge of all of the positions which give them power over the livelihood of others. And naturally, these types of positions engender a sense of excessive expectations in those who are vested in such positions.

What is meant by "the administrators of the political order" are none other than the ladies and gentlemen who are present here. Each of you has been entrusted with a section of the government, and each of you must therefore be on your guard about this "inner circle" that surrounds you and me. You should not wonder whose inner circle you belong to; rather, it is you yourselves who each have his or her own inner circles which you have to be on your guard against. The instructions are addressed to you. One of the many things which causes these inner circle types to deviate from that which is right is that they are listened to and respected by other people on account of the positions that they hold or because of the fact that they are immune from prosecution. Suppose that the son or brother or close friend of such and such a high official goes to the office of some other official – a minister, for example – and asks for something. Well, the minister will grant him his request; I mean without your having written a letter of recommendation for him or having put in a good word for him. This is something that must be rectified.

You are a good person yourself, but this person who is related to you in some way or has been appointed to his position by you or is your close relative goes to others in positions of authority in the state and obtains concessions on your credit or by riding on your coattail, as it were.

Suppose he goes to the Central Bank and demands a certain sum [as a loan]. Would the head of the Central Bank dare to turn down the son or brother of so and so? Or he goes to the Ministry of Trade and asks that approvals be given for such and such a trade deal. Or he goes to the Ministry of Oil or to the State Department (or Foreign Office) and demands to be positioned on some mission abroad. Will anyone dare to stand in his way? Because they imagine that there is a high official behind such requests and demands. His Eminence states, "Cut off the means of their influence." (فَاحسِم مادَّة أُولَئِكَ بِقَطعِ). Make a proclamation to the effect that if my son or my brother or anyone else who is within my inner circle comes to you and asks you for something, do not on any account comply with their demands unless it be presented through the normal channels. Make this announcement to all other governmental officials who hold positions of authority, not to accept whatever it is that they ask of you, if you are approached in such a way. And let such people know that if they do anything illegal, they will be subject to prosecution like everyone else. This kind of behavior and attitude must be cut off at its roots. It must not be allowed to fester and grow among one's inner circle.

Then His Eminence provides some examples in order to flesh out the details: "Bestow no fiefs upon any of your entourage or relatives, nor let them covet from you the acquisition of a landed estate" (وَ لا تُقطِعَنَّ لِاَحَدٍ مِن حاشِيَتِكَ وَ حامَّتِكَ قَطيعَةً). *Hāshia* means those who surround you, your entourage, and *hāma* means your relatives and those who are close to you: your sons and daughters, your sons in law, your brothers and other close relatives. His Eminence instructs [Mālik] not to bestow fiefs (*qat'iya*) to any of these, where *qat'iya* means a tenure of land subject to feudal obligations which it was customary for feudal lords to hand out. Of course what it means here is not the fiefdoms which were common in Russia and Europe where serfs were legally bound to a landed estate and required to perform labor for the lord of that estate in exchange for a personal allotment of land. It was not like that in our regions. But there was this phenomenon where [the king, or sultan or governor of a province] would entrust a large tract of land to the trust of someone else [in exchange for military services in protection of the realm], and where the recipient could keep a portion of the tax revenue. His Eminence tells us never to bestow fiefs (*qaṭīʿa*) to any of our sons and close relatives.

Of course fiefs existed in those days, whereas they no longer exist today. And so the equivalent today would be not to bestow positions of high responsibility to them, and not to make them the managing directors of a company or of a state-run concern. And this applies just as much to close friends as it does to one's family; the prohibition is not necessarily limited to one's kith and kin. For there are some close friends to whom one is closer than one's own relatives; they are one's confidants or "bosom buddies". It makes no difference: the instruction is never to give any of these people anything, and never to entrust them with any position of responsibility. In other words, think of this as a red line: no positions, no companies to run, no concessions, no government contracts, or any other advantage. Let them go and find their own way in the world during the few years of your tenure in a position of responsibility.

"Nor let them covet from you the acquisition of a landed estate which would bring loss to the people bordering upon it in [terms of] a water supply or a common undertaking, the burden of which would be imposed upon them" (في شِرْبٍ أَو عَمَلٍ مُشْتَرَكٍ يَحمِلونَ مَؤُونَتَهُ عَلَى غَيرِهِم). There were common water supplies in those days, and someone who was within a high official's inner circle would go and take more than his share of the water; or there might be some joint venture, and the person would drag his feet and not pull his own weight. His Eminence instructs us not to provide our inner circle with the opportunity to do such things. Naturally, these instances have different examples in our own time. For example, paying taxes, where such people either do not pay their taxes at all or underpay and let others shoulder the majority of the tax burden on a property where they are a shareholder. And so on.

"And if you do make such bestowals… its benefit would be for those [who acquired the fiefs or other favors] and not for you, and its fault

would be upon you in this world and in the world to come." (فَيَكونَ مَهنَأً ذلِكَ
لَهُم دونَكَ وَ عَيبُهُ عَلَيكَ فِي الدُّنيا وَ الآخِرَةِ). His Eminence then goes on to say,
"Impose that which is right (*al-haqq*) upon whomsoever it is incumbent,
whether he be related to you or not" (وَ ٱلزِم الحَقَّ مَن لَزِمَهُ مِنَ القَريبِ وَ البَعيدِ). If,
for example, there is the right of a retributory warrant (*ḍimān*), either in
the form of a *dīya* (financial compensation) or a *qiṣāṣ* (comparable
retribution); or if the state has a right of collecting an unpaid tax, "impose
that which is right (*al-haqq*) upon him".

"Be patient in this and look to your [ultimate] account (*muḥtasib*),
however this may affect your relatives and favorites. Desire the ultimate
end in that of it [imposing the right] which weighs heavily against you, for
its outcome will be praiseworthy (وَ كُن في ذلِكَ صابِراً مُحتَسِباً واقِعاً ذلِكَ مِن قَرابَتِكَ
وَ خاصَّتِكَ حَيثُ وَقَعَ). What His Eminence means is to put your trust in God
🕮 and to do it on His account, as it were, and bring forbearance to bear as
it is not an easy task to hold your relatives and close ones to account. And
of course it is something that is easier said than done. And entrust your
fate in God's 🕮 hands, and allow whatever fate that is to befall your friends
and relatives to befall them; it makes no difference: surrender to God's 🕮
will, as many before you have failed in this difficult trial. I can tell you that
many a contender has failed here, and they are unable to withstand [the
pressure of the job's requirements] when it comes to themselves or their
loved ones. And it sometimes can be the case where a person does indeed
withstand the pressure, but then others will pile more pressure on by saying
things like, "Sir, they treated you and your sons and daughters so
disgracefully; how do you allow such behavior? Why do you exercise such
forbearance and restraint in the face of such treatment?" They apply
pressure from within, and this is what makes one give in. Thus, it is a very
difficult job indeed, and that is why the Commander of the Faithful
focuses on this issue and tells Mālik Ashtar [to do what needs to be done]
"however this may affect your relatives and favorites" (واقِعاً ذلِكَ مِن قَرابَتِكَ وَ
خاصَّتِكَ حَيثُ وَقَعَ).

Imam Ali continues in a consoling tone, as if in consolation for the great and demanding work that Mālik Ashtar is about to undertake, and for the difficulties and hardships which he will have to endure. "Desire the ultimate end in that of imposing that which is right which weighs heavily against you, for its outcome will be praiseworthy" (وَ ابتَغِ عاقِبَتَهُ بِما يَثقُلُ عَلَيكَ مِنهُ فَإِنَّ مَغَبَّةَ ذلِكَ مَحمودَةٌ). The pressures and heavy burdens that you will be bearing as a result of being vested in this office accrue as a result of the ultimate end that you are after, so bear them with patience and longanimity. Yearn for the ultimate end of this action, which is a good and praiseworthy end. Know that you will not lose as a result of this tenure. Endure these pressures knowing that when all is said and done, you will have profited from it. And needless to say, the profit that is being spoken of here is in two parts, one of which is an other-worldly profit, and the other part of which pertains to this world. So let us experience these hardships and endure these pressures to some extent and then see if we feel profited by it. If we do this, we will gain the trust of the people. A purity [of purpose] will be seen in those in positions of authority within the order and the light of this purity will naturally be reflected in and shine within the souls of the people. When such an action is taken by anyone in positions of authority, it will completely transform the entire political climate within our society.

"If any of your subjects should suspect you of an injustice, explain to them your justification. By your explanation turn their suspicions away from yourself" (وَ إِن ظَنَّتِ الرَّعِيَّةُ بِكَ حَيفاً فَأَصحِر لَهُم بِعُذرِكَ وَ اعدِل عَنكَ ظُنونَهُم بِإِصحارِكَ). Another one of the pieces of advice which Imam Ali gives to Mālik Ashtar is that if ever you should become the subject of a misunderstanding on the part of the people, you should provide them with you explanation of the matter quickly. In other words, it should not be the case that if some people say that we just came and spent money from the public purse and even stole some of it for ourselves, that we should react by saying to hell with them, we did no such thing. When people raise concerns, we should not ignore them. We should go before the people, tell them that what they are saying is not the case, and explain the truth to them: that this is not the case, and no such thing has happened. Explain away all the rumors that arise and "turn their suspicions away from yourself" by your explanations.

"Thereby you train your soul (*nafs*), act kindly to your subjects and justify [yourself] in a manner to attain your need, i.e., setting them on the way of that which is right" (وَ إِعذاراً تَبلُغُ بِهِ حاجَتَكَ مِن تَقويمِهِم عَلَى الحَقِّ فَإِنَّ في ذلِكَ رِياضَةً مِنكَ لِنَفسِكَ وَ رِفقاً بِرَعِيَّتِكَ). This will benefit both you and the people. The benefit for you is that, because being under suspicion and coming out and explaining the misunderstanding away is a difficult task, it will train your soul to know that you will always be able to justify your deeds, and that you must be answerable to the people for your mistakes. It is an exercise in austerity, and the very act of undertaking such an exercise diverts one away from error. On the other hand, it is beneficial for the people because it unruffles their feathers and it is a balm on their wounds. And all this will enable you to set the people on the path of that which is right, i.e. to make progress in improving the lives of the people.

What I would like to add as a commentary on the words of this noble man to the friends here present is that firstly, one of the things that solves these problems [that we have] is for those who are in positions of authority in the political order to live lives of simplicity. I beseech the gentlemen here to take this matter perfectly seriously. In other words, you should plan your lives in accordance with this [request]. Fight the tendency to want to live out your lives like so many aristocrats! You are not of the aristocratic class! We [in the Islamic social order] do not have an aristocratic class as the phrase is understood in the world. "The nobility of the Islamic community carry Qurans." (أشرافُ أُمَّتي حَمَلَةُ القُرآنِ). The [Islamic] nobility (*ashāb al-layl*) are those who stay awake at night either for the purpose of devotion or in order to work for the benefit of others. We do not have an aristocratic class in the sense that is understood in the world where there are a bunch of people who are in charge of running the country who live lives of extravagance and unimaginable wealth and overindulgence. Aristocracy as so defined is a terrible phenomenon and we are free of it. But the tendency toward aristocratic lifestyles does indeed exist, and it is something which we must resist. This is something which I insist upon.

Now, all that having been said, it is possible for there to be differences within our lives; it is possible that the life of one of us is better and more comfortable than that of his other friends and colleagues. Well, tastes and habits and circumstances vary. I do not want to draw a line on one side of which is a lifestyle that is acceptable and on the other side of which is one that is not. There are limits, after all. But pretense to an aristocratic lifestyle is a great sin and is perhaps a greater sin than living an aristocratic life itself, but one that is hidden from public view and not in the limelight. This is the point that I would like to make: let us not fan the flames of this desire to live like aristocrats by pretending to do so! Well, sit down and go to work in the various ministries, in your personal lives, and in what can be seen in the hustle and bustle of everyday life, so that the middle classes and those who live a less-than-average life no longer feel at a distance from you in terms of your lifestyles. Do this in order to dissociate yourselves from the carpetbaggers who have taken advantage of the situation after the revolution to fill their bags, and to demonstrate that you are not a part of them. Therefore, do not promote an aristocratic lifestyle, but wage war against it, especially before the cameras and in front of the gaze of the people.

"[Never reject a peace to which your enemy calls you and in which is God's ﷻ pleasure, for in peace there is ease for your soldiers, relaxation from your cares and security for your land. But] be cautious, very cautious, with your enemy after [having made] peace with him, for the enemy may have drawn near in order to take advantage of [your] negligence. Therefore be prudent and have doubts about trusting your enemy in this [matter]" (فَإِنَّ العَدُوَّ رُبَّما قارَبَ لِيَتَغَفَّلَ فَخُذ بِالحَزمِ وَ اتَّهِم في ذلِكَ حُسنَ الظَّنِّ). O Mālik! The enemy sometimes draws close to you in order to catch you unawares. Therefore, act with prudence, wisdom, and great care when confronting the enemy. The last part of the sentence means to put aside trusting your enemy, for there is no room for good will with an enemy which cannot be seen. Rather, one should be suspicious and on one's guard. The Islamic *ommat* (Arabic: *ummah*) and the authorities of the Islamic governmental order are duty-bound to confront the enemy carefully and with precision and vigor wherever signs of the enemy can be seen. The concern and matter of a community is not an individual concern such that someone can say that he foregoes the enmity of the enemy. What is at issue and at stake is the welfare of the entire community and its entire history. The people who are responsible for administering the Islamic social order must not allow the enemy to infiltrate the community, either in the order's governmental offices, in its various key posts, or in the form of deceptive and duplicitous foreign friends. Because the enemy will strike at a moment which is opportune for them and not for us. And that is why it is necessary for the Islamic community to recognize its enemies.

Verses from the Quran continue this line of thought:

وَكَذَٰلِكَ جَعَلْنَا لِكُلِّ نَبِيٍّ عَدُوًّا شَيَاطِينَ الْإِنسِ وَالْجِنِّ يُوحِي بَعْضُهُمْ إِلَىٰ بَعْضٍ زُخْرُفَ الْقَوْلِ غُرُورًا ۚ وَلَوْ شَاءَ رَبُّكَ مَا فَعَلُوهُ ۖ فَذَرْهُمْ وَمَا يَفْتَرُونَ ﴿١١٢﴾ وَلِتَصْغَىٰ إِلَيْهِ أَفْئِدَةُ الَّذِينَ لَا يُؤْمِنُونَ بِالْآخِرَةِ وَلِيَرْضَوْهُ وَلِيَقْتَرِفُوا مَا هُم مُّقْتَرِفُونَ ﴿١١٣﴾

[6:112] And thus it is that against every prophet We have set up as enemies the evil forces from among humans as well as from among invisible beings that whisper unto one another glittering half-truths meant to delude the mind. But they could not do this unless thy Sustainer had so willed: stand, therefore, aloof from them and from all their false imagery! [6:113] Yet, to the end that the hearts of those who do not believe in the life to come might incline towards Him, and that in Him they might find contentment, and that they might earn whatever they can earn [of merit] …

Which means that the enemies teach each other false words in order to ruin the environment of Islamic society, and in order to undermine the confidence of people. God ﷻ orders the Prophet ﷺ to leave them be and to stay away from their slander; that is, leave them alone and continue on your path.

If someone is accused of something or is defamed and slandered, if he is to accomplish anything, he should not pay any attention and should continue his journey. But those who do not have proper faith in the Day of Judgment and the Hereafter, listen to and accept what the enemies invent and like what they say. And they will end up with the same fate which will befall the enemy when it comes to God's ﷻ turn to judge.

Because the letter is long, I have had to be selective, and have chosen those passages which I thought we are most in need of hearing. His Eminence says, "Beware of being pleased with yourself" (وَ اِیّاكَ وَ الإعجابَ بِنَفسِكَ وَ الثِّقَةَ بِما یُعجِبُكَ مِنها). *A'jāba bi nafsika* means being pleased with oneself and His Eminence warns Mālik not to fall into this trap. One sometimes sees good traits within oneself: one's intelligence, one's bodily strength, a powerful memory storing a vast amount of knowledge, the power of one's rhetoric or the pleasant sound of one's voice, attractive looks, and so on. Once you recognize that the feeling of being pleased with yourself exists in you – which means that this pleasure hides your faults – then know that this is a dangerous pass; this is that same feeling which His Eminence is warning us about.

It might be the case that you think to yourself that you see one or more of these merits in yourself and think, what of it? After all, I did graduate first in my class, for example, in such and such a course; or I performed such and such a sensitive task with distinction! What should I do? Ignore these distinctions? No, acknowledge all of your distinctions, but also acknowledge all of your defects and shortcomings and negative points right alongside your merits and distinctions. What makes a person self-satisfied is the way in which he sums up the entirety of his personality. We tend to see all our own good points and to ignore those that are bad, shameful, and disgraceful. And this results in an overall evaluation which amounts to one who is self-satisfied and enamored with himself; which of course is problematic. Thus, it is imperative that we see our weaknesses along with our strengths.

"Do not rely on that part of yourself which pleases you and which loves lavish praise" (وَ ايّاكَ وَ الإعجابَ بِنَفسِكَ وَ الثِّقَةَ بِما يعجِبُكَ مِنها). In other words, do not necessarily believe that this merit does indeed exist in you. Sometimes a person might think that he has certain merits, whereas this is nothing but an illusion, because he has compared himself with a person who is at a lower level, and given himself a higher comparative score; whereas if he were to be compared to others who are at a higher level, he would not score well at all. Therefore, do not be so sure about what you see in yourself.

"Beware of ... the love of lavish praise, for these are among Satan's surest opportunities to efface what there might be of the good that the righteous person has done" (وَ حُبِّ الإطراءِ فَإِنَّ ذلِكَ مِن أوثَقِ فُرَصِ الشَّيطانِ في نَفسِهِ لِيَمحَقَ ما يَكونُ مِن إحسانِ المُحسِنينَ). Satan will come and destroy those good deeds, and take away the effects of those good and righteous acts from you.

Following this is an important passage where we are advised: "Beware of reproaching (*mann*) your subjects in your good-doing [for their insufficient acknowledgment of their debt to you]" (ايّاكَ وَ المَنَّ عَلَى رَعِيَّتِكَ بِإحسانِكَ). Do not look for praise for the work that you do for the people, because it was a duty of yours which you duly performed. "Do not overstate the deeds that you have performed" (أوِ التَّزَيُّدَ فيما كانَ مِن فِعلِكَ). Sometimes one does something, then exaggerates the merits of what he has done to several times its true value. "And do not break your promises" (أو أن تَعِدَهُم فَتُتبِعَ مَوعِدَكَ بِخُلفِكَ). Be persistent in striving to fulfill that which you have promised the people you will do; i.e. consider yourself committed to the promises you make. Do not take the attitude of one who thinks, "Well, we tried, but it just wasn't meant to be". No: insist on accomplishing what you have promised. Of course it sometimes happens that an emergency situation arises [that is out of your hands], and that is a different case. But you should do all that is within your power to keep the promises that you have made; and do not do so with an attitude of expecting to be thanked or praised for having performed your duty. "For reproach voids good-doing, overstatement takes away the light of the truth and breaking one's promises results in the hatred of God ﷻ and men" (وَ فَإِنَّ المَنَّ يُبطِلُ الإحسانَ

(التَّزَيُّدَ يَذهَبُ بِنورِ الحَقِّ وَ الخُلفَ يوجِبُ المَقتَ عِندَ اللهِ وَ النّاسِ).

Imam Ali says that we are not to exaggerate the merits of the work that we do, nor to do it with the expectation of thanks and praise. And if we have promised to do something for the people, that we should do it. He then says that if you do reproach the people for not praising you or thanking you for merely performing your duty, that this will have the effect of annulling the benefit of that good deed for you; and exaggeration will snuff out the light of truth. I.e. even the amount of truth that exists will be dimmed in the eyes of the people. And if you break your promises, this is something that is hateful in the eyes of God ﷻ as well as of mankind. "God ﷻ the Sublimely Exalted has said, [61:3] *Most loathsome is it in the sight of God ﷻ that you say that which you do not do!*" And while it is true that these are words which the Commander of the Faithful has addressed to Mālik Ashtar, but at the same time, they are addressed to all of us as well.

"Beware of hurrying to [accomplish] affairs before their [proper] time" (وَ اِيّاكَ وَ العَجَلَةَ بِالأمورِ قَبلَ آوانِها). In one of his sermons, the Commander of the Faithful compares hurrying to do something before its time to picking unripe fruit, stating concerning anyone who does so that it is as if they have sown and tended to and harvested [a field] for someone else in that they reap no benefit from it. If you sow seeds on someone else's land, he will reap the rewards, not you. And if you sow seeds or plant saplings on your own land and tend to them, but reap any fruit that it might yield before its time and before it can be of any use, then you have wasted all of your efforts. He tells us not to hurry in that sermon, and repeats that advice here, where he goes on to say that we "should not neglect work when it is possible to perform it and not to delay it" (آو التَّسَقُّطَ فيها عِندَ إِمكانِها). Nor should we "stubbornly persist in them when they become impracticable (أَوِ اللَّجَاجَةَ فِيهَا إِذَا تَنَكَّرَت). For example, we might have thought of a project, brought our reasons for why it is a good idea to bear, started it, and expended much effort and energy in its pursuit. Still, there were dissenting voices who thought it was not a good idea, whose advice we decided not to heed. And now we have reached an impasse with the project where it has become evident that the dissenting voices were correct. This is where one must recant his words and his position. There is no shame in that. Thus, we should not persist in our obstinacy when it is clear that we are on the wrong track. "And neither should we show hesitation or weakness when it becomes clear that performing something is necessary" (أَوِ الوَهنَ عَنها إِذَا استَوضَحَت). So we must "put everything in its place and perform every action at its appropriate time."

Let us appreciate the value of these words, God ۞ willing. And of course these words are addressed to myself, first and foremost, and only secondarily to you who are its audience. And I repeat that I pray God ۞ that these words have an effect on me. And if we appreciate the value of these words and gain something from them, God ۞ willing, and learn from them, then we will have become the beneficiaries of a truly great benefit. That is, the greatest of the tasks before us are those which His Eminence Imam Ali has mentioned here in his epistle. And of course this epistle and this instruction is very strange indeed. Despite its frequent recitation and translation into different languages, I know that most government officials have not read the Epistle carefully from beginning to end or contemplated its contents with care. Truly, we must sit and read this *Epistle* with the same deliberation and care with which we read the Quran. Of course, the Arabic text of the *Nahj ul-Balāgha* is difficult, because it has many beautiful linguistic expressions and rhetorical devices [which are unfamiliar to us]. That is where the difference lies compared to the other expressions that we find in the rest of the *hadith* report corpus. And that is why it is difficult to read the *Nahj ul-Balāgha* and to understand its meaning, unless one has a mastery of classical Arabic. Therefore, it is necessary to refer to its translations, or to bilingual editions which must be read with great care. Each section of this *Epistle* must be read with great care. Sometimes meanings are hidden or latent in a single one of its words. Therefore, it is necessary to refer to its translation into the text according to the translation. Truly, when one contemplates the depths of the meanings hidden within this *Epistle,* one feels a sense of inferiority compared to its greatness.

Well, this was the content of what we said on the occasion of the month of Ramadan. We are minutes away from the time designated to break our fasts. Dear brothers and honored sisters; you are the top officials of the country and the heaviest loads are weighing on your shoulders. Truly, if we were to take a tally, among the ordinary tasks that a person can undertake in life, nothing could be more demanding than the tasks which you and I have accepted. It is a vocation which entails both intellectual pressure as well as physical stress, and has a heavy burden of responsibility both towards our fellow countrymen as well as before God ﷻ. If, God ﷻ forbid, we are not able to receive the reward of the Divine in the work which we have taken on, then all of these burdens and pressures and hardships which we endure will be for naught.

Endeavor to ensure that God ﷻ is satisfied with the great burden of responsibility which you have shouldered, for if God ﷻ is not pleased with your performance, even if all of the world is pleased – which of course they will never be: (إِنَّ رِضَا النَّاسِ لَايُملَكُ) it is not possible to obtain the satisfaction of all of the people – even then, it will be to no avail. This is also a truism: that one cannot obtain the complete satisfaction of all of the people. There will always be some who remain unsatisfied, some who are ungrateful, some who do not understand a given situation, and others who understand but who deny its reality anyway. These things exist. And in this midst, there might be some who are satisfied. But even if we assume for the sake of the argument that it was possible to obtain everyone's satisfaction, then, truly, this would not suffice [as a recompense] of all of these burdens and pressures and hardships which we endure. Someone who has taken on such a heavy burden of responsibility and who carries that burden with such difficulty; and who faces such grave consequences if he or she should falter for a brief moment – how can the obtaining of everyone's satisfaction possibly save him from his great concerns and the great trials and tribulations which he or she has to face? Unless it be that God 🌼 is pleased with one's performance. Indeed, it is only God's 🌼 satisfaction which must be the objective of our every effort and exertion. The Commander of the Faithful thought like this and his intention was that his appointees and agent and those who worked for him should be like this also. If God 🌼 accepts this from us, we consider ourselves to be one of the agents and employees of that great nobleman. Of course, we do not consider ourselves to be at the level of Mālek Ashtar and Ammār Yāser and Muhammad b. Abu Bakr; but at a lower level. After all, is seems that that great nobleman has appointed us to the mission which we face today. And as a matter of fact, the *Epistle* which His Eminence has addressed to Mālek Ashtar is just as equally addressed to us. It is our duty to take each and every one of the instructions which are given to Mālek Ashtar as our own. And the first instance is fearing God 🌼 and having *taqwā*.

May God 🌼 grand you success in all of your endeavors. And when we sit down to break our fasts, God 🌼 willing, let us continue this conversation where all of the discussion does not necessarily have to relate to the world to come, but can be more down to earth as well.

3 Imam Ali's Epistle to Mālik Ashtar

Imam Ali wrote these instructions to al-Ashtar al-Nakha'i [1] when he appointed him governor of Egypt and its provinces at the time the rule of Muhammad ibn Abi Bakr was in turmoil. It is the longest set of instructions in the *Nahj ul-balaghah*. Among all his letters it embraces the largest number of good qualities.

1 Introduction [2]

In the Name of God 🕮, the Merciful, the Compassionate

This is that with which 'Ali, the servant of God 🕮 and Commander of the Faithful, charged Malik ibn al-Harith al-Ashtar in his instructions to him when he appointed him governor of Egypt: to collect its land tax, [3] to war against its enemies, to improve the condition of the people and to engender prosperity in its regions. He charged him to fear God 🕮, to prefer obedience to Him (over all else) and to follow what He has directed in His Book-both the acts He has made obligatory and those He recommends [4] - for none attains felicity but he who follows His directions, and none is overcome by wretchedness but he who denies them and lets them slip by. (He charged him) to help God-glory be to Him-with his heart, his hand and his tongue, [5] for He-majestic is His Name-has promised to help him who exalts Him. [6]

And he charged him to break the passions of his soul and restrain it in its recalcitrance, for the soul incites to evil, except inasmuch as God ☙ has mercy. [7]

2 Commands and Instructions Concerning Righteous Action in the Affairs of the State

Know, O Malik, that I am sending you to a land where governments, just and unjust, have existed before you. People will look upon your affairs in the same way that you were wont to look upon the affairs of the rulers before you. They will speak about you as you were wont to speak about those rulers. And the righteous are only known by that which God ☙ causes to pass concerning them on the tongues of His servants. So let the dearest of your treasuries be the treasury of righteous action. Control your desire and restrain your soul from what is not lawful to you, for restraint of the soul is for it to be equitous in what it likes and dislikes. Infuse your heart with mercy, love and kindness for your subjects. Be not in face of them a voracious animal, counting them as easy prey, for they are of two kinds: either they are your brothers in religion or your equals in creation. Error catches them unaware, deficiencies overcome them, (evil deeds) are committed by them intentionally and by mistake. So grant them your pardon and your forgiveness to the same extent that you hope God ☙ will grant you His pardon and His forgiveness. For you are above them, and he who appointed you is above you, and God ☙ is above him who appointed you. God ☙ has sought from you the fulfillment of their requirements and He is trying you with them.

Set yourself not up to war against God ☙, [8] for you have no power against His vengeance, nor are you able to dispense with His pardon and His mercy. Never be regretful of pardon or rejoice at punishment, and never hasten (to act) upon an impulse if you can find a better course. Never say, "I am invested with authority, I give orders and I am obeyed," for surely that is corruption in the heart, enfeeblement of the religion and an approach to changes (in fortune). If the authority you possess engender in you pride or arrogance, then reflect upon the tremendousness of the dominion of God ﷻ above you and His power over you in that in which you yourself have no control. This will subdue your recalcitrance, restrain your violence and restore in you what has left you of the power of your reason. Beware of vying with God ﷻ in His tremendousness and likening yourself to Him in His exclusive power, for God ﷻ abases every tyrant and humiliates all who are proud.

See that justice is done towards God ﷻ [9] and justice is done towards the people by yourself, your own family and those whom you favor among your subjects. For if you do not do so, you have worked wrong. And as for him who wrongs the servants of God ﷻ, God ﷻ is his adversary, not to speak of His servants. God ﷻ renders null and void the argument of whosoever contends with Him. Such a one will be God's ﷻ enemy until he desists or repents. Nothing is more conducive to the removal of God's ﷻ blessing and the hastening of His vengeance than to continue in wrongdoing, for God ﷻ harkens to the call of the oppressed and He is ever on the watch against the wrongdoers. [10]

Let the dearest of your affairs be those which are middlemost in rightfulness, [11] most inclusive in justice and most comprehensive in (establishing) the content of the subjects. For the discontent of the common people invalidates the content of favorites, and the discontent of favorites is pardoned at (the achievement of) the content of the masses. Moreover, none of the subjects is more burdensome upon the ruler in ease and less of a help to him in trial than his favorites. (None are) more disgusted by equity, more importunate in demands, less grateful upon bestowal, slower to pardon (the ruler upon his) withholding (favor) and more deficient in patience at the misfortunes of time than the favorites. Whereas the support of religion, the solidarity of Muslims and preparedness in the face of the enemy lie only with the common people of the community, so let your inclination and affection be toward them. Let the farthest of your subjects from you and the most hateful to you be he who most seeks out the faults of men. For men possess faults, which the ruler more than anyone else should conceal. So do not uncover those of them which are hidden from you, for it is only encumbent upon you to remedy what appears before you. God ☙ will judge what is hidden from you. So veil imperfection to the extent you are able; God ☙ will veil that of yourself which you would like to have veiled from your subjects. Loose from men the knot of every resentment, sever from yourself the cause of every animosity, and ignore all that which does not become your station. Never hasten to believe the slanderer, for the slanderer is a deceiver, even if he seems to be a sincere advisor.

Bring not into your consultation a miser, who might turn you away from liberality and promise you poverty; [12] nor a coward, who might enfeeble you in your affairs; nor a greedy man, who might in his lust deck out oppression to you as something fair. Miserliness, cowardliness and greed are diverse temperaments which have in common distrust in God ☙. [13]

Truly the worst of your viziers are those who were the viziers of the evil (rulers) before you and shared with them in their sins. Let them not be among your retinue, for they are aides of the sinners and brothers of the wrongdoers. You will find the best of substitutes for them from among those who possess the like of their ideas and effectiveness but are not encumbranced by the like of their sins and crimes; who have not aided a wrongdoer in his wrongs nor a sinner in his sins. These will be a lighter burden upon you, a better aid, more inclined toward you in sympathy and less intimate with people other than you. So choose these men as your special companions in privacy and at assemblies. Then let the most influential among them be he who speaks most to you with the bitterness of the truth and supports you least inactivities which God ☙ dislikes in His friends, however this strikes your pleasure. Cling to men of piety and veracity. Then accustom them not to lavish praise upon you nor to (try to) gladden you by (attributing to you) a vanity you did not do, [14] for the lavishing of abundant praise causes arrogance and draws (one) close to pride.

Never let the good-doer and the evil-doer possess an equal station before you, for that would cause the good-doer to abstain from his good-doing and habituate the evil-doer to his evildoing. Impose upon each of them what he has imposed upon himself. [15]

Know that there is nothing more conducive to the ruler's trusting his subjects than that he be kind towards them, lighten their burdens and abandon coercing them in that in which they possess not the ability. So in this respect you should attain a situation in which you can confidently trust your subjects, for trusting (them) will sever from you lasting strain.[16] And surely he who most deserves your trust is he who has done well when you have tested him, and he who most deserves your mistrust is he who has done badly when you have tested him. Abolish no proper custom (sunnah) which has been acted upon by the leaders of this community, through which harmony has been strengthened and because of which the subjects have prospered. Create no new custom which might in any way prejudice the customs of the past, lest their reward belong to him who originated them, and the burden be upon you to the extent that you have abolished them.

Study much with men of knowledge ('*ulama*') and converse much with sages (*hukama*') concerning the consolidation of that which causes the state of your land to prosper and the establishment of that by which the people before you remained strong. [17]

3 Concerning the Classes of Men

Know that subjects are of various classes, none of which can be set aright without the others and none of which is independent from the others. Among them are (I.) the soldiers of God 🌟, (2.) secretaries for the common people and the people of distinction, [18] executors of justice [19] and administrators of equity and kindness, [20] (3.) payers of *jizyah* [21] and land tax, namely the people of protective covenants [22] and the Muslims, (4.) merchants and craftsmen and (5.) the lowest class, the needy and wretched. For each of them God 🕮 has designated a portion, and commensurate with each portion He has established obligatory acts (*faridah*) in His Book and the Sunnah of His Prophet-may God 🕮 bless him and his household and give them peace-as a covenant from Him maintained by us. [23]

Now soldiers, by the leave of God 🕮, are the fortresses of the subjects, the adornment of rulers, the might of religion and the means to security. The subjects have no support but them, and the soldiers in their turn have no support but the land tax which God 🕮 has extracted for them, (a tax) by which they are given the power to war against their enemy and upon which they depend for that which puts their situation in order and meets their needs. Then these two classes (soldiers and taxpayers) have no support but the third class, the judges, administrators and secretaries, for they draw up contracts, [24] gather yields, and are entrusted with private and public affairs. And all of these have no support but the merchants and craftsmen, through the goods which they bring together and the markets which they set up. They provide for the needs (of the first three classes) by acquiring with their own hands those (goods) to which the resources of others do not attain. Then there is the lowest class, the needy and wretched, those who have the right to aid and assistance. With God 🕮 there is plenty for each (of the classes). Each has a claim upon the ruler to the extent that will set it aright. But the ruler will not truly accomplish what God 🕮 has enjoined upon him in this respect except by resolutely striving, by recourse to God's 🕮 help, by reconciling himself to what the truth requires and by being patient in the face of it in what is easy for him or burdensome.

(I.) Appoint as commander from among your troops that person who is in your sight the most sincere in the way of God 🙶 and His Prophet 🙶 and of your Imam, [25] who is purest of heart and most outstanding in intelligence, who is slow to anger, relieved to pardon, gentle to the weak and harsh with the strong and who is not stirred to action by severity nor held back by incapacity. Then hold fast to men of noble descent and those of righteous families and good precedents, then to men of bravery, courage, generosity and magnanimity, for they are encompassed by nobility and embraced by honor.

Then inspect the affairs of the soldiers [26] as parents inspect their own child. Never let anything through which you have strengthened them distress you, and disdain not a kindness you have undertaken for them, even if it be small, for it will invite them to counsel you sincerely and trust you. Do not leave aside the examination of their minor affairs while depending upon (the examination of) the great, for there is a place where they will profit from a trifling kindness, and an occasion in which they cannot do without the great.

Among the chiefs of your army favor most him who assists the soldiers with his aid and bestows upon them what is at his disposal to the extent that suffices both them and the members of their families left behind. [27] Then their concern in battle with the enemy will be a single concern, for your kind inclination toward them will incline their hearts to you. [28] Verily the foremost delight of the eye for rulers is the establishment of justice in the land and the appearance of love for them among the subjects. [29] But surely the subjects' love will not appear without the well-being of their breasts, and their sincerity (toward rulers) will not become free from blemishes unless they watch over their rulers, find their governments of little burden and cease to hope that their period (of rule) will soon come to an end. Therefore let their hopes be expanded, and persist in praising them warmly and taking into account the (good) accomplishments of everyone among them who has accomplished, for frequent mention of their good deeds will encourage the bold and rouse the indolent, God 🕮 willing.

Then recognize in every man that which he has accomplished, attribute not one man's accomplishment to another and fall not short (of attributing) to him the full extent of his accomplishment. Let not a man's eminence invite you to consider as great an accomplishment which was small, nor a man's lowliness to consider as small an accomplishment which was great.

Refer to God 🕮 and His Messenger any concerns which distress you and any matters which are obscure for you, for God-high be He exalted-has said to a people whom He desired to guide, "O believers, obey God 🕮, and obey the Messenger and those in authority among you. If you should quarrel on anything, refer it to God 🕮 and the Messenger" (IV, 59). To refer to God 🕮 is to adhere to the clear text of His Book, [30] while to refer to the Prophet 🕮 is to adhere to his uniting (*al-jami'ah*) Sunnah, not the dividing (*al-mufarriq*). [31]

(2a.) Then choose to judge (*al-hukm*) among men him who in your sight is the most excellent of subjects, i.e., one who is not beleaguered by (complex) affairs, who is not rendered ill-tempered by the litigants, [32] who does not persist in error, who is not distressed by returning to the truth when he recognizes it, whose soul does not descend to any kind of greed, who is not satisfied with an inferior understanding (of a thing) short of the more thorough, who hesitates most in (acting in the face of) obscurities, who adheres most to arguments, who is the least to become annoyed at the petition of the litigants, who is the most patient (in waiting) for the facts to become clear and who is the firmest when the verdict has become manifest; a man who does not become conceited when praise is lavished upon him and who is not attracted by temptation. But such (men) are rare.

Thereupon investigate frequently his execution of the law (*qada'*) and grant generously to him that which will eliminate his lacks and through which his need for men will decrease. Bestow upon him that station near to you to which none of your other favorites may aspire, that by it he may be secure from (character) assassination before you by men of importance. [33] (In sum) study that (i.e., the selection of judges) with thorough consideration, for this religion was prisoner in the hands of the wicked, who acted with it out of caprice and used it to seek (the pleasures of) the present world. [34]

(2b.) Then look into the affairs of your administrators. Employ them (only after) having tested (them) and appoint them not with favoritism or arbitrariness, for these two (attributes) embrace different kinds of oppression and treachery. [35] Among them look for people of experience and modesty [36] from righteous families foremost in Islam, [37] for they are nobler in moral qualities, more genuine in dignity and less concerned with ambitious designs, and they perceive more penetratingly the consequences of affairs. Then bestow provisions upon them liberally, for that will empower them to set themselves aright and to dispense with consuming what is under their authority; and it is an argument against them if they should disobey your command or sully your trust.

Then investigate their actions. Dispatch truthful and loyal observers (to watch) over them, for your investigation of their affairs in secret will incite them to carry out their trust faithfully and to act kindly toward the subjects. Be heedful of aides. If one of them should extend his hand in a treacherous act, concerning which the intelligence received against him from your observers concurs, and if you are satisfied with that as a witness, subject him to corporeal punishment and seize him for what befell from his action. Then install him in a position of degradation, brand him with treachery and gird him with the shame of accusation.

(3.) Investigate the situation of the land tax in a manner that will rectify the state of those who pay it, for in the correctness of the land tax and the welfare of the taxpayers is the welfare of others. The welfare of others will not be achieved except through them, for the people, all of them, are dependent upon the land tax and those who pay it. Let your care for the prosperity of the earth be deeper than your care for the collecting of land tax, for it will not be gathered except in prosperity. Whoever exacts land tax without prosperity has desolated the land and destroyed the servants (of God ﷻ). His affairs will remain in order but briefly.

So if your subjects complain of burden, [38] of blight, of the cutting off of irrigation water, of lack of rain, or of the transformation of the earth through its being inundated by a flood or ruined by drought, lighten (their burden) to the extent you wish their affairs to be rectified. And let not anything by which you have lightened their burden weigh heavily against you, for it is a store which they will return to you by bringing about prosperity in your land and embellishing your rule. You will gain their fairest praise and pride yourself at the spreading forth of justice among them. You will be able to depend upon the increase in their strength (resulting) from what you stored away with them when you gave them ease; and upon their trust, since you accustomed them to your justice toward them through your kindness to them. Then perhaps matters will arise which afterwards they will undertake gladly if in these you depend upon them, for prosperity will carry that with which you burden it. Truly the destruction of the earth only results from the destitution of its inhabitants, and its inhabitants become destitute only when rulers concern themselves with amassing (wealth), when they have misgivings about the endurance (of their own rule) [39] and when they profit little from warning examples.

(4) Then examine the state of your secretaries and put the best of them in charge of your affairs. [40] Assign those of your letters in which you insert your stratagems and secrets to him among them most generously endowed with the aspects of righteous moral qualities, a person whom high estate does not make reckless, that because of it he might be so bold as to oppose you in the presence of an assembly. (He should be someone) whom

negligence will not hinder from delivering to you the letters of your administrators, nor from issuing their answers properly for you in that which he takes for you and bestows in your stead; a person who will not weaken a contract which he binds for you, nor will he be incapable of dissolving what has been contracted to your loss; a man who is not ignorant of the extent of his own value in affairs, for he who is ignorant of his own value is even more ignorant of the value of others.

Let not your choosing of them be in accordance with your own discernment, confidence and good opinion, for men make themselves known to the discernment of rulers by dissimulating and serving them well, even though beyond this there may be nothing of sincere counsel and loyalty. Rather examine them in that with which they were entrusted by the righteous before you. Depend upon him who has left the fairest impression upon the common people and whose countenance is best known for trustworthiness. This will be proof of your sincerity toward God ﷻ and toward him whose affair has been entrusted to you.

Appoint to the head of each of your concerns a chief from among these men, (a person) who is neither overpowered when these concerns are great nor disturbed when they are many. Whatever fault of your secretaries you overlook will come to be attached to you. (4.) Then make merchants and craftsmen-those who are permanently fixed, those who move about with their wares and those who profit from (the labor of) their own body [41]-your own concern, and urge others to do so, [42] for they are the bases of benefits and the means of attaining conveniences. They bring (benefits and conveniences) from remote and inaccessible places in the land, sea, plains and mountains, and from places where men neither gather together nor dare to go. (The merchants and craftsmen) are a gentleness from which there is no fear of calamity and a pacifity from which there is no worry of disruption. [43] Examine their affairs in your presence and in every corner of your land.

But know, nevertheless, that in many of them is shameful miserliness, detestable avarice, hoarding of benefits and arbitrariness in sales. This is a source of loss to all and a stain upon rulers. So prohibit hoarding (*ihtikar*), for the Messenger of God-may God ☙ bless him and his household and give them peace-prohibited it. [44] Let selling be an openhanded selling, with justly balanced scales and prices which do not prejudice either party, buyer or seller. [45] As for him who lets himself be tempted to hoard after you have forbidden him (to do so), make an example of him and punish him, but not excessively.

(5.) Then (fear) God ☙, (fear) God ☙ regarding the lowest class, the wretched, needy, suffering and disabled who have no means at their disposal, for in this class there is he who begs and he who is needy (but does not beg). Be heedful for God's ☙ sake of those rights of theirs which He has entrusted to you. Set aside for them a share of your treasury (*bayt al-mal*) and in every town a share of the produce of the lands of Islam taken as booty (*sawafi al-islam*), [46] for to the farthest away of them belongs the equivalent of what belongs to the nearest. [47] You are bound to observe the right of each of them, so be not distracted from them by arrogance, for you will not be excused if, to attend to the very important affair, you neglect the trifling, So avert not your solicitude from them and turn not your face away from them in contempt.

Investigate the affairs of those (of the lowest class) who are unable to gain access to you, those upon whom eyes disdain to gaze and whom men regard with scorn. Appoint to attend exclusively to them a person whom you trust from among the God ☙ fearing and humble, and let him submit to you their affairs. Then act toward them in a manner that will absolve you before God ☙ on the day that you meet Him. [48] For among the subjects these are more in need of equity than others. In the case of each of them prepare your excuse with God ☙ by accomplishing for him his rightfully due (*al-haqq*). Take upon yourself the upkeep of the orphans and aged from among those who have no means at their disposal and do not exert themselves in begging. (All of) this is a heavy burden upon rulers. The truth (*al-haqq*), all of it, is a heavy burden. But God ☙ may lighten it for people who seek the final end, who admonish their souls to be patient and trust in the truth of God's 🌸 promise to them.

4 Commands and Prohibitions in Malik al-Ashtar's Best Interest

Set aside for those who have requests (*hajat*) from you a portion (of your time) in which you yourself are free to (attend) to them. Hold an open audience for them and therein be humble before God 🌸 who created you. Keep the soldiers and aides who are your bodyguards and police away from them so that their spokesman may address you without stammering (in fear), for I heard the Messenger of God-may God 🌸 bless him and his household and give them peace-say not (only) on one occasion, "No community shall be sanctified within which the rightfully due of the weak may not be taken from the strong without stammering (by the weak)". Furthermore suffer them to be coarse and faltering of speech and become not annoyed and angry with them. For that God 🌸 will outspread the wings of His mercy over you and make binding for you the reward of having obeyed Him. Bestow what you bestow in a pleasant manner and refrain (from granting requests when you must) gracefully and while asking pardon.

Then there are certain of your affairs which you must take in hand personally. Among them is giving an ear to your administrators when your secretaries have been unable to find the correct solution, and among them is attending to the requests of men when presented to you because the breasts of your aides have been straitened by them. [49]

Each day perform the work of that day, for to each belongs what is proper to it. Set aside for yourself in what is between you and God 🌸 the most excellent of these hours and the fullest of these portions, even though all of them belong to God 🌸 if in them your intention is correct and because of them the subjects remain secure. In making your religion sincerely God's 🌸 perform especially His obligations (*fara'id*), [50] which pertain only to Him. So give to God 🕮 of your body in your night and your day, and complete in a perfect manner, neither defectively nor deficiently, what brings you near to God 🕮, no matter what may befall your body (as a result). [51]

When you stand to lead men in the canonical prayers, neither drive (them) away (by praying too lengthily) nor mar (the prayer by performing it too quickly or faultily), for among men there are some who are ill and others who are needy. I asked the Messenger of God-may God 🕮 bless him and his household and give them peace-when he sent me to the Yemen, "How shall I lead them in prayer?" He said, "Lead them in prayer as the weakest of them prays, and be merciful to the believers." Furthermore, prolong not your seclusion (*ihtijab*) from your subjects, for rulers' seclusion from subjects is a kind of constraint and (results in) a lack of knowledge of affairs. Seclusion from them cuts rulers off from the knowledge of that from which they have been secluded. Then the great appears to them as small and the small as great. The beautiful appears as ugly and the ugly as beautiful. And the truth becomes stained with falsehood. The ruler is only a man. He does not know the affairs which men hide from him. There are no marks upon the truth by which the various kinds of veracity might be distinguished from falsehood.

Again, you are one of only two men: either you give generously in the way of the truth-then why seclude yourself from carrying out a valid obligation or performing a noble deed? Or else you are afflicted by niggardliness-then, then how quickly will men refrain from petitioning you when they despair of your generosity? Moreover, most requests men present to you are those which impose no burden upon you, such as a complaint against a wrong or the seeking of equity in a transaction.

Then surely the ruler has favorites and intimates, among whom there is a certain arrogation, transgression and lack of equity in transactions. Remove the substance of these (qualities) by cutting off the means of obtaining these situations. Bestow no fiefs upon any of your entourage or relatives, nor let them covet from you the acquisition of a landed estate [52] which would bring loss to the people bordering upon it in (terms of) a water supply or a common undertaking, the burden of which would be imposed upon them. [53] Its benefit would be for those (who acquired the fiefs) and not for you, and its fault would be upon you in this world and the next.

Impose the right (*al-ḥaqq*) upon whomsoever it is incumbent, whether he be related to you or not. [54] Be patient in this and look to your (ultimate) account (*muḥtasib*), [55] however this may affect your relatives and favorites. Desire she ultimate end in that of it (imposing the right) which weighs heavily against you, for its outcome will be praiseworthy.

If any of your subjects should suspect you of an injustice, explain to them your justification. By your explanation turn their suspicions away from yourself. Thereby you train your soul (*nafs*), act kindly to your subjects and justify (yourself) in a manner to attain your need, i.e., setting them in the way of the truth. Never reject a peace to which your enemy calls you and in which is God's 🙻 pleasure, for in peace there is ease for your soldiers, relaxation from your cares and security for your land. But be cautious, very cautious, with your enemy after (having made) peace with him, for the enemy may have drawn near in order to take advantage of (your) negligence. Therefore, be prudent and have doubts about trusting your enemy in this (matter).

If you bind an agreement between yourself and your enemy or cloth him in a protective covenant (*dhimmah*), guard your agreement in good faith and tend to your covenant with fidelity. Make of yourself a shield before what you have granted, [56] for men do not unite more firmly in any of the obligations (imposed upon them) by God 🙻 than in attaching importance to fidelity in agreements, [57] despite the division among their sects and the diversity of their opinions. The idolators (*al-mushrikūn*) had already adhered to that (honoring agreements) among themselves before the Muslims, by reason of the evil consequences of treachery that they had seen. So never betray your protective covenant, never break your agreement and never deceive your enemy, for none is audacious before God ﷻ but a wretched fool. God ﷻ has made His agreement and His protective covenant a security which He has spread among the servants by His mercy, and a sanctuary in whose impregnability they may rest and in whose proximity they may spread forth. [58] Within it there is no corruption, treachery or deceit.

Make not an agreement in which you allow deficiencies and rely not upon ambiguity of language [59] after confirmation and finalization (of the agreement). Let not the straitness of an affair in which an agreement before God ﷻ is binding upon you invite you to seek its abrogation unjustly. For your patience in the straitness of an affair, hoping for its solution and the blessing of its outcome, is better than an act of treachery. You would fear the act's consequence and (you would fear) that a liability before God ﷻ will encompass you, a liability from which you will not be exempted in this world or the next.

Beware of blood and spilling it unlawfully, for nothing is more deserving of vengeance (from God ﷻ), greater in its consequence or more likely to (bring about) a cessation of blessing and the cutting off of (one's appointed) term than shedding blood unjustly. God ﷻ -glory be to Him- on the Day of Resurrection will begin judgment among His servants over the blood they have spilt. [60] So never strengthen your rule by shedding unlawful blood, for that is among the factors which weaken and enfeeble it, nay, which overthrow and transfer it. You have no excuse before God ﷻ and before me for intentional killing, for in that there is bodily retaliation. [61] If you are stricken by error, and your whip, your sword or your hand should exceed their bounds in punishment- for in striking with the fists and all that exceeds it there is killing -never let the arrogance of your authority prevent you from paying the relatives of the killed their rightfully due (*al-ḥaqq*). [62]

Beware of being pleased with yourself, [63] of reliance upon that of yourself which pleases you and of the love of lavish praise, for these are among Satan's surest opportunities to efface what there might be of the good-doers' good-doing.

Beware of reproaching (*mann*) your subjects in your good-doing (for their insufficient acknowledgment of their debt to you), of overstating the deeds you have done and of making promises to them followed by non-observance. For reproach voids good- doing, [64] overstatement takes away the light of the truth and non- observance results in the hatred of God 🌸 and men. God-may He be exalted-has said, "Very hateful is it to God 🌸, that you say what you do not" (LXI, 3).

Beware of hurrying to (accomplish) affairs before their (proper) time, of neglecting them when they are possible, of stubborn persistence in them when they are impracticable and of weakness in them when they have become clear. So put everything in its place and perform every action at its time.

Beware of arrogating for yourself that in which men are equal; and of negligence in that which is of concern after it has become manifest to the eyes (of men), for these things will be held against you for (the benefit of) others ; [65] and (beware of negligence) of the fact that little remains until the coverings of affairs are lifted from you and justice is demanded from you for the wronged. [66]

Control the ardor of your pride, the violence of your strength, the force of your hand and the edge of your tongue. Be on thy guard against all these by restraining impulses and delaying force until your anger has subsided and you have mastered (your own) power of choice. But you will not gain control over that from your soul until you multiply your concern for remembering the return unto your Lord.

Incumbent upon you is to recall the just governments, the excellent customs, the Sunnah of our Prophet-may God 🌸 bless him and his household and give them peace-and the obligations (promulgated) in the Book of God 🌸, which preceded you among those of earlier times. Take as the model for your action what you have observed us to perform of them, and strive to your utmost to follow what I have instructed you in these my instructions. I trust in them to act as my argument against you so that you shall have no cause for your soul's hastening to its caprice. [67] I ask God ﷻ by the amplitude of His mercy, and His tremendous power to grant every desire, to bestow upon me and you in that wherein is His pleasure success in presenting Him and His creatures with a clear justification (for our actions). (May He bestow) excellent praise from among His servants, fair influence in the land, completion of blessings and manifold increase in honor. And (I ask) that He seal (the lives of) me and you with felicity (*al-sa'adah*) and martyrdom (*al-shahadah*). "Unto Him we are returning" (II, I56). Peace be upon the Messenger of God-may God ﷻ bless him and his good and pure household and grant them abundant peace. *Wa-l-salam.*

5 Endnotes:

[1] See the article "al-Ashtar" in the new Encyclopedia of Islam.

[2] The division into parts and the headings of parts two, three and four are taken from the commentary of Ibn Maytham.

[3]   The land tax (*kharaj*) was collected on the basis of the land's produce. See the Encyclopedia of Islam (new edition), vol. 3, pp. I030-s6.

[4]   Fara'id wa sunan. The first very often refer to those acts which are commanded by God ﷻ such as the five daily prayers, fasting during the month of Ramadan, etc.-in which case they are contrasted with the sunan, meaning the commands of the Prophet ﷺ, which are divided into the commands he gave orally (*qawl*), the acts he performed (*fi'l*) and the acts he allowed others to perform without criticising or protesting (*iqrar*). Here, however, since both kinds of acts are said to be mentioned in the Quran, the meaning is as translated.

[5]   " 'With his heart', or through firm belief; 'with his hand', or through holy war and exertion in His path; and 'with his tongue', or through speaking the truth, commanding the good and forbidding the evil" (Ibn Abi-l-Hadid, vol. I7, p. 3I)

[6]   Cf. Quran XLVII, 7, "O believers, if you help God 🕮, He will help you and confirm your feet", and other similar verses, such as XXII, 40.

[7]   Nearly a direct quotation from Quran XII, 53: "Surely the soul incites to evil, except inasmuch as my Lord has mercy."

[8]   "I.e., oppose Him not through acts of disobedience" (Ibn Abi-l-Hadid, vol I7, p- 33)

[9]   "i.e., Perform for Him the worship which He has made incumbent upon you and the requirements of intelligence and tradition" (Ibn Abi-l-Hadid, vol. I7, p- 35)-

[10]   Cf. Quran LXXXIX, I4: "Surely the Lord is ever on the watch."

[11]   *Awsatuha fi-l-haqq*, reference to the "golden mean". Here some of the commentators mention Aristotle and refer to such hadiths of the Prophet 🕮 as "The best of affairs is their middlemost." See for example T. al-Fakiki, al-Ra'i wa-l-ra'iyyah, vol. 2, Najaf, I940, pp. I08-II.

[12]   According to Ibn Abi-l-Hadid, this sentence is based upon the following Quranic verse: "The devil promises you poverty and bids you unto indecency; but God 🕮 promises you His pardon and His bounty" (II, 268). He explains that the commentators of the Quran say that here "indecency" (*al-fahsha'*) means "miserliness" (*al-bukhl*), and that the meaning of
"promises you poverty" is that he makes you believe you will become poor if you are generous with your wealth (vol. I7, p. 4I)

[13]   Ibn Abi-l-Hadid comments that if man trusts God 🕮 with certainty and sincerity, he will know that his life-span, his daily provision, his wealth and his poverty are foreordained and that nothing occurs but by God's 🕮 decree (vol. I7, p. 4I). Ibn Maytham points out that "distrust in God 🕮 begins with lack of knowledge (marifah) of Him." A person ignorant of His generosity and bounty will not know that He rewards what is expended in His path; hence he will be miserly in order to avoid poverty. He makes similar remarks concerning the qualities of cowardliness and greed.

[14]   According to Ibn Maytham this sentence is part of the description of those favorites who should be most influential. It means that the ruler "should train and discipline them by forbidding them from praising him lavishly or trying to make him happy by a false statement in which they attribute to him an act which he did not do and by this attribution cause him to be blameworthy." He then quotes the following verse of the Quran: "Reckon not that those who rejoice in what they have brought, and love to be praised for what they have not done-do not reckon them secure from chastisement" (III, I88).

[15]   "The evil-doer has imposed upon himself worthiness for punishment and the good-doer worthiness for reward" (Muhammad 'Abduh, vol. 3, p. 98).

[16]   Ibn Abi-l-Hadid comments on this passage as follows: "Whoever does good toward you will trust you and whoever does evil will shy away from you. This is because when you do good to someone and repeat it, you will come to believe that he likes you, and this belief will in turn lead to your liking him, for man by his very nature likes anyone who likes him. Then when you like him, you will feel secure with him and trust him. The reverse is true when you do evil toward someone . . ." (vol. I7, p. 47).

[17]   "He commands him to multiply his study with the men of knowledge, i.e., he should increase his study of the injunctions of the Shar'iah and the laws of religion; and he should increase his discussions with sages, or those whose knowledge is from God 🅰 Himself (al-'arifun billah) and who know the secrets of His servants and His land" (Ibn Maytham).

[18]   The secretaries (*kuttab*) are "those who are in charge of the ruler's own affairs and who write letters for him to his administrators and commanders. They take care of making arrangements and running the government administration (diwan)" (Ibn Abi-l-Hadid, vol. I7, p. 76).

[19]   Qudat al-adl, i.e. judges.

[20]   Administrators (*'ummal*) are government officials concerned with the affairs of "the general public, alms, religious endowments, the common

interest, etc." (Ibn Abi-l-Hadid, vol. I7, p. 69). For the meaning of the term 'amil (singular of *'ummal*) throughout Islamic history see the Encyclopedia of Islam (new edition), vol. I, p. 435.

[21]   Jizyah is the head tax upon "People of the Book"-followers of revealed religions other than Islam-who live under Muslim rule.

[22]   *Ahl al-dhimmah.* In other words the "People of the Book" who live in Muslim lands and are accorded hospitality and protection by Islam on condition of acknowledging Islamic political domination and paying the jizyah.

[23]   The covenant between man and God ✿ (*'ahd*) is frequently mentioned in the Quran and plays a central role in Islamic thought. Some representative Quranic verses are the following: "Only men possessed of minds remember, who fulfill God's ✿ covenant. . ." (XIII, 20); "And fulfill the covenant; surely the covenant shall be questioned of" (XVII, 34); "Made I not a covenant with you Children of Adam, that you should not serve Satan . . . and that you should serve Me?" (XXXVI, 59-60).

[24]   One commentator remarks as follows: "Land tax is only paid in accordance with an agreement between the owners of the land and the ruler, so it is necessary that the documents be drawn up. Furthermore officials have to collect the land tax from the land owners according to the terms of the contract. Here it is possible that disputes arise between the government officials and the landowners, so it will be necessary to refer to judges to solve these disputes." Mirza Habiballah al-Hashimi, *Minjaj al-bara'ah fi sharh nahj al-balaghah*, Tehran, I389/I969-70, vol. 20, p. 200.

[25]   I.e., Imam 'Ali himself.

[26]   "Of the soldiers" is a translation of the pronoun "their", and some question remains as to whether the pronoun does not in fact refer to the commanders. "If you say, 'But the soldiers of the army are not mentioned in the preceding section, only the commanders ,' I will answer, 'On the contrary, they were mentioned where he says "The weak and the strong" ' " (Ibn Abi-l-Hadid, vol. I7, p. 53)

[27]   *Khuluf* (plural of *khalf*) are the women, children and weak left behind when the men go on a journey.

[28]   Kind inclination toward the army means choosing for them the best of commanders, which will, in turn, cause them to love the ruler (Ibn Maytham).

[29]   According to Ibn al-Hadid, the context indicates that the word "subjects" refers specifically to the army. Al-Hashimi disagrees and states that 'Ali does in fact mean all the subjects. He mentions them in the section on soldiers because the soldiers have to keep order m the land among the subjects (vol. 20, p. 222-2).

[30]   See above, p. 56, note 48.

[31]   The commentators explain this as meaning that people should follow that part of the Sunnah of the Prophet ﷺ upon which all are agreed, not that concerning which there is a difference of opinion.

[32]   *Tamhakuhu-l-khusum.* According to Ibn Abi-l-Hadid, the verb here means to "make cantankerous or obstinate" (vol. 17, p. 59). Ibn Maytham, however, interprets the passage to mean that the judge should be someone "who is not overcome in his attempt to ascertain the truth by the obstinacy of the litigants. It has been said that this is an allusion to the person with whom the litigants are satisfied."

[33]   Muhammad 'Abduh explains that when the judge is given an elevated position, the ruler's favorites as well as the common people will be in awe of him and no one will dare slander him, out of fear of the ruler and respect for the person held in such high esteem by him (vol. 3, p. 105).

[34]   Ibn Abi-l-Hadid: "His words refer to the judges and rulers appointed by 'Uthman, for during his reign they did not judge rightfully but in accordance with caprice and in order to seek this world. Some people say that this happened because 'Uthman-may God's ﷺ mercy be upon him-was weak and his relatives were able to gain mastery over him. They disrupted the affairs of state without his knowledge, so the sin is upon them and 'Uthman is guiltless of what they were doing" (vol. 17, p. 60). See *Shi'ite Islam*, pp. 46-48.

[35]   Ibn Abi-l-Hadid reads *hum* for *hum'a*, i.e.: "For they (the administrators) are embraced by different kinds of oppression and treachery", and he interprets the sentence to refer to the administrators who served under the three caliphs before 'Ali. Al-Hashmi offers a number of arguments in support of this interpretation, Minhaj al-bara'ah vol. 20, pp. 246-9.

[36]   "Experience (*tajribah*) alone is not sufficient if the administrator is not endowed with modesty (*haya'*), for modesty is the basis of manliness (*muru'ah*). As the Prophet ﷺ said, 'Modesty brings only good', and 'Whoso has not modesty has not religion and will not enter Paradise' . . ." (al-Fakiki, *al-Ra'iwa l-ra'iyyah*, vol. 2, p. 38).

[37]   I.e., those families who were first to enter Islam. "This is because.... righteousness of family determines the way men are raised, and being foremost in Islam indicates nobility of character . . ." (Ibid., p. 39).

[38]   Whether as the result of the land tax itself or the oppression of the tax collectors (Ibn Abi-l-Hadid, vol. I7, p. 72).

[39]   Ibn Abi-l-Hadid offers two possible explanations of this clause. According to the first the words "*su' zannihim bi-l-baqa*" would have to be translated "they think wrongly about endurance", which means that they think their own existence will endure and they forget death and dissolution. In the translation however, I have followed the second interpretation, which he explains as meaning "They imagine they will be deposed and replaced, so they seize upon opportunities, appropriate wealth and show no concern for the prosperity of the land" (vol- I7v p- 73)

[40]   "Know that the secretary alluded to by the Commander of the Faithful is he who nowadays is commonly called the 'vizier', for he is entrusted with the management of the affairs of the ruler's person and in all of them is his deputy. The letters of the administrators come to him and their answers are issued by him. He puts the (affairs of the) administrators in order and is supervisor over them. In fact he is the 'secretary of the secretaries' and for this reason is known as the vizier in the absolute sense. It is said that the secretary has three prerogatives before

the king: to remove the veil from him (i.e., he has access to his personal affairs, even in the harem), to accuse traitors before him and to make secrets known to him . . ." (Ibn Abi-l-Hadid, vol. I7, p. 79).

[41]   Ibn Abi-l-Hadid explains that the first two of these groups are merchants -those who have shops and those who travel with their wares- and the third group are the craftsman (vol. I7, p. 84).

[42]   The translation of this sentence is rather free and follows Ibn Abi-l-Hadid's first interpretation. He adds that it is also permissible to read the sentence as follows: "Accept counsel (from me) for the good of merchants and craftsmen and counsel (others) concerning them" (vol. I7, pp. 83-4).

[43]   This is a literal translation of a passage which Ibn Abi-l-Hadid explains as follows: "Than the Imam says, 'Surely they are a gentleness', that is to say, merchants and craftsman are so. He seeks Malik al-Ashtar's sympathy and favor for them and he says they are not like taxcollectors and commanders of the army, for they have to be sustained, protected and taken care of, the more so since there is no fear of calamity from them, neither in property where they might be disloyal (as in the case of the taxcollectors) nor in the government where they might work corruption (as in the case of the commanders of the army)" (vol. I7, p. 84).

[44]   "According to the Sixth Imam, Ja'far al-Sadiq (founder of the Ja'fari, i.e. Twelve-Imami

Shi'ite, school of law), 'It is reprehensible (*makruh*) to hoard and to leave men with nothing. And it is said that it is forbidden (haram), and this latter view is more correct. As was said by the Prophet 🕮 of God 🕮, "Mercy is upon him who imports, and curses upon him who hoards". Surely hoarding is forbidden under two conditions: First, that food-i.e. wheat, barley, dates, raisins, clarified butter, or salt-be held back seeking an increase in price. Second, if there is no other distributor to be found . . .'." Quoted in al-Fakiki, *Al RaT wa-lra'iyyah*, vol 2, p. I65.

[45]   Cf. Quran LXXXIII, I-2: "Woe to the stinters who, when they measure against the people, take full measure, but, when they measure for them or weigh for them, they skimp."

[46]   Reference to the principle alluded to in the following verse of the Quran (VIII, 4I): "Know that, whatever booty you take, the fifth of it is God's ✿ and the Messenger's and the near kinsman's and the orphan's and for the needy and the traveler".

[47]   "In other words, all poor Muslims are equal in their shares, there is no 'farthest away' or

'nearest'. Prefer not him who is near to you or to one of your favorites over him who is far from you and without any connection to you or reason for you to turn toward him. It is also possible that he means that the produce of tbe land taken as booty in a certain area should not be distributed only to the needy of that area, for the right to the produce of the land is the same whether a person is far from that land or resides in it" (Ibn Abi-l-Hadid, vo1. I7v pp. 86-7)-

[48]   The "meeting with God" is mentioned in a number of Quranic verses, such as the following: "They indeed are losers who deny their meeting with God" (VI, 3I).

[49]   " 'The breasts of aides are straitened' by expediting the removal of grievances. They love to postpone attending to them, either in order to seek personal gain or to demonstrate their own authority" (Muhammad 'Abduh, vol. 3, p- II4)

[50]   i.e. the obligatory acts such as the five daily prayers.

[51]   The references to the body are due especially to the particularly physical nature of the daily canonical prayers. Ibn Abi-l-Hadid explains the last clause as meaning, "Even if that wearies you and impairs your body and your strength" (vol I7, p. 90).

[52]   The words "acquisition of a landed estate" (*i'tiqad ;uqdah*) might be translated literally as the "binding of a contract". The commentators, such as Ibn Abi-l-Hadid (vol. I7, p. 97) Ibn Maytham and Muhammad 'Abduh (vol 3, p. II)explain it as translated (*iqtina' day'ah* or *tamlik day'ah*).

[53]   "His words . . . explain the methods of cutting off the causes referred to: the bestowal of a fief upon one of the entourage or a relative, and his desire to acquire a landed estate which will harm those people bordering upon it in terms of the water supply or a common undertaking- such as a building, etc.-while he imposes the burden of the undertaking on man, are the causes of the above- mentioned situations . . ." (Ibn Maytham).

[54]   Or "whether near (*qarib*) to you or far away (*ba'id*)." I.e., whoever he might be, bring the person who has committed a wrong to justice.

[55]   I.e., realize that you will be rewarded in the next world.

[56]   "That is, even if you yourself should perish, act without treachery" (Ibn Abi-l-Hadid, vol. I7, p. I07).

[57]   The importance of observing covenants and agreements is referred to frequently in the Quran. See for example, XVI, 9I: "Fulfill God's covenant, when you make covenant, and break not the oaths after they have been confirmed . . .". See also VI, I53; XIIL 20; XVII, 34 et al.

[58]   According to Ibn Abi-l-Hadid (vol. I7) p. I09)) "in whose proximity they may spread forth" means "while dwelling in its proximity they may disperse in search of their needs and desires". 'Abduh explains the verb translated here as "spread forth" (*yastafid'un*) to mean "swiftly take refuge" (vol. 3, p. II8), but the first interpretation seems more likely.

[59]   Lahn qawl, "color of words". Ibn Maytham explains this expression as meaning "ambiguity, dissimulation or allusion." Ibn Abi-l-Hadid's explanation is similar: "He forbids him when making an agreement between himself and his enemy to break it by relying upon a hidden interpretation or the tenor of the words, or by saying, 'Surely I meant such and such, I did not have the apparent sense of the words in mind' " (vol. I7, p. I09).

[60]   Ibn Abi-l-Hadid cites the following hadith of the Prophet: "On the Day of Resurrection the first thing which God will judge upon among the servants is blood which has been spilled" (vol. I7, p. III).

[61]   "Then he advises him that intentional killing involves retaliation, and he says 'bodily retaliation'. In other words, intentional killing makes the destruction of the physical body necessary, just as you have destroyed the body of the person killed. The Imam's intention is to frighten him with these words, and they are more effective than if he had merely said, 'surely in that there is retaliation' " (Ibn Abi-l-Hadid, vol. I73 p. III).

[62]   Like retaliation in cases of intentional murder, compensation in cases of unintentional killing are determined by the Shari'ah. Cf. Quran IV, 92-3: "It belongs not to a believer to slay a believer, except it be by error. If any slays a believer by error, then let him free a believing slave, and bloodwit is to be paid to his family unless they forego it as a freewill offering. If he belong to a people at enmity with you and is a believer, let the slayer set free a believing slave. If he belong to a people joined with you by a compact, then bloodwit is to be paid to his family and the slayer shall set free a believing slave . . . And whoso slays a believer wilfully, his recompense is Gehenna . . .".

[63]   Ibn Abi-l-Hadid cites several sayings of the Prophet 🕌, including the following: "There are three mortal perils: yielding to niggardliness, following caprice and being pleased with oneself" (vol. I7, p. II4).

[64]   Cf. Quran II, 264: '4'0 believers, void not your freewill offerings with reproach and injury."

[65]   Ibn Abi-l-Hadid comments: For example, if it is pointed out to the commander that one of his favorites is performing a reprehensible act in secret, and if he then ignores that act, this will be to the benefit of the person doing the act, but not to his own benefit (vol. I75 p. II6). [66] Cf. Quran L, I9-22: "And death's agony comes in truth; that is what thou wast shunning! . . . 'Thou wast heedless of this; therefore We have now removed from thee thy covering, and so thy sight today is piercing'." Ibn Maytham remarks that when the veils of affairs are lifted from man at death, he sees the reality of these affairs and what God 🌿 has prepared for him of good and evil: "The day every soul shall find what it has done of good brought forward, and what it has done of evil . . ." (Quran III, 30).

[67] Cf. Quran LXXIX, 40-I: "*But as for him who feared the Station of his Lord and forbade the soul its caprice, surely Paradise shall be the refuge.*"

4 Imam Ali's Epistle to Malik Ashtar (Arabic)

حديث:

و من كتاب له (عليه السلام)كتبه للأشتر النخعي لما ولاه على مصر و أعمالها حين اضطرب أمر أميرها محمد بن أبي بكر، و هو أطول عهد كتبه و أجمعه للمحاسن

بِسْمِ اللَّهِ الرَّحْمَنِ الرَّحِيمِ ، هَذَا مَا أَمَرَ بِهِ عَبْدُ اللَّهِ عَلِيٌّ أَمِيرُ الْمُؤْمِنِينَ مَالِكَ بْنَ الْحَارِثِ الْأَشْتَرَ فِي عَهْدِهِ إِلَيْهِ حِينَ وَلَّاهُ مِصْرَ جِبَايَةَ خَرَاجِهَا وَ جِهَادَ عَدُوِّهَا وَ اسْتِصْلَاحَ أَهْلِهَا وَ عِمَارَةَ بِلَادِهَا.

أَمَرَهُ بِتَقْوَى اللَّهِ وَ إِيثَارِ طَاعَتِهِ وَ اتِّبَاعِ مَا أَمَرَ بِهِ فِي كِتَابِهِ مِنْ فَرَائِضِهِ وَ سُنَنِهِ الَّتِي لَا يَسْعَدُ أَحَدٌ إِلَّا بِاتِّبَاعِهَا وَ لَا يَشْقَى إِلَّا مَعَ جُحُودِهَا وَ إِضَاعَتِهَا وَ أَنْ يَنْصُرَ اللَّهَ سُبْحَانَهُ بِقَلْبِهِ وَ يَدِهِ وَ لِسَانِهِ فَإِنَّهُ جَلَّ اسْمُهُ قَدْ تَكَفَّلَ بِنَصْرِ مَنْ نَصَرَهُ وَ إِعْزَازِ مَنْ أَعَزَّهُ وَ أَمَرَهُ أَنْ يَكْسِرَ نَفْسَهُ مِنَ الشَّهَوَاتِ وَ يَزَعَهَا عِنْدَ الْجَمَحَاتِ فَإِنَّ النَّفْسَ أَمَّارَةٌ بِالسُّوءِ إِلَّا مَا رَحِمَ اللَّهُ ثُمَّ اعْلَمْ يَا مَالِكُ أَنِّي قَدْ وَجَّهْتُكَ إِلَى بِلَادٍ قَدْ جَرَتْ عَلَيْهَا دُوَلٌ قَبْلَكَ مِنْ عَدْلٍ وَ جَوْرٍ وَ أَنَّ النَّاسَ يَنْظُرُونَ مِنْ أُمُورِكَ فِي مِثْلِ مَا كُنْتَ تَنْظُرُ فِيهِ مِنْ أُمُورِ الْوُلَاةِ قَبْلَكَ وَ يَقُولُونَ فِيكَ مَا كُنْتَ تَقُولُ فِيهِمْ وَ إِنَّمَا يُسْتَدَلُّ عَلَى الصَّالِحِينَ بِمَا يُجْرِي اللَّهُ لَهُمْ عَلَى أَلْسُنِ عِبَادِهِ فَلْيَكُنْ أَحَبَّ الذَّخَائِرِ إِلَيْكَ ذَخِيرَةُ الْعَمَلِ الصَّالِحِ فَامْلِكْ هَوَاكَ وَ شُحَّ بِنَفْسِكَ عَمَّا لَا يَحِلُّ لَكَ فَإِنَّ الشُّحَّ بِالنَّفْسِ الْإِنْصَافُ مِنْهَا فِيمَا أَحَبَّتْ أَوْ كَرِهَتْ.

167

وَ أَشْعِرْ قَلْبَكَ الرَّحْمَةَ لِلرَّعِيَّةِ وَ الْمَحَبَّةَ لَهُمْ وَ اللُّطْفَ بِهِمْ وَ لَا تَكُونَنَّ عَلَيْهِمْ سَبُعاً ضَارِياً تَغْتَنِمُ أَكْلَهُمْ فَإِنَّهُمْ صِنْفَانِ إِمَّا أَخٌ لَكَ فِي الدِّينِ وَ إِمَّا نَظِيرٌ لَكَ فِي الْخَلْقِ يَفْرُطُ مِنْهُمُ الزَّلَلُ وَ تَعْرِضُ لَهُمُ الْعِلَلُ وَ يُؤْتَى عَلَى أَيْدِيهِمْ فِي الْعَمْدِ وَ الْخَطَإِ فَأَعْطِهِمْ مِنْ عَفْوِكَ وَ صَفْحِكَ مِثْلَ الَّذِي تُحِبُّ وَ تَرْضَى أَنْ يُعْطِيَكَ اللَّهُ مِنْ عَفْوِهِ وَ صَفْحِهِ فَإِنَّكَ فَوْقَهُمْ وَ وَالِي الْأَمْرِ عَلَيْكَ فَوْقَكَ وَ اللَّهُ فَوْقَ مَنْ وَلَّاكَ وَ قَدِ اسْتَكْفَاكَ أَمْرَهُمْ وَ ابْتَلَاكَ بِهِمْ وَ لَا تَنْصِبَنَّ نَفْسَكَ لِحَرْبِ اللَّهِ فَإِنَّهُ لَا يَدَ لَكَ بِنِقْمَتِهِ وَ لَا غِنَى بِكَ عَنْ عَفْوِهِ وَ رَحْمَتِهِ وَ لَا تَنْدَمَنَّ عَلَى عَفْوٍ وَ لَا تَبْجَحَنَّ بِعُقُوبَةٍ وَ لَا تُسْرِعَنَّ إِلَى بَادِرَةٍ وَجَدْتَ مِنْهَا مَنْدُوحَةً وَ لَا تَقُولَنَّ إِنِّي مُؤَمَّرٌ آمُرُ فَأُطَاعُ فَإِنَّ ذَلِكَ إِدْغَالٌ فِي الْقَلْبِ وَ مَنْهَكَةٌ لِلدِّينِ وَ تَقَرُّبٌ مِنَ الْغِيَرِ وَ إِذَا أَحْدَثَ لَكَ مَا أَنْتَ فِيهِ مِنْ سُلْطَانِكَ أُبَّهَةً أَوْ مَخِيلَةً فَانْظُرْ إِلَى عِظَمِ مُلْكِ اللَّهِ فَوْقَكَ وَ قُدْرَتِهِ مِنْكَ عَلَى مَا لَا تَقْدِرُ عَلَيْهِ مِنْ نَفْسِكَ فَإِنَّ ذَلِكَ يُطَامِنُ إِلَيْكَ مِنْ طِمَاحِكَ وَ يَكُفُّ عَنْكَ مِنْ غَرْبِكَ وَ يَفِيءُ إِلَيْكَ بِمَا عَزَبَ عَنْكَ مِنْ عَقْلِكَ.

إِيَّاكَ وَ مُسَامَاةَ اللَّهِ فِي عَظَمَتِهِ وَ التَّشَبُّهَ بِهِ فِي جَبَرُوتِهِ فَإِنَّ اللَّهَ يُذِلُّ كُلَّ جَبَّارٍ وَ يُهِينُ كُلَّ مُخْتَالٍ أَنْصِفِ اللَّهَ وَ أَنْصِفِ النَّاسَ مِنْ نَفْسِكَ وَ مِنْ خَاصَّةِ أَهْلِكَ وَ مَنْ لَكَ فِيهِ هَوًى مِنْ رَعِيَّتِكَ فَإِنَّكَ إِلَّا تَفْعَلْ تَظْلِمْ وَ مَنْ ظَلَمَ عِبَادَ اللَّهِ كَانَ اللَّهُ خَصْمَهُ دُونَ عِبَادِهِ وَ مَنْ خَاصَمَهُ اللَّهُ أَدْحَضَ حُجَّتَهُ وَ كَانَ لِلَّهِ حَرْباً حَتَّى يَنْزِعَ أَوْ يَتُوبَ وَ لَيْسَ شَيْءٌ أَدْعَى إِلَى تَغْيِيرِ نِعْمَةِ اللَّهِ وَ تَعْجِيلِ نِقْمَتِهِ مِنْ إِقَامَةٍ عَلَى ظُلْمٍ فَإِنَّ اللَّهَ سَمِيعٌ دَعْوَةَ الْمُضْطَهَدِينَ وَ هُوَ لِلظَّالِمِينَ بِالْمِرْصَادِ.

وَ لْيَكُنْ أَحَبُّ الْأُمُورِ إِلَيْكَ أَوْسَطُهَا فِي الْحَقِّ وَ أَعَمُّهَا فِي الْعَدْلِ وَ أَجْمَعُهَا لِرِضَى الرَّعِيَّةِ فَإِنَّ سُخْطَ الْعَامَّةِ يُجْحِفُ بِرِضَى الْخَاصَّةِ وَ إِنَّ سُخْطَ الْخَاصَّةِ يُغْتَفَرُ مَعَ رِضَى الْعَامَّةِ وَ لَيْسَ أَحَدٌ مِنَ الرَّعِيَّةِ أَثْقَلَ عَلَى الْوَالِي مَئُونَةً فِي الرَّخَاءِ وَ أَقَلَّ مَعُونَةً لَهُ فِي الْبَلَاءِ وَ أَكْرَهَ لِلْإِنْصَافِ وَ أَسْأَلَ بِالْإِلْحَافِ وَ أَقَلَّ شُكْراً عِنْدَ الْإِعْطَاءِ وَ أَبْطَأَ عُذْراً عِنْدَ الْمَنْعِ وَ أَضْعَفَ صَبْراً عِنْدَ مُلِمَّاتِ الدَّهْرِ مِنْ أَهْلِ الْخَاصَّةِ وَ إِنَّمَا عِمَادُ الدِّينِ وَ جِمَاعُ الْمُسْلِمِينَ وَ الْعُدَّةُ لِلْأَعْدَاءِ الْعَامَّةُ مِنَ الْأُمَّةِ فَلْيَكُنْ صِغْوُكَ لَهُمْ وَ مَيْلُكَ مَعَهُمْ.

وَ لْيَكُنْ أَبْعَدَ رَعِيَّتِكَ مِنْكَ وَ أَشْنَأَهُمْ عِنْدَكَ أَطْلَبُهُمْ لِمَعَايِبِ النَّاسِ فَإِنَّ فِي النَّاسِ عُيُوباً الْوَالِي أَحَقُّ مَنْ سَتَرَهَا فَلَا تَكْشِفَنَّ عَمَّا غَابَ عَنْكَ مِنْهَا فَإِنَّمَا عَلَيْكَ تَطْهِيرُ مَا ظَهَرَ لَكَ وَ اللَّهُ يَحْكُمُ عَلَى مَا غَابَ عَنْكَ فَاسْتُرِ الْعَوْرَةَ مَا اسْتَطَعْتَ يَسْتُرِ اللَّهُ مِنْكَ مَا تُحِبُّ سَتْرَهُ مِنْ رَعِيَّتِكَ أَطْلِقْ عَنِ النَّاسِ عُقْدَةَ كُلِّ حِقْدٍ وَ اقْطَعْ عَنْكَ سَبَبَ كُلِّ

وِتْرٍ وَ تَغَابَ عَنْ كُلِّ مَا لَا يَضِحُ لَكَ وَ لَا تَعْجَلَنَّ إِلَى تَصْدِيقِ سَاعٍ فَإِنَّ السَّاعِيَ غَاشٌّ وَ إِنْ تَشَبَّهَ بِالنَّاصِحِينَ.

وَ لَا تُدْخِلَنَّ فِي مَشْوَرَتِكَ بَخِيلًا يَعْدِلُ بِكَ عَنِ الْفَضْلِ وَ يَعِدُكَ الْفَقْرَ وَ لَا جَبَاناً يُضَعِّفُكَ عَنِ الْأُمُورِ وَ لَا حَرِيصاً يُزَيِّنُ لَكَ الشَّرَهَ بِالْجَوْرِ فَإِنَّ الْبُخْلَ وَ الْجُبْنَ وَ الْحِرْصَ غَرَائِزُ شَتَّى يَجْمَعُهَا سُوءُ الظَّنِّ بِاللهِ إِنَّ شَرَّ وُزَرَائِكَ مَنْ كَانَ لِلْأَشْرَارِ قَبْلَكَ وَزِيراً وَ مَنْ شَرِكَهُمْ فِي الْآثَامِ فَلَا يَكُونَنَّ لَكَ بِطَانَةً فَإِنَّهُمْ أَعْوَانُ الْأَثَمَةِ وَ إِخْوَانُ الظَّلَمَةِ وَ أَنْتَ وَاجِدٌ مِنْهُمْ خَيْرَ الْخَلَفِ مِمَّنْ لَهُ مِثْلُ آرَائِهِمْ وَ نَفَاذِهِمْ وَ لَيْسَ عَلَيْهِ مِثْلُ آصَارِهِمْ وَ أَوْزَارِهِمْ وَ آثَامِهِمْ مِمَّنْ لَمْ يُعَاوِنْ ظَالِماً عَلَى ظُلْمِهِ وَ لَا آثِماً عَلَى إِثْمِهِ أُولَئِكَ أَخَفُّ عَلَيْكَ مَئُونَةً وَ أَحْسَنُ لَكَ مَعُونَةً وَ أَحْنَى عَلَيْكَ عَطْفاً وَ أَقَلُّ لِغَيْرِكَ إِلْفاً فَاتَّخِذْ أُولَئِكَ خَاصَّةً لِخَلَوَاتِكَ وَ حَفَلَاتِكَ ثُمَّ لْيَكُنْ آثَرُهُمْ عِنْدَكَ أَقْوَلَهُمْ بِمُرِّ الْحَقِّ لَكَ وَ أَقَلَّهُمْ مُسَاعَدَةً فِيمَا يَكُونُ مِنْكَ مِمَّا كَرِهَ اللهُ لِأَوْلِيَائِهِ وَاقِعاً ذَلِكَ مِنْ هَوَاكَ حَيْثُ وَقَعَ.

وَ الْصَقْ بِأَهْلِ الْوَرَعِ وَ الصِّدْقِ ثُمَّ رُضْهُمْ عَلَى أَلَّا يُطْرُوكَ وَ لَا يَبْجَحُوكَ بِبَاطِلٍ لَمْ تَفْعَلْهُ فَإِنَّ كَثْرَةَ الْإِطْرَاءِ تُحْدِثُ الزَّهْوَ وَ تُدْنِي مِنَ الْعِزَّةِ وَ لَا يَكُونَنَّ الْمُحْسِنُ وَ الْمُسِيءُ عِنْدَكَ بِمَنْزِلَةٍ سَوَاءٍ فَإِنَّ فِي ذَلِكَ تَزْهِيداً لِأَهْلِ الْإِحْسَانِ فِي الْإِحْسَانِ وَ تَدْرِيباً لِأَهْلِ الْإِسَاءَةِ عَلَى الْإِسَاءَةِ وَ أَلْزِمْ كُلًّا مِنْهُمْ مَا أَلْزَمَ نَفْسَهُ وَ اعْلَمْ أَنَّهُ لَيْسَ شَيْءٌ بِأَدْعَى إِلَى حُسْنِ ظَنِّ رَاعٍ بِرَعِيَّتِهِ مِنْ إِحْسَانِهِ إِلَيْهِمْ وَ تَخْفِيفِهِ الْمَئُونَاتِ عَلَيْهِمْ وَ تَرْكِ اسْتِكْرَاهِهِ إِيَّاهُمْ عَلَى مَا لَيْسَ لَهُ قِبَلَهُمْ فَلْيَكُنْ مِنْكَ فِي ذَلِكَ أَمْرٌ يَجْتَمِعُ لَكَ بِهِ حُسْنُ الظَّنِّ بِرَعِيَّتِكَ فَإِنَّ حُسْنَ الظَّنِّ يَقْطَعُ عَنْكَ نَصَباً طَوِيلًا وَ إِنَّ أَحَقَّ مَنْ حَسُنَ ظَنُّكَ بِهِ لَمَنْ حَسُنَ بَلَاؤُكَ عِنْدَهُ وَ إِنَّ أَحَقَّ مَنْ سَاءَ ظَنُّكَ بِهِ لَمَنْ سَاءَ بَلَاؤُكَ عِنْدَهُ وَ لَا تَنْقُضْ سُنَّةً صَالِحَةً عَمِلَ بِهَا صُدُورُ هَذِهِ الْأُمَّةِ وَ اجْتَمَعَتْ بِهَا الْأُلْفَةُ وَ صَلَحَتْ عَلَيْهَا الرَّعِيَّةُ وَ لَا تُحْدِثَنَّ سُنَّةً تَضُرُّ بِشَيْءٍ مِنْ مَاضِي تِلْكَ السُّنَنِ فَيَكُونَ الْأَجْرُ لِمَنْ سَنَّهَا وَ الْوِزْرُ عَلَيْكَ بِمَا نَقَضْتَ مِنْهَا وَ أَكْثِرْ مُدَارَسَةَ الْعُلَمَاءِ وَ مُنَاقَشَةَ الْحُكَمَاءِ فِي تَثْبِيتِ مَا صَلَحَ عَلَيْهِ أَمْرُ بِلَادِكَ وَ إِقَامَةِ مَا اسْتَقَامَ بِهِ النَّاسُ قَبْلَكَ.

وَ اعْلَمْ أَنَّ الرَّعِيَّةَ طَبَقَاتٌ لَا يَصْلُحُ بَعْضُهَا إِلَّا بِبَعْضٍ وَ لَا غِنَى بِبَعْضِهَا عَنْ بَعْضٍ فَمِنْهَا جُنُودُ اللهِ وَ مِنْهَا كُتَّابُ الْعَامَّةِ وَ الْخَاصَّةِ وَ مِنْهَا قُضَاةُ الْعَدْلِ وَ مِنْهَا عُمَّالُ الْإِنْصَافِ وَ الرِّفْقِ وَ مِنْهَا أَهْلُ الْجِزْيَةِ وَ الْخَرَاجِ مِنْ أَهْلِ الذِّمَّةِ وَ مُسْلِمَةِ النَّاسِ وَ مِنْهَا التُّجَّارُ وَ أَهْلُ الصِّنَاعَاتِ وَ مِنْهَا الطَّبَقَةُ السُّفْلَى مِنْ ذَوِي الْحَاجَةِ وَ الْمَسْكَنَةِ وَ كُلٌّ قَدْ سَمَّى اللهُ لَهُ سَهْمَهُ وَ وَضَعَ عَلَى حَدِّهِ فَرِيضَةً فِي كِتَابِهِ أَوْ سُنَّةِ نَبِيِّهِ (صلى الله عليه وآله) عَهْداً مِنْهُ عِنْدَنَا مَحْفُوظاً فَالْجُنُودُ بِإِذْنِ اللهِ حُصُونُ الرَّعِيَّةِ وَ زَيْنُ الْوُلَاةِ وَ عِزُّ الدِّينِ وَ سُبُلُ الْأَمْنِ وَ لَيْسَ تَقُومُ الرَّعِيَّةُ إِلَّا بِهِمْ ثُمَّ لَا قِوَامَ لِلْجُنُودِ إِلَّا بِمَا يُخْرِجُ

اللهُ لَهُمْ مِنَ الْخَرَاجِ الَّذِي يَقْوَوْنَ بِهِ عَلَى جِهَادِ عَدُوِّهِمْ وَ يَعْتَمِدُونَ عَلَيْهِ فِيمَا يُصْلِحُهُمْ وَ يَكُونُ مِنْ وَرَاءِ حَاجَتِهِمْ ثُمَّ لَا قِوَامَ لِهَذَيْنِ الصِّنْفَيْنِ إِلَّا بِالصِّنْفِ الثَّالِثِ مِنَ الْقُضَاةِ وَ الْعُمَّالِ وَ الْكُتَّابِ لِمَا يُحْكِمُونَ مِنَ الْمَعَاقِدِ وَ يَجْمَعُونَ مِنَ الْمَنَافِعِ وَ يُؤْتَمَنُونَ عَلَيْهِ مِنْ خَوَاصِّ الْأُمُورِ وَ عَوَامِّهَا وَ لَا قِوَامَ لَهُمْ جَمِيعاً إِلَّا بِالتُّجَّارِ وَ ذَوِي الصِّنَاعَاتِ فِيمَا يَجْتَمِعُونَ عَلَيْهِ مِنْ مَرَافِقِهِمْ وَ يُقِيمُونَهُ مِنْ أَسْوَاقِهِمْ وَ يَكْفُونَهُمْ مِنَ التَّرَفُّقِ بِأَيْدِيهِمْ مَا لَا يَبْلُغُهُ رِفْقُ غَيْرِهِمْ ثُمَّ الطَّبَقَةُ السُّفْلَى مِنْ أَهْلِ الْحَاجَةِ وَ الْمَسْكَنَةِ الَّذِينَ يَحِقُّ رِفْدُهُمْ وَ مَعُونَتُهُمْ وَ فِي اللَّهِ لِكُلٍّ سَعَةٌ وَ لِكُلٍّ عَلَى الْوَالِي حَقٌّ بِقَدْرِ مَا يُصْلِحُهُ وَ لَيْسَ يَخْرُجُ الْوَالِي مِنْ حَقِيقَةِ مَا أَلْزَمَهُ اللَّهُ مِنْ ذَلِكَ إِلَّا بِالِاهْتِمَامِ وَ الِاسْتِعَانَةِ بِاللَّهِ وَ تَوْطِينِ نَفْسِهِ عَلَى لُزُومِ الْحَقِّ وَ الصَّبْرِ عَلَيْهِ فِيمَا خَفَّ عَلَيْهِ أَوْ ثَقُلَ.

فَوَلِّ مِنْ جُنُودِكَ أَنْصَحَهُمْ فِي نَفْسِكَ لِلَّهِ وَ لِرَسُولِهِ وَ لِإِمَامِكَ وَ أَنْقَاهُمْ جَيْباً وَ أَفْضَلَهُمْ حِلْماً مِمَّنْ يُبْطِئُ عَنِ الْغَضَبِ وَ يَسْتَرِيحُ إِلَى الْعُذْرِ وَ يَرْأَفُ بِالضُّعَفَاءِ وَ يَنْبُو عَلَى الْأَقْوِيَاءِ وَ مِمَّنْ لَا يُثِيرُهُ الْعُنْفُ وَ لَا يَقْعُدُ بِهِ الضَّعْفُ ثُمَّ الْصَقْ بِذَوِي الْمُرُوءَاتِ وَ الْأَحْسَابِ وَ أَهْلِ الْبُيُوتَاتِ الصَّالِحَةِ وَ السَّوَابِقِ الْحَسَنَةِ ثُمَّ أَهْلِ النَّجْدَةِ وَ الشَّجَاعَةِ وَ السَّخَاءِ وَ السَّمَاحَةِ فَإِنَّهُمْ جِمَاعٌ مِنَ الْكَرَمِ وَ شُعَبٌ مِنَ الْعُرْفِ ثُمَّ تَفَقَّدْ مِنْ أُمُورِهِمْ مَا يَتَفَقَّدُ الْوَالِدَانِ مِنْ وَلَدِهِمَا وَ لَا يَتَفَاقَمَنَّ فِي نَفْسِكَ شَيْءٌ قَوَّيْتَهُمْ بِهِ وَ لَا تَحْقِرَنَّ لُطْفاً تَعَاهَدْتَهُمْ بِهِ وَ إِنْ قَلَّ فَإِنَّهُ دَاعِيَةٌ لَهُمْ إِلَى بَذْلِ النَّصِيحَةِ لَكَ وَ حُسْنِ الظَّنِّ بِكَ وَ لَا تَدَعْ تَفَقُّدَ لَطِيفِ أُمُورِهِمُ اتِّكَالًا عَلَى جَسِيمِهَا فَإِنَّ لِلْيَسِيرِ مِنْ لُطْفِكَ مَوْضِعاً يَنْتَفِعُونَ بِهِ وَ لِلْجَسِيمِ مَوْقِعاً لَا يَسْتَغْنُونَ عَنْهُ وَ لْيَكُنْ آثَرُ رُءُوسِ جُنْدِكَ عِنْدَكَ مَنْ وَاسَاهُمْ فِي مَعُونَتِهِ وَ أَفْضَلَ عَلَيْهِمْ مِنْ جِدَتِهِ بِمَا يَسَعُهُمْ وَ يَسَعُ مَنْ وَرَاءَهُمْ مِنْ خُلُوفِ أَهْلِيهِمْ حَتَّى يَكُونَ هَمُّهُمْ هَمّاً وَاحِداً فِي جِهَادِ الْعَدُوِّ فَإِنَّ عَطْفَكَ عَلَيْهِمْ يَعْطِفُ قُلُوبَهُمْ عَلَيْكَ وَ إِنَّ أَفْضَلَ قُرَّةِ عَيْنِ الْوُلَاةِ اسْتِقَامَةُ الْعَدْلِ فِي الْبِلَادِ وَ ظُهُورُ مَوَدَّةِ الرَّعِيَّةِ وَ إِنَّهُ لَا تَظْهَرُ مَوَدَّتُهُمْ إِلَّا بِسَلَامَةِ صُدُورِهِمْ وَ لَا تَصِحُّ نَصِيحَتُهُمْ إِلَّا بِحِيطَتِهِمْ عَلَى وُلَاةِ الْأُمُورِ وَ قِلَّةِ اسْتِثْقَالِ دُوَلِهِمْ وَ تَرْكِ اسْتِبْطَاءِ انْقِطَاعِ مُدَّتِهِمْ فَافْسَحْ فِي آمَالِهِمْ وَ وَاصِلْ فِي حُسْنِ الثَّنَاءِ عَلَيْهِمْ وَ تَعْدِيدِ مَا أَبْلَى ذَوُو الْبَلَاءِ مِنْهُمْ فَإِنَّ كَثْرَةَ الذِّكْرِ لِحُسْنِ أَفْعَالِهِمْ تَهُزُّ الشُّجَاعَ وَ تُحَرِّضُ النَّاكِلَ إِنْ شَاءَ اللَّهُ ثُمَّ اعْرِفْ لِكُلِّ امْرِئٍ مِنْهُمْ مَا أَبْلَى وَ لَا تَضُمَّنَّ بَلَاءَ امْرِئٍ إِلَى غَيْرِهِ وَ لَا تُقَصِّرَنَّ بِهِ دُونَ غَايَةِ بَلَائِهِ وَ لَا يَدْعُوَنَّكَ شَرَفُ امْرِئٍ إِلَى أَنْ تُعَظِّمَ مِنْ بَلَائِهِ مَا كَانَ صَغِيراً وَ لَا ضَعَةُ امْرِئٍ إِلَى أَنْ تَسْتَصْغِرَ مِنْ بَلَائِهِ مَا كَانَ عَظِيماً وَ ارْدُدْ إِلَى اللَّهِ وَ رَسُولِهِ مَا يُضْلِعُكَ مِنَ الْخُطُوبِ وَ يَشْتَبِهُ عَلَيْكَ مِنَ الْأُمُورِ فَقَدْ قَالَ اللَّهُ تَعَالَى لِقَوْمٍ أَحَبَّ إِرْشَادَهُمْ يَا أَيُّهَا الَّذِينَ آمَنُوا أَطِيعُوا اللَّهَ وَ أَطِيعُوا الرَّسُولَ وَ أُولِي الْأَمْرِ مِنْكُمْ فَإِنْ تَنَازَعْتُمْ فِي شَيْءٍ فَرُدُّوهُ إِلَى

اللهِ وَ الرَّسُولِ فَالرَّدُّ إِلَى اللهِ الْأَخْذُ بِمُحْكَمِ كِتَابِهِ وَ الرَّدُّ إِلَى الرَّسُولِ الْأَخْذُ بِسُنَّتِهِ الْجَامِعَةِ غَيْرِ الْمُفَرِّقَةِ.

ثُمَّ اخْتَرْ لِلْحُكْمِ بَيْنَ النَّاسِ أَفْضَلَ رَعِيَّتِكَ فِي نَفْسِكَ مِمَّنْ لَا تَضِيقُ بِهِ الْأُمُورُ وَ لَا تُمَحِّكُهُ الْخُصُومُ وَ لَا يَتَمَادَى فِي الزَّلَّةِ وَ لَا يَحْصَرُ مِنَ الْفَيْءِ إِلَى الْحَقِّ إِذَا عَرَفَهُ وَ لَا تُشْرِفُ نَفْسُهُ عَلَى طَمَعٍ وَ لَا يَكْتَفِي بِأَدْنَى فَهْمٍ دُونَ أَقْصَاهُ وَ أَوْقَفَهُمْ فِي الشُّبُهَاتِ وَ آخَذَهُمْ بِالْحُجَجِ وَ أَقَلَّهُمْ تَبَرُّماً بِمُرَاجَعَةِ الْخَصْمِ وَ أَصْبَرَهُمْ عَلَى تَكَشُّفِ الْأُمُورِ وَ أَصْرَمَهُمْ عِنْدَ اتِّضَاحِ الْحُكْمِ مِمَّنْ لَا يَزْدَهِيهِ إِطْرَاءٌ وَ لَا يَسْتَمِيلُهُ إِغْرَاءٌ وَ أُولَئِكَ قَلِيلٌ ثُمَّ أَكْثِرْ تَعَاهُدَ قَضَائِهِ وَ افْسَحْ لَهُ فِي الْبَذْلِ مَا يُزِيلُ عِلَّتَهُ وَ تَقِلُّ مَعَهُ حَاجَتُهُ إِلَى النَّاسِ وَ أَعْطِهِ مِنَ الْمَنْزِلَةِ لَدَيْكَ مَا لَا يَطْمَعُ فِيهِ غَيْرُهُ مِنْ خَاصَّتِكَ لِيَأْمَنَ بِذَلِكَ اغْتِيَالَ الرِّجَالِ لَهُ عِنْدَكَ فَانْظُرْ فِي ذَلِكَ نَظَراً بَلِيغاً فَإِنَّ هَذَا الدِّينَ قَدْ كَانَ أَسِيراً فِي أَيْدِي الْأَشْرَارِ يُعْمَلُ فِيهِ بِالْهَوَى وَ تُطْلَبُ بِهِ الدُّنْيَا.

ثُمَّ انْظُرْ فِي أُمُورِ عُمَّالِكَ فَاسْتَعْمِلْهُمُ اخْتِبَاراً وَ لَا تُوَلِّهِمْ مُحَابَاةً وَ أَثَرَةً فَإِنَّهُمَا جِمَاعٌ مِنْ شُعَبِ الْجَوْرِ وَ الْخِيَانَةِ وَ تَوَخَّ مِنْهُمْ أَهْلَ التَّجْرِبَةِ وَ الْحَيَاءِ مِنْ أَهْلِ الْبُيُوتَاتِ الصَّالِحَةِ وَ الْقَدَمِ فِي الْإِسْلَامِ الْمُتَقَدِّمَةِ فَإِنَّهُمْ أَكْرَمُ أَخْلَاقاً وَ أَصَحُّ أَعْرَاضاً وَ أَقَلُّ فِي الْمَطَامِعِ إِشْرَاقاً وَ أَبْلَغُ فِي عَوَاقِبِ الْأُمُورِ نَظَراً ثُمَّ أَسْبِغْ عَلَيْهِمُ الْأَرْزَاقَ فَإِنَّ ذَلِكَ قُوَّةٌ لَهُمْ عَلَى اسْتِصْلَاحِ أَنْفُسِهِمْ وَ غِنًى لَهُمْ عَنْ تَنَاوُلِ مَا تَحْتَ أَيْدِيهِمْ وَ حُجَّةٌ عَلَيْهِمْ إِنْ خَالَفُوا أَمْرَكَ أَوْ ثَلَمُوا أَمَانَتَكَ ثُمَّ تَفَقَّدْ أَعْمَالَهُمْ وَ ابْعَثِ الْعُيُونَ مِنْ أَهْلِ الصِّدْقِ وَ الْوَفَاءِ عَلَيْهِمْ فَإِنَّ تَعَاهُدَكَ فِي السِّرِّ لِأُمُورِهِمْ حَدْوَةٌ لَهُمْ عَلَى اسْتِعْمَالِ الْأَمَانَةِ وَ الرِّفْقِ بِالرَّعِيَّةِ وَ تَحَفَّظْ مِنَ الْأَعْوَانِ فَإِنْ أَحَدٌ مِنْهُمْ بَسَطَ يَدَهُ إِلَى خِيَانَةٍ اجْتَمَعَتْ بِهَا عَلَيْهِ عِنْدَكَ أَخْبَارُ عُيُونِكَ اكْتَفَيْتَ بِذَلِكَ شَاهِداً فَبَسَطْتَ عَلَيْهِ الْعُقُوبَةَ فِي بَدَنِهِ وَ أَخَذْتَهُ بِمَا أَصَابَ مِنْ عَمَلِهِ ثُمَّ نَصَبْتَهُ بِمَقَامِ الْمَذَلَّةِ وَ وَسَمْتَهُ بِالْخِيَانَةِ وَ قَلَّدْتَهُ عَارَ التُّهَمَةِ.

وَ تَفَقَّدْ أَمْرَ الْخَرَاجِ بِمَا يُصْلِحُ أَهْلَهُ فَإِنَّ فِي صَلَاحِهِ وَ صَلَاحِهِمْ صَلَاحاً لِمَنْ سِوَاهُمْ وَ لَا صَلَاحَ لِمَنْ سِوَاهُمْ إِلَّا بِهِمْ لِأَنَّ النَّاسَ كُلَّهُمْ عِيَالٌ عَلَى الْخَرَاجِ وَ أَهْلِهِ وَ لْيَكُنْ نَظَرُكَ فِي عِمَارَةِ الْأَرْضِ أَبْلَغَ مِنْ نَظَرِكَ فِي اسْتِجْلَابِ الْخَرَاجِ لِأَنَّ ذَلِكَ لَا يُدْرَكُ إِلَّا بِالْعِمَارَةِ وَ مَنْ طَلَبَ الْخَرَاجَ بِغَيْرِ عِمَارَةٍ أَخْرَبَ الْبِلَادَ وَ أَهْلَكَ الْعِبَادَ وَ لَمْ يَسْتَقِمْ أَمْرُهُ إِلَّا قَلِيلاً فَإِنْ شَكَوْا ثِقَلاً أَوْ عِلَّةً أَوِ انْقِطَاعَ شِرْبٍ أَوْ بَالَّةٍ أَوْ إِحَالَةَ أَرْضٍ اغْتَمَرَهَا غَرَقٌ أَوْ أَجْحَفَ بِهَا عَطَشٌ خَفَّفْتَ عَنْهُمْ بِمَا تَرْجُو أَنْ يَصْلُحَ بِهِ أَمْرُهُمْ وَ لَا يَثْقُلَنَّ عَلَيْكَ شَيْءٌ خَفَّفْتَ بِهِ الْمَئُونَةَ عَنْهُمْ فَإِنَّهُ ذُخْرٌ يَعُودُونَ بِهِ عَلَيْكَ فِي عِمَارَةِ بِلَادِكَ وَ تَزْيِينِ وِلَايَتِكَ مَعَ اسْتِجْلَابِكَ حُسْنَ ثَنَائِهِمْ وَ تَبَجُّحِكَ بِاسْتِفَاضَةِ الْعَدْلِ فِيهِمْ مُعْتَمِداً فَضْلَ قُوَّتِهِمْ بِمَا ذَخَرْتَ عِنْدَهُمْ مِنْ إِجْمَامِكَ لَهُمْ وَ الثِّقَةِ مِنْهُمْ بِمَا عَوَّدْتَهُمْ مِنْ

عَدْلِكَ عَلَيْهِمْ وَ رِفْقِكَ بِهِمْ فَرُبَّمَا حَدَثَ مِنَ الْأُمُورِ مَا إِذَا عَوَّلْتَ فِيهِ عَلَيْهِمْ مِنْ بَعْدُ احْتَمَلُوهُ طَيِّبَةً أَنْفُسُهُمْ بِهِ فَإِنَّ الْعُمْرَانَ مُحْتَمِلٌ مَا حَمَّلْتَهُ وَ إِنَّمَا يُؤْتَى خَرَابُ الْأَرْضِ مِنْ إِعْوَازِ أَهْلِهَا وَ إِنَّمَا يُعْوِزُ أَهْلُهَا لِإِشْرَافِ أَنْفُسِ الْوُلَاةِ عَلَى الْجَمْعِ وَ سُوءِ ظَنِّهِمْ بِالْبَقَاءِ وَ قِلَّةِ انْتِفَاعِهِمْ بِالْعِبَرِ.

ثُمَّ انْظُرْ فِي حَالِ كُتَّابِكَ فَوَلِّ عَلَى أُمُورِكَ خَيْرَهُمْ وَ اخْصُصْ رَسَائِلَكَ الَّتِي تُدْخِلُ فِيهَا مَكَايِدَكَ وَ أَسْرَارَكَ بِأَجْمَعِهِمْ لِوُجُوهِ صَالِحِ الْأَخْلَاقِ مِمَّنْ لَا تُبْطِرُهُ الْكَرَامَةُ فَيَجْتَرِئَ بِهَا عَلَيْكَ فِي خِلَافٍ لَكَ بِحَضْرَةِ مَلَإٍ وَ لَا تَقْصُرُ بِهِ الْغَفْلَةُ عَنْ إِيرَادِ مُكَاتَبَاتِ عُمَّالِكَ عَلَيْكَ وَ إِصْدَارِ جَوَابَاتِهَا عَلَى الصَّوَابِ عَنْكَ فِيمَا يَأْخُذُ لَكَ وَ يُعْطِي مِنْكَ وَ لَا يُضْعِفُ عَقْداً اعْتَقَدَهُ لَكَ وَ لَا يَعْجِزُ عَنْ إِطْلَاقِ مَا عُقِدَ عَلَيْكَ وَ لَا يَجْهَلُ مَبْلَغَ قَدْرِ نَفْسِهِ فِي الْأُمُورِ فَإِنَّ الْجَاهِلَ بِقَدْرِ نَفْسِهِ يَكُونُ بِقَدْرِ غَيْرِهِ أَجْهَلَ ثُمَّ لَا يَكُنِ اخْتِيَارُكَ إِيَّاهُمْ عَلَى فِرَاسَتِكَ وَ اسْتِنَامَتِكَ وَ حُسْنِ الظَّنِّ مِنْكَ فَإِنَّ الرِّجَالَ يَتَعَرَّضُونَ لِفِرَاسَاتِ الْوُلَاةِ بِتَصَنُّعِهِمْ وَ حُسْنِ خِدْمَتِهِمْ وَ لَيْسَ وَرَاءَ ذَلِكَ مِنَ النَّصِيحَةِ وَ الْأَمَانَةِ شَيْءٌ وَ لَكِنِ اخْتَبِرْهُمْ بِمَا وُلُّوا لِلصَّالِحِينَ قَبْلَكَ فَاعْمِدْ لِأَحْسَنِهِمْ كَانَ فِي الْعَامَّةِ أَثَراً وَ أَعْرَفِهِمْ بِالْأَمَانَةِ وَجْهاً فَإِنَّ ذَلِكَ دَلِيلٌ عَلَى نَصِيحَتِكَ لِلَّهِ وَ لِمَنْ وُلِّيتَ أَمْرَهُ وَ اجْعَلْ لِرَأْسِ كُلِّ أَمْرٍ مِنْ أُمُورِكَ رَأْساً مِنْهُمْ لَا يَقْهَرُهُ كَبِيرُهَا وَ لَا يَتَشَتَّتُ عَلَيْهِ كَثِيرُهَا وَ مَهْمَا كَانَ فِي كُتَّابِكَ مِنْ عَيْبٍ فَتَغَابَيْتَ عَنْهُ أُلْزِمْتَهُ.

ثُمَّ اسْتَوْصِ بِالتُّجَّارِ وَ ذَوِي الصِّنَاعَاتِ وَ أَوْصِ بِهِمْ خَيْراً الْمُقِيمِ مِنْهُمْ وَ الْمُضْطَرِبِ بِمَالِهِ وَ الْمُتَرَفِّقِ بِبَدَنِهِ فَإِنَّهُمْ مَوَادُّ الْمَنَافِعِ وَ أَسْبَابُ الْمَرَافِقِ وَ جُلَّابُهَا مِنَ الْمَبَاعِدِ وَ الْمَطَارِحِ فِي بَرِّكَ وَ بَحْرِكَ وَ سَهْلِكَ وَ جَبَلِكَ وَ حَيْثُ لَا يَلْتَئِمُ النَّاسُ لِمَوَاضِعِهَا وَ لَا يَجْتَرِئُونَ عَلَيْهَا فَإِنَّهُمْ سِلْمٌ لَا تُخَافُ بَائِقَتُهُ وَ صُلْحٌ لَا تُخْشَى غَائِلَتُهُ وَ تَفَقَّدْ أُمُورَهُمْ بِحَضْرَتِكَ وَ فِي حَوَاشِي بِلَادِكَ وَ اعْلَمْ مَعَ ذَلِكَ أَنَّ فِي كَثِيرٍ مِنْهُمْ ضِيقاً فَاحِشاً وَ شُحّاً قَبِيحاً وَ احْتِكَاراً لِلْمَنَافِعِ وَ تَحَكُّماً فِي الْبِيَاعَاتِ وَ ذَلِكَ بَابُ مَضَرَّةٍ لِلْعَامَّةِ وَ عَيْبٌ عَلَى الْوُلَاةِ فَامْنَعْ مِنَ الِاحْتِكَارِ فَإِنَّ رَسُولَ اللَّهِ (صلى الله عليه وآله) مَنَعَ مِنْهُ وَ لْيَكُنِ الْبَيْعُ بَيْعاً سَمْحاً بِمَوَازِينِ عَدْلٍ وَ أَسْعَارٍ لَا تُجْحِفُ بِالْفَرِيقَيْنِ مِنَ الْبَائِعِ وَ الْمُبْتَاعِ فَمَنْ قَارَفَ حُكْرَةً بَعْدَ نَهْيِكَ إِيَّاهُ فَنَكِّلْ بِهِ وَ عَاقِبْ فِي غَيْرِ إِسْرَافٍ.

ثُمَّ اللَّهَ اللَّهَ فِي الطَّبَقَةِ السُّفْلَى مِنَ الَّذِينَ لَا حِيلَةَ لَهُمْ مِنَ الْمَسَاكِينِ وَ الْمُحْتَاجِينَ وَ أَهْلِ الْبُؤْسَى وَ الزَّمْنَى فَإِنَّ فِي هَذِهِ الطَّبَقَةِ قَانِعاً وَ مُعْتَرّاً وَ احْفَظْ لِلَّهِ مَا اسْتَحْفَظَكَ مِنْ حَقِّهِ فِيهِمْ وَ اجْعَلْ لَهُمْ قِسْماً مِنْ بَيْتِ مَالِكَ وَ قِسْماً مِنْ غَلَّاتِ صَوَافِي الْإِسْلَامِ فِي كُلِّ بَلَدٍ فَإِنَّ لِلْأَقْصَى مِنْهُمْ مِثْلَ الَّذِي لِلْأَدْنَى وَ كُلٌّ قَدِ اسْتُرْعِيتَ حَقَّهُ وَ لَا يَشْغَلَنَّكَ عَنْهُمْ بَطَرٌ فَإِنَّكَ لَا تُعْذَرُ بِتَضْيِيعِكَ التَّافِهَ لِإِحْكَامِكَ الْكَثِيرَ الْمُهِمَّ فَلَا

تُشْخِصْ هَمَّكَ عَنْهُمْ وَ لَا تُصَعِّرْ خَدَّكَ لَهُمْ وَ تَفَقَّدْ أُمُورَ مَنْ لَا يَصِلُ إِلَيْكَ مِنْهُمْ مِمَّنْ تَقْتَحِمُهُ الْعُيُونُ وَ تَحْقِرُهُ الرِّجَالُ فَفَرِّغْ لِأُولَئِكَ ثِقَتَكَ مِنْ أَهْلِ الْخَشْيَةِ وَ التَّوَاضُعِ فَلْيَرْفَعْ إِلَيْكَ أُمُورَهُمْ ثُمَّ اعْمَلْ فِيهِمْ بِالْإِعْذَارِ إِلَى اللَّهِ يَوْمَ تَلْقَاهُ فَإِنَّ هَؤُلَاءِ مِنْ بَيْنِ الرَّعِيَّةِ أَحْوَجُ إِلَى الْإِنْصَافِ مِنْ غَيْرِهِمْ وَ كُلٌّ فَأَعْذِرْ إِلَى اللَّهِ فِي تَأْدِيَةِ حَقِّهِ إِلَيْهِ وَ تَعَهَّدْ أَهْلَ الْيُتْمِ وَ ذَوِي الرِّقَّةِ فِي السِّنِّ مِمَّنْ لَا حِيلَةَ لَهُ وَ لَا يَنْصِبُ لِلْمَسْأَلَةِ نَفْسَهُ وَ ذَلِكَ عَلَى الْوُلَاةِ ثَقِيلٌ وَ الْحَقُّ كُلُّهُ ثَقِيلٌ وَ قَدْ يُخَفِّفُهُ اللَّهُ عَلَى أَقْوَامٍ طَلَبُوا الْعَاقِبَةَ فَصَبَّرُوا أَنْفُسَهُمْ وَ وَثِقُوا بِصِدْقِ مَوْعُودِ اللَّهِ لَهُمْ وَ اجْعَلْ لِذَوِي الْحَاجَاتِ مِنْكَ قِسْماً تُفَرِّغُ لَهُمْ فِيهِ شَخْصَكَ وَ تَجْلِسُ لَهُمْ مَجْلِساً عَامّاً فَتَتَوَاضَعُ فِيهِ لِلَّهِ الَّذِي خَلَقَكَ وَ تُقْعِدُ عَنْهُمْ جُنْدَكَ وَ أَعْوَانَكَ مِنْ أَحْرَاسِكَ وَ شُرَطِكَ حَتَّى يُكَلِّمَكَ مُتَكَلِّمُهُمْ غَيْرَ مُتَتَعْتِعٍ فَإِنِّي سَمِعْتُ رَسُولَ اللَّهِ (صلى الله عليه وآله) يَقُولُ فِي غَيْرِ مَوْطِنٍ لَنْ تُقَدَّسَ أُمَّةٌ لَا يُؤْخَذُ لِلضَّعِيفِ فِيهَا حَقُّهُ مِنَ الْقَوِيِّ غَيْرَ مُتَتَعْتِعٍ ثُمَّ احْتَمِلِ الْخُرْقَ مِنْهُمْ وَ الْعِيَّ وَ نَحِّ عَنْهُمُ الضِّيقَ وَ الْأَنَفَ يَبْسُطِ اللَّهُ عَلَيْكَ بِذَلِكَ أَكْنَافَ رَحْمَتِهِ وَ يُوجِبْ لَكَ ثَوَابَ طَاعَتِهِ وَ أَعْطِ مَا أَعْطَيْتَ هَنِيئاً وَ امْنَعْ فِي إِجْمَالٍ وَ إِعْذَارٍ.

ثُمَّ أُمُورٌ مِنْ أُمُورِكَ لَا بُدَّ لَكَ مِنْ مُبَاشَرَتِهَا مِنْهَا إِجَابَةُ عُمَّالِكَ بِمَا يَعْيَا عَنْهُ كُتَّابُكَ وَ مِنْهَا إِصْدَارُ حَاجَاتِ النَّاسِ يَوْمَ وُرُودِهَا عَلَيْكَ بِمَا تَحْرَجُ بِهِ صُدُورُ أَعْوَانِكَ وَ أَمْضِ لِكُلِّ يَوْمٍ عَمَلَهُ فَإِنَّ لِكُلِّ يَوْمٍ مَا فِيهِ وَ اجْعَلْ لِنَفْسِكَ فِيمَا بَيْنَكَ وَ بَيْنَ اللَّهِ أَفْضَلَ تِلْكَ الْمَوَاقِيتِ وَ أَجْزَلَ تِلْكَ الْأَقْسَامِ وَ إِنْ كَانَتْ كُلُّهَا لِلَّهِ إِذَا صَلَحَتْ فِيهَا النِّيَّةُ وَ سَلِمَتْ مِنْهَا الرَّعِيَّةُ وَ لْيَكُنْ فِي خَاصَّةِ مَا تُخْلِصُ بِهِ لِلَّهِ دِينَكَ إِقَامَةُ فَرَائِضِهِ الَّتِي هِيَ لَهُ خَاصَّةً فَأَعْطِ اللَّهَ مِنْ بَدَنِكَ فِي لَيْلِكَ وَ نَهَارِكَ وَ وَفِّ مَا تَقَرَّبْتَ بِهِ إِلَى اللَّهِ مِنْ ذَلِكَ كَامِلًا غَيْرَ مَثْلُومٍ وَ لَا مَنْقُوصٍ بَالِغاً مِنْ بَدَنِكَ مَا بَلَغَ وَ إِذَا قُمْتَ فِي صَلَاتِكَ لِلنَّاسِ فَلَا تَكُونَنَّ مُنَفِّراً وَ لَا مُضَيِّعاً فَإِنَّ فِي النَّاسِ مَنْ بِهِ الْعِلَّةُ وَ لَهُ الْحَاجَةُ وَ قَدْ سَأَلْتُ رَسُولَ اللَّهِ (صلى الله عليه وآله) حِينَ وَجَّهَنِي إِلَى الْيَمَنِ كَيْفَ أُصَلِّي بِهِمْ فَقَالَ صَلِّ بِهِمْ كَصَلَاةِ أَضْعَفِهِمْ وَ كُنْ بِالْمُؤْمِنِينَ رَحِيماً وَ أَمَّا بَعْدُ فَلَا تُطَوِّلَنَّ احْتِجَابَكَ عَنْ رَعِيَّتِكَ فَإِنَّ احْتِجَابَ الْوُلَاةِ عَنِ الرَّعِيَّةِ شُعْبَةٌ مِنَ الضِّيقِ وَ قِلَّةُ عِلْمٍ بِالْأُمُورِ وَ الِاحْتِجَابُ مِنْهُمْ يَقْطَعُ عَنْهُمْ عِلْمَ مَا احْتَجَبُوا دُونَهُ فَيَصْغُرُ عِنْدَهُمُ الْكَبِيرُ وَ يَعْظُمُ الصَّغِيرُ وَ يَقْبُحُ الْحَسَنُ وَ يَحْسُنُ الْقَبِيحُ وَ يُشَابُ الْحَقُّ بِالْبَاطِلِ وَ إِنَّمَا الْوَالِي بَشَرٌ لَا يَعْرِفُ مَا تَوَارَى عَنْهُ النَّاسُ بِهِ مِنَ الْأُمُورِ وَ لَيْسَتْ عَلَى الْحَقِّ سِمَاتٌ تُعْرَفُ بِهَا ضُرُوبُ الصِّدْقِ مِنَ الْكَذِبِ وَ إِنَّمَا أَنْتَ أَحَدُ رَجُلَيْنِ إِمَّا امْرُؤٌ سَخَتْ نَفْسُكَ بِالْبَذْلِ فِي الْحَقِّ فَفِيمَ احْتِجَابُكَ مِنْ وَاجِبِ حَقٍّ تُعْطِيهِ أَوْ فِعْلٍ كَرِيمٍ تُسْدِيهِ أَوْ مُبْتَلًى بِالْمَنْعِ فَمَا أَسْرَعَ كَفَّ النَّاسِ عَنْ مَسْأَلَتِكَ إِذَا أَيِسُوا مِنْ بَذْلِكَ مَعَ أَنَّ أَكْثَرَ حَاجَاتِ النَّاسِ إِلَيْكَ مِمَّا لَا مَئُونَةَ فِيهِ عَلَيْكَ مِنْ شَكَاةِ مَظْلِمَةٍ أَوْ طَلَبِ إِنْصَافٍ فِي مُعَامَلَةٍ.

ثُمَّ إِنَّ لِلْوَالِي خَاصَّةً وَ بِطَانَةً فِيهِمُ اسْتِئْثَارٌ وَ تَطَاوُلٌ وَ قِلَّةُ إِنْصَافٍ فِي مُعَامَلَةٍ فَاحْسِمْ مَادَّةَ أُولَئِكَ بِقَطْعِ أَسْبَابِ تِلْكَ الْأَحْوَالِ وَ لَا تُقْطِعَنَّ لِأَحَدٍ مِنْ حَاشِيَتِكَ وَ حَامَّتِكَ قَطِيعَةً وَ لَا يَطْمَعَنَّ مِنْكَ فِي اعْتِقَادِ عُقْدَةٍ تَضُرُّ بِمَنْ يَلِيهَا مِنَ النَّاسِ فِي شِرْبٍ أَوْ عَمَلٍ مُشْتَرَكٍ يَحْمِلُونَ مَئُونَتَهُ عَلَى غَيْرِهِمْ فَيَكُونَ مَهْنَأُ ذَلِكَ لَهُمْ دُونَكَ وَ عَيْبُهُ عَلَيْكَ فِي الدُّنْيَا وَ الْآخِرَةِ وَ أَلْزِمِ الْحَقَّ مَنْ لَزِمَهُ مِنَ الْقَرِيبِ وَ الْبَعِيدِ وَ كُنْ فِي ذَلِكَ صَابِراً

مُحْتَسِباً وَاقِعاً ذَلِكَ مِنْ قَرَابَتِكَ وَ خَاصَّتِكَ حَيْثُ وَقَعَ وَ ابْتَغِ عَاقِبَتَهُ بِمَا يَثْقُلُ عَلَيْكَ مِنْهُ فَإِنَّ مَغَبَّةَ ذَلِكَ مَحْمُودَةٌ وَ إِنْ ظَنَّتِ الرَّعِيَّةُ بِكَ حَيْفاً فَأَصْحِرْ لَهُمْ بِعُذْرِكَ وَ اعْدِلْ عَنْكَ ظُنُونَهُمْ بِإِصْحَارِكَ فَإِنَّ فِي ذَلِكَ رِيَاضَةً مِنْكَ لِنَفْسِكَ وَ رِفْقاً بِرَعِيَّتِكَ وَ إِعْذَاراً تَبْلُغُ بِهِ حَاجَتَكَ مِنْ تَقْوِيمِهِمْ عَلَى الْحَقِّ.

وَ لَا تَدْفَعَنَّ صُلْحاً دَعَاكَ إِلَيْهِ عَدُوُّكَ وَ لِلَّهِ فِيهِ رِضاً فَإِنَّ فِي الصُّلْحِ دَعَةً لِجُنُودِكَ وَ رَاحَةً مِنْ هُمُومِكَ وَ أَمْناً لِبِلَادِكَ وَ لَكِنِ الْحَذَرَ كُلَّ الْحَذَرِ مِنْ عَدُوِّكَ بَعْدَ صُلْحِهِ فَإِنَّ الْعَدُوَّ رُبَّمَا قَارَبَ لِيَتَغَفَّلَ فَخُذْ بِالْحَزْمِ وَ اتَّهِمْ فِي ذَلِكَ حُسْنَ الظَّنِّ وَ إِنْ عَقَدْتَ بَيْنَكَ وَ بَيْنَ عَدُوِّكَ عُقْدَةً أَوْ أَلْبَسْتَهُ مِنْكَ ذِمَّةً فَحُطْ عَهْدَكَ بِالْوَفَاءِ وَ ارْعَ ذِمَّتَكَ بِالْأَمَانَةِ وَ اجْعَلْ نَفْسَكَ جُنَّةً دُونَ مَا أَعْطَيْتَ فَإِنَّهُ لَيْسَ مِنْ فَرَائِضِ اللَّهِ شَيْءٌ النَّاسُ أَشَدُّ عَلَيْهِ اجْتِمَاعاً مَعَ تَفَرُّقِ أَهْوَائِهِمْ وَ تَشَتُّتِ آرَائِهِمْ مِنْ تَعْظِيمِ الْوَفَاءِ بِالْعُهُودِ وَ قَدْ لَزِمَ ذَلِكَ الْمُشْرِكُونَ فِيمَا بَيْنَهُمْ دُونَ الْمُسْلِمِينَ لِمَا اسْتَوْبَلُوا مِنْ عَوَاقِبِ الْغَدْرِ فَلَا تَغْدِرَنَّ بِذِمَّتِكَ وَ لَا تَخِيسَنَّ بِعَهْدِكَ وَ لَا تَخْتِلَنَّ عَدُوَّكَ فَإِنَّهُ لَا يَجْتَرِئُ عَلَى اللَّهِ إِلَّا جَاهِلٌ شَقِيٌّ وَ قَدْ جَعَلَ اللَّهُ عَهْدَهُ وَ ذِمَّتَهُ أَمْناً أَفْضَاهُ بَيْنَ الْعِبَادِ بِرَحْمَتِهِ وَ حَرِيماً يَسْكُنُونَ إِلَى مَنَعَتِهِ وَ يَسْتَفِيضُونَ إِلَى جِوَارِهِ فَلَا إِدْغَالَ وَ لَا مُدَالَسَةَ وَ لَا خِدَاعَ فِيهِ وَ لَا تَعْقِدْ عَقْداً تُجَوِّزُ فِيهِ الْعِلَلَ وَ لَا تُعَوِّلَنَّ عَلَى لَحْنِ قَوْلٍ بَعْدَ التَّأْكِيدِ وَ التَّوْثِقَةِ وَ لَا يَدْعُوَنَّكَ ضِيقُ أَمْرٍ لَزِمَكَ فِيهِ عَهْدُ اللَّهِ إِلَى طَلَبِ انْفِسَاخِهِ بِغَيْرِ الْحَقِّ فَإِنَّ صَبْرَكَ عَلَى ضِيقِ أَمْرٍ تَرْجُو انْفِرَاجَهُ وَ فَضْلَ عَاقِبَتِهِ خَيْرٌ مِنْ غَدْرٍ تَخَافُ تَبِعَتَهُ وَ أَنْ تُحِيطَ بِكَ مِنَ اللَّهِ فِيهِ طِلْبَةٌ لَا تَسْتَقْبِلُ فِيهَا دُنْيَاكَ وَ لَا آخِرَتَكَ.

إِيَّاكَ وَ الدِّمَاءَ وَ سَفْكَهَا بِغَيْرِ حِلِّهَا فَإِنَّهُ لَيْسَ شَيْءٌ أَدْعَى لِنِقْمَةٍ وَ لَا أَعْظَمَ لِتَبِعَةٍ وَ لَا أَحْرَى بِزَوَالِ نِعْمَةٍ وَ انْقِطَاعِ مُدَّةٍ مِنْ سَفْكِ الدِّمَاءِ بِغَيْرِ حَقِّهَا وَ اللَّهُ سُبْحَانَهُ مُبْتَدِئٌ بِالْحُكْمِ بَيْنَ الْعِبَادِ فِيمَا تَسَافَكُوا مِنَ الدِّمَاءِ يَوْمَ الْقِيَامَةِ فَلَا تُقَوِّيَنَّ سُلْطَانَكَ بِسَفْكِ دَمٍ حَرَامٍ فَإِنَّ ذَلِكَ مِمَّا يُضْعِفُهُ وَ يُوهِنُهُ بَلْ يُزِيلُهُ وَ يَنْقُلُهُ وَ لَا عُذْرَ لَكَ عِنْدَ اللَّهِ وَ لَا عِنْدِي فِي قَتْلِ الْعَمْدِ لِأَنَّ فِيهِ قَوَدَ الْبَدَنِ وَ إِنِ ابْتُلِيتَ بِخَطَإٍ وَ أَفْرَطَ عَلَيْكَ سَوْطُكَ أَوْ سَيْفُكَ أَوْ يَدُكَ بِالْعُقُوبَةِ فَإِنَّ فِي الْوَكْزَةِ فَمَا فَوْقَهَا مَقْتَلَةً فَلَا تَطْمَحَنَّ بِكَ نَخْوَةُ سُلْطَانِكَ عَنْ أَنْ تُؤَدِّيَ إِلَى أَوْلِيَاءِ الْمَقْتُولِ حَقَّهُمْ.

174

وَ إِيَّاكَ وَ الْإِعْجَابَ بِنَفْسِكَ وَ الثِّقَةَ بِمَا يُعْجِبُكَ مِنْهَا وَ حُبَّ الْإِطْرَاءِ فَإِنَّ ذَلِكَ مِنْ أَوْثَقِ فُرَصِ الشَّيْطَانِ فِي نَفْسِهِ لِيَمْحَقَ مَا يَكُونُ مِنْ إِحْسَانِ الْمُحْسِنِينَ.

وَ إِيَّاكَ وَ الْمَنَّ عَلَى رَعِيَّتِكَ بِإِحْسَانِكَ أَوِ التَّزَيُّدَ فِيمَا كَانَ مِنْ فِعْلِكَ أَوْ أَنْ تَعِدَهُمْ فَتُتْبِعَ مَوْعِدَكَ بِخُلْفِكَ فَإِنَّ الْمَنَّ يُبْطِلُ الْإِحْسَانَ وَ التَّزَيُّدَ يَذْهَبُ بِنُورِ الْحَقِّ وَ الْخُلْفَ يُوجِبُ الْمَقْتَ عِنْدَ اللَّهِ وَ النَّاسِ قَالَ اللَّهُ تَعَالَى كَبُرَ مَقْتاً عِنْدَ اللَّهِ أَنْ تَقُولُوا مَا لَا تَفْعَلُونَ.

وَ إِيَّاكَ وَ الْعَجَلَةَ بِالْأُمُورِ قَبْلَ أَوَانِهَا أَوِ التَّسَقُّطَ فِيهَا عِنْدَ إِمْكَانِهَا أَوِ اللَّجَاجَةَ فِيهَا إِذَا تَنَكَّرَتْ أَوِ الْوَهْنَ عَنْهَا إِذَا اسْتَوْضَحَتْ فَضَعْ كُلَّ أَمْرٍ مَوْضِعَهُ وَ أَوْقِعْ كُلَّ أَمْرٍ مَوْقِعَهُ.

وَ إِيَّاكَ وَ الِاسْتِئْثَارَ بِمَا النَّاسُ فِيهِ أُسْوَةٌ وَ التَّغَابِيَ عَمَّا تُعْنَى بِهِ مِمَّا قَدْ وَضَحَ لِلْعُيُونِ فَإِنَّهُ مَأْخُوذٌ مِنْكَ لِغَيْرِكَ وَ عَمَّا قَلِيلٍ تَنْكَشِفُ عَنْكَ أَغْطِيَةُ الْأُمُورِ وَ يُنْتَصَفُ مِنْكَ لِلْمَظْلُومِ امْلِكْ حَمِيَّةَ أَنْفِكَ وَ سَوْرَةَ حَدِّكَ وَ سَطْوَةَ يَدِكَ وَ غَرْبَ لِسَانِكَ وَ احْتَرِسْ مِنْ كُلِّ ذَلِكَ بِكَفِّ الْبَادِرَةِ وَ تَأْخِيرِ السَّطْوَةِ حَتَّى يَسْكُنَ غَضَبُكَ فَتَمْلِكَ الِاخْتِيَارَ وَ لَنْ تَحْكُمَ ذَلِكَ مِنْ نَفْسِكَ حَتَّى تُكْثِرَ هُمُومَكَ بِذِكْرِ الْمَعَادِ إِلَى رَبِّكَ وَ الْوَاجِبُ عَلَيْكَ أَنْ تَتَذَكَّرَ مَا مَضَى لِمَنْ تَقَدَّمَكَ مِنْ حُكُومَةٍ عَادِلَةٍ أَوْ سُنَّةٍ فَاضِلَةٍ أَوْ أَثَرٍ عَنْ نَبِيِّنَا (صلى الله عليه وآله) أَوْ فَرِيضَةٍ فِي كِتَابِ اللَّهِ فَتَقْتَدِيَ بِمَا شَاهَدْتَ مِمَّا عَمِلْنَا بِهِ فِيهَا وَ تَجْتَهِدَ لِنَفْسِكَ فِي اتِّبَاعِ مَا عَهِدْتُ إِلَيْكَ فِي عَهْدِي هَذَا وَ اسْتَوْثَقْتُ بِهِ مِنَ الْحُجَّةِ لِنَفْسِي عَلَيْكَ لِكَيْلَا تَكُونَ لَكَ عِلَّةٌ عِنْدَ تَسَرُّعِ نَفْسِكَ إِلَى هَوَاهَا وَ أَنَا أَسْأَلُ اللَّهَ بِسَعَةِ رَحْمَتِهِ وَ عَظِيمِ قُدْرَتِهِ عَلَى إِعْطَاءِ كُلِّ رَغْبَةٍ أَنْ يُوَفِّقَنِي وَ إِيَّاكَ لِمَا فِيهِ رِضَاهُ مِنَ الْإِقَامَةِ عَلَى الْعُذْرِ الْوَاضِحِ إِلَيْهِ وَ إِلَى خَلْقِهِ مَعَ حُسْنِ الثَّنَاءِ فِي الْعِبَادِ وَ جَمِيلِ الْأَثَرِ فِي الْبِلَادِ وَ تَمَامِ النِّعْمَةِ وَ تَضْعِيفِ الْكَرَامَةِ وَ أَنْ يَخْتِمَ لِي وَ لَكَ بِالسَّعَادَةِ وَ الشَّهَادَةِ إِنَّا إِلَيْهِ رَاجِعُونَ وَ السَّلَامُ عَلَى رَسُولِ اللَّهِ صَلَّى اللَّهُ عَلَيْهِ وَ آلِهِ وَ سَلَّمَ الطَّيِّبِينَ الطَّاهِرِينَ وَ سَلَّمَ تَسْلِيماً كَثِيراً وَ السَّلَامُ.

متن عربي نامه ۵۳ حضرت علي (ع) به مالك اشتر 53-و من آتاب له (عليه السلام) آتبه للأشتر النخعي لما ولاه على مصر و أعمالها حين اضطرب أمر أميرها محمد بن أبي بكر، و هو أطول عهد آتبه و أجمعه للمحاسن :بِسْمِ اللَّهِ الرَّحْمَنِ الرَّحِيمِ ، هَذَا مَا أَمَرَ بِهِ عَبْدُ اللَّهِ عَلِيٌّ أَمِيرُ الْمُؤْمِنِينَ مَالِكَ بْنَ الْحَارِثِ الْأَشْتَرَ فِي عَهْدِهِ إِلَيْهِ حِينَ وَلَّاهُ مِصْرَ جِبَايَةَ خَرَاجِهَا وَ جِهَادَ عَدُوِّهَا وَ اسْتِصْلَاحَ أَهْلِهَا وَ عِمَارَةَ بِلَادِهَا أَمَرَهُ بِتَقْوَى اللَّهِ وَ إِيثَارِ طَاعَتِهِ وَ اتِّبَاعِ مَا أَمَرَ بِهِ فِي كِتَابِهِ مِنْ فَرَائِضِهِ وَ سُنَنِهِ الَّتِي لَا

يَسْعَدُ أَحَدٌ إِلَّا بِاتِّبَاعِهَا وَ لَا يَشْقَى إِلَّا مَعَ جُحُودِهَا وَ إِضَاعَتِهَا وَ أَنْ يَنْصُرَ اللَّهَ
سُبْحَانَهُ بِقَلْبِهِ وَ يَدِهِ وَ لِسَانِهِ فَإِنَّهُ جَلَّ اسْمُهُ قَدْ تَكَفَّلَ بِنَصْرِ مَنْ نَصَرَهُ وَ إِعْزَازِ مَنْ
أَعَزَّهُ وَ أَمَرَهُ أَنْ يَكْسِرَ نَفْسَهُ مِنَ الشَّهَوَاتِ وَ يَزَعَهَا عِنْدَ الْجَمَحَاتِ فَإِنَّ النَّفْسَ أَمَّارَةٌ
بِالسُّوءِ إِلَّا مَا رَحِمَ اللَّهُ ثُمَّ اعْلَمْ يَا مَالِكُ أَنِّي قَدْ وَجَّهْتُكَ إِلَى بِلَادٍ قَدْ جَرَتْ عَلَيْهَا
دُوَلٌ قَبْلَكَ مِنْ عَدْلٍ وَ جَوْرٍ وَ أَنَّ النَّاسَ يَنْظُرُونَ مِنْ أُمُورِكَ فِي مِثْلِ مَا أَنْتَ تَنْظُرُ
فِيهِ مِنْ أُمُورِ الْوُلَاةِ قَبْلَكَ وَ يَقُولُونَ فِيكَ مَا أَنْتَ تَقُولُ فِيهِمْ وَ إِنَّمَا يُسْتَدَلُّ عَلَى
الصَّالِحِينَ بِمَا يُجْرِي اللَّهُ لَهُمْ عَلَى أَلْسُنِ عِبَادِهِ فَلْيَكُنْ أَحَبَّ الذَّخَائِرِ إِلَيْكَ ذَخِيرَةُ الْعَمَلِ
الصَّالِحِ فَامْلِكْ هَوَاكَ وَ شُحَّ بِنَفْسِكَ عَمَّا لَا يَحِلُّ لَكَ فَإِنَّ الشُّحَّ بِالنَّفْسِ الْإِنْصَافُ
مِنْهَا فِيمَا أَحَبَّتْ أَوْ أَرِهَتْ وَ أَشْعِرْ قَلْبَكَ الرَّحْمَةَ لِلرَّعِيَّةِ وَ الْمَحَبَّةَ لَهُمْ وَ اللُّطْفَ بِهِمْ
وَ لَا تَكُونَنَّ عَلَيْهِمْ سَبُعاً ضَارِياً تَغْتَنِمُ أَكْلَهُمْ فَإِنَّهُمْ صِنْفَانِ إِمَّا أَخٌ لَكَ فِي الدِّينِ وَ إِمَّا
نَظِيرٌ لَكَ فِي الْخَلْقِ يَفْرُطُ مِنْهُمُ الزَّلَلُ وَ تَعْرِضُ لَهُمُ الْعِلَلُ وَ يُؤْتَى عَلَى أَيْدِيهِمْ فِي
الْعَمْدِ وَ الْخَطَإِ فَأَعْطِهِمْ مِنْ عَفْوِكَ وَ صَفْحِكَ مِثْلَ الَّذِي تُحِبُّ وَ تَرْضَى أَنْ يُعْطِيَكَ
اللَّهُ مِنْ عَفْوِهِ وَ صَفْحِهِ فَإِنَّكَ فَوْقَهُمْ وَ وَالِي الْأَمْرِ عَلَيْكَ فَوْقَكَ وَ اللَّهُ فَوْقَ مَنْ وَلَّاكَ
وَ قَدِ اسْتَكْفَاكَ أَمْرَهُمْ وَ ابْتَلَاكَ بِهِمْ وَ لَا تَنْصِبَنَّ نَفْسَكَ لِحَرْبِ اللَّهِ فَإِنَّهُ لَا يَدَ لَكَ
بِنِقْمَتِهِ وَ لَا غِنَى بِكَ عَنْ عَفْوِهِ وَ رَحْمَتِهِ وَ لَا تَنْدَمَنَّ عَلَى عَفْوٍ وَ لَا تَبْجَحَنَّ بِعُقُوبَةٍ
وَ لَا تُسْرِعَنَّ إِلَى بَادِرَةٍ وَجَدْتَ مِنْهَا مَنْدُوحَةً وَ لَا تَقُولَنَّ إِنِّي مُؤَمَّرٌ آمُرُ فَأُطَاعُ فَإِنَّ
ذَلِكَ إِدْغَالٌ فِي الْقَلْبِ وَ مَنْهَكَةٌ لِلدِّينِ وَ تَقَرُّبٌ مِنَ الْغِيَرِ وَ إِذَا أَحْدَثَ لَكَ مَا أَنْتَ
فِيهِ مِنْ سُلْطَانِكَ أُبَّهَةً أَوْ مَخِيلَةً فَانْظُرْ إِلَى عِظَمِ مُلْكِ اللَّهِ فَوْقَكَ وَ قُدْرَتِهِ مِنْكَ عَلَى
مَا لَا تَقْدِرُ عَلَيْهِ مِنْ نَفْسِكَ فَإِنَّ ذَلِكَ يُطَامِنُ إِلَيْكَ مِنْ طِمَاحِكَ وَ يَكُفُّ عَنْكَ مِنْ
غَرْبِكَ وَ يَفِيءُ إِلَيْكَ بِمَا عَزَبَ عَنْكَ مِنْ عَقْلِكَ إِيَّاكَ وَ مُسَامَاةَ اللَّهِ فِي عَظَمَتِهِ وَ
التَّشَبُّهَ بِهِ فِي جَبَرُوتِهِ فَإِنَّ اللَّهَ يُذِلُّ كُلَّ مُخْتَالٍ وَ يُهِينُ كُلَّ جَبَّارٍ أَنْصِفِ اللَّهَ وَ أَنْصِفِ
النَّاسَ مِنْ نَفْسِكَ وَ مِنْ خَاصَّةِ أَهْلِكَ وَ مَنْ لَكَ فِيهِ هَوًى مِنْ رَعِيَّتِكَ فَإِنَّكَ إِلَّا
تَفْعَلْ تَظْلِمْ وَ مَنْ ظَلَمَ عِبَادَ اللَّهِ أَانَ اللَّهُ خَصْمَهُ دُونَ عِبَادِهِ وَ مَنْ خَاصَمَهُ اللَّهُ أَدْحَضَ
حُجَّتَهُ وَ أَانَ لِلَّهِ حَرْباً حَتَّى يَنْزِعَ أَوْ يَتُوبَ وَ لَيْسَ شَيْءٌ أَدْعَى إِلَى تَغْيِيرِ نِعْمَةِ اللَّهِ وَ
تَعْجِيلِ نِقْمَتِهِ مِنْ إِقَامَةٍ عَلَى ظُلْمٍ فَإِنَّ اللَّهَ سَمِيعٌ دَعْوَةَ الْمُضْطَهَدِينَ وَ هُوَ لِلظَّالِمِينَ
بِالْمِرْصَادِ وَ لْيَكُنْ أَحَبَّ الْأُمُورِ إِلَيْكَ أَوْسَطُهَا فِي الْحَقِّ وَ أَعَمُّهَا فِي الْعَدْلِ وَ أَجْمَعُهَا
لِرِضَى الرَّعِيَّةِ فَإِنَّ سُخْطَ الْعَامَّةِ يُجْحِفُ بِرِضَى الْخَاصَّةِ وَ إِنَّ سُخْطَ الْخَاصَّةِ يُغْتَفَرُ
مَعَ رِضَى الْعَامَّةِ وَ لَيْسَ أَحَدٌ مِنَ الرَّعِيَّةِ أَثْقَلَ عَلَى الْوَالِي مَئُونَةً فِي الرَّخَاءِ وَ أَقَلَّ مَعُونَةً
لَهُ فِي الْبَلَاءِ وَ أَكْرَهَ لِلْإِنْصَافِ وَ أَسْأَلَ بِالْإِلْحَافِ وَ أَقَلَّ شُكْراً عِنْدَ الْإِعْطَاءِ وَ أَبْطَأَ
عُذْراً عِنْدَ الْمَنْعِ وَ أَضْعَفَ صَبْراً عِنْدَ مُلِمَّاتِ الدَّهْرِ مِنْ أَهْلِ الْخَاصَّةِ وَ إِنَّمَا عِمَادُ
الدِّينِ وَ جِمَاعُ الْمُسْلِمِينَ وَ الْعُدَّةُ لِلْأَعْدَاءِ الْعَامَّةُ مِنَ الْأُمَّةِ فَلْيَكُنْ صِغْوُكَ لَهُمْ وَ مَيْلُكَ
مَعَهُمْ وَ لْيَكُنْ أَبْعَدَ رَعِيَّتِكَ مِنْكَ وَ أَشْنَأَهُمْ عِنْدَكَ أَطْلَبُهُمْ لِمَعَايِبِ النَّاسِ فَإِنَّ فِي

النَّاسِ عُيُوباً الْوَالِي أَحَقُّ مَنْ سَتَرَهَا فَلَا تَكْشِفَنَّ عَمَّا غَابَ عَنْكَ مِنْهَا فَإِنَّمَا عَلَيْكَ تَطْهِيرُ مَا ظَهَرَ لَكَ وَ اللَّهُ يَحْكُمُ عَلَى مَا غَابَ عَنْكَ فَاسْتُرِ الْعَوْرَةَ مَا اسْتَطَعْتَ يَسْتُرِ اللَّهُ مِنْكَ مَا تُحِبُّ سَتْرَهُ مِنْ رَعِيَّتِكَ أَطْلِقْ عَنِ النَّاسِ عُقْدَةَ كُلِّ حِقْدٍ وَ اقْطَعْ عَنْكَ سَبَبَ كُلِّ وِتْرٍ وَ تَغَابَ عَنْ كُلِّ مَا لَا يَضِحُ لَكَ وَ لَا تَعْجَلَنَّ إِلَى تَصْدِيقِ سَاعٍ فَإِنَّ السَّاعِيَ غَاشٌّ وَ إِنْ تَشَبَّهَ بِالنَّاصِحِينَ وَ لَا تُدْخِلَنَّ فِي مَشُورَتِكَ بَخِيلًا يَعْدِلُ بِكَ عَنِ الْفَضْلِ وَ يَعِدُكَ الْفَقْرَ وَ لَا جَبَاناً يُضْعِفُكَ عَنِ الْأُمُورِ وَ لَا حَرِيصاً يُزَيِّنُ لَكَ الشَّرَهَ بِالْجَوْرِ فَإِنَّ الْبُخْلَ وَ الْجُبْنَ وَ الْحِرْصَ غَرَائِزُ شَتَّى يَجْمَعُهَا سُوءُ الظَّنِّ بِاللَّهِ إِنَّ شَرَّ وُزَرَائِكَ مَنْ كَانَ لِلْأَشْرَارِ قَبْلَكَ وَزِيراً وَ مَنْ شَرِكَهُمْ فِي الْآثَامِ فَلَا يَكُونَنَّ لَكَ بِطَانَةً فَإِنَّهُمْ أَعْوَانُ الْأَثَمَةِ وَ إِخْوَانُ الظَّلَمَةِ وَ أَنْتَ وَاجِدٌ مِنْهُمْ خَيْرَ الْخَلَفِ مِمَّنْ لَهُ مِثْلُ آرَائِهِمْ وَ نَفَاذِهِمْ وَ لَيْسَ عَلَيْهِ مِثْلُ آصَارِهِمْ وَ أَوْزَارِهِمْ مِمَّنْ لَمْ يُعَاوِنْ ظَالِماً عَلَى ظُلْمِهِ وَ لَا آثِماً عَلَى إِثْمِهِ أُولَئِكَ أَخَفُّ عَلَيْكَ مَئُونَةً وَ أَحْسَنُ لَكَ مَعُونَةً وَ أَحْنَى عَلَيْكَ عَطْفاً وَ أَقَلُّ لِغَيْرِكَ إِلْفاً فَاتَّخِذْ أُولَئِكَ خَاصَّةً لِخَلَوَاتِكَ وَ حَفَلَاتِكَ ثُمَّ لْيَكُنْ آثَرُهُمْ عِنْدَكَ أَقْوَلَهُمْ بِمُرِّ الْحَقِّ لَكَ وَ أَقَلَّهُمْ مُسَاعَدَةً فِيمَا يَكُونُ مِنْكَ مِمَّا أَرِهَ اللَّهُ لِأَوْلِيَائِهِ وَاقِعاً ذَلِكَ مِنْ هَوَاكَ حَيْثُ وَقَعَ وَ الْصَقْ بِأَهْلِ الْوَرَعِ وَ الصِّدْقِ ثُمَّ رُضْهُمْ عَلَى أَلَّا يُطْرُوكَ وَ لَا يَبْجَحُوكَ بِبَاطِلٍ لَمْ تَفْعَلْهُ فَإِنَّ أَثَرَةَ الْإِطْرَاءِ تُحْدِثُ الزَّهْوَ وَ تُدْنِي مِنَ الْعِزَّةِ وَ لَا يَكُونَنَّ الْمُحْسِنُ وَ الْمُسِيءُ عِنْدَكَ بِمَنْزِلَةٍ سَوَاءٍ فَإِنَّ فِي ذَلِكَ تَزْهِيداً لِأَهْلِ الْإِحْسَانِ فِي الْإِحْسَانِ وَ تَدْرِيباً لِأَهْلِ الْإِسَاءَةِ عَلَى الْإِسَاءَةِ وَ أَلْزِمْ كُلًّا مِنْهُمْ مَا أَلْزَمَ نَفْسَهُ وَ اعْلَمْ أَنَّهُ لَيْسَ شَيْءٌ بِأَدْعَى إِلَى حُسْنِ ظَنِّ رَاعٍ بِرَعِيَّتِهِ مِنْ إِحْسَانِهِ إِلَيْهِمْ وَ تَخْفِيفِهِ الْمَئُونَاتِ عَلَيْهِمْ وَ تَرْكِ اسْتِكْرَاهِهِ إِيَّاهُمْ عَلَى مَا لَيْسَ لَهُ قِبَلَهُمْ فَلْيَكُنْ مِنْكَ فِي ذَلِكَ أَمْرٌ يَجْتَمِعُ لَكَ بِهِ حُسْنُ الظَّنِّ بِرَعِيَّتِكَ فَإِنَّ حُسْنَ الظَّنِّ يَقْطَعُ عَنْكَ نَصَباً طَوِيلًا وَ إِنَّ أَحَقَّ مَنْ حَسُنَ ظَنُّكَ بِهِ لَمَنْ حَسُنَ بَلَاؤُكَ عِنْدَهُ وَ إِنَّ أَحَقَّ مَنْ سَاءَ ظَنُّكَ بِهِ لَمَنْ سَاءَ بَلَاؤُكَ عِنْدَهُ وَ لَا تَنْقُضْ سُنَّةً صَالِحَةً عَمِلَ بِهَا صُدُورُ هَذِهِ الْأُمَّةِ وَ اجْتَمَعَتْ بِهَا الْأُلْفَةُ وَ صَلَحَتْ عَلَيْهَا الرَّعِيَّةُ وَ لَا تُحْدِثَنَّ سُنَّةً تَضُرُّ بِشَيْءٍ مِنْ مَاضِي تِلْكَ السُّنَنِ فَيَكُونُ الْأَجْرُ لِمَنْ سَنَّهَا وَ الْوِزْرُ عَلَيْكَ بِمَا نَقَضْتَ مِنْهَا وَ أَكْثِرْ مُدَارَسَةَ الْعُلَمَاءِ وَ مُنَاقَشَةَ الْحُكَمَاءِ فِي تَثْبِيتِ مَا صَلَحَ عَلَيْهِ أَمْرُ بِلَادِكَ وَ إِقَامَةِ مَا اسْتَقَامَ بِهِ النَّاسُ قَبْلَكَ وَ اعْلَمْ أَنَّ الرَّعِيَّةَ طَبَقَاتٌ لَا يَصْلُحُ بَعْضُهَا إِلَّا بِبَعْضٍ وَ لَا غِنَى بِبَعْضِهَا عَنْ بَعْضٍ فَمِنْهَا جُنُودُ اللَّهِ وَ مِنْهَا كُتَّابُ الْعَامَّةِ وَ الْخَاصَّةِ وَ مِنْهَا قُضَاةُ الْعَدْلِ وَ مِنْهَا عُمَّالُ الْإِنْصَافِ وَ الرِّفْقِ وَ مِنْهَا أَهْلُ الْجِزْيَةِ وَ الْخَرَاجِ مِنْ أَهْلِ الذِّمَّةِ وَ مُسْلِمَةِ النَّاسِ وَ مِنْهَا التُّجَّارُ وَ أَهْلُ الصِّنَاعَاتِ وَ مِنْهَا الطَّبَقَةُ السُّفْلَى مِنْ ذَوِي الْحَاجَةِ وَ الْمَسْكَنَةِ وَ كُلٌّ قَدْ سَمَّى اللَّهُ لَهُ سَهْمَهُ وَ وَضَعَ عَلَى حَدِّهِ فَرِيضَةً فِي كِتَابِهِ أَوْ سُنَّةِ نَبِيِّهِ (صلى الله عليه وآله) عَهْداً مِنْهُ عِنْدَنَا مَحْفُوظاً فَالْجُنُودُ بِإِذْنِ اللَّهِ حُصُونُ الرَّعِيَّةِ وَ زَيْنُ الْوُلَاةِ وَ عِزُّ الدِّينِ وَ سُبُلُ الْأَمْنِ وَ لَيْسَ تَقُومُ الرَّعِيَّةُ إِلَّا بِهِمْ ثُمَّ

لَا قِوَامَ لِلْجُنُودِ إِلَّا بِمَا يُخْرِجُ اللَّهُ لَهُمْ مِنَ الْخَرَاجِ الَّذِي يَقْوَوْنَ بِهِ عَلَى جِهَادِ عَدُوِّهِمْ وَ يَعْتَمِدُونَ عَلَيْهِ فِيمَا يُصْلِحُهُمْ وَ يَكُونُ مِنْ وَرَاءِ حَاجَتِهِمْ ثُمَّ لَا قِوَامَ لِهَذَيْنِ الصِّنْفَيْنِ إِلَّا بِالصِّنْفِ الثَّالِثِ مِنَ الْقُضَاةِ وَ الْعُمَّالِ وَ الْكُتَّابِ لِمَا يُحْكِمُونَ مِنَ الْمَعَاقِدِ وَ يَجْمَعُونَ مِنَ الْمَنَافِعِ وَ يُؤْتَمَنُونَ عَلَيْهِ مِنْ خَوَاصِّ الْأُمُورِ وَ عَوَامِّهَا وَ لَا قِوَامَ لَهُمْ جَمِيعاً إِلَّا بِالتُّجَّارِ وَ ذَوِي الصِّنَاعَاتِ فِيمَا يَجْتَمِعُونَ عَلَيْهِ مِنْ مَرَافِقِهِمْ وَ يُقِيمُونَهُ مِنْ أَسْوَاقِهِمْ وَ يَكْفُونَهُمْ مِنَ التَّرَفُّقِ بِأَيْدِيهِمْ مَا لَا يَبْلُغُهُ رِفْقُ غَيْرِهِمْ ثُمَّ الطَّبَقَةُ السُّفْلَى مِنْ أَهْلِ الْحَاجَةِ وَ الْمَسْكَنَةِ الَّذِينَ يَحِقُّ رِفْدُهُمْ وَ مَعُونَتُهُمْ وَ فِي اللَّهِ لِكُلٍّ سَعَةٌ وَ لِكُلٍّ عَلَى الْوَالِي حَقٌّ بِقَدْرِ مَا يُصْلِحُهُ وَ لَيْسَ يَخْرُجُ الْوَالِي مِنْ حَقِيقَةِ مَا أَلْزَمَهُ اللَّهُ مِنْ ذَلِكَ إِلَّا بِالِاهْتِمَامِ وَ الِاسْتِعَانَةِ بِاللَّهِ وَ تَوْطِينِ نَفْسِهِ عَلَى لُزُومِ الْحَقِّ وَ الصَّبْرِ عَلَيْهِ فِيمَا خَفَّ عَلَيْهِ أَوْ ثَقُلَ فَوَلِّ مِنْ جُنُودِكَ أَنْصَحَهُمْ فِي نَفْسِكَ لِلَّهِ وَ لِرَسُولِهِ وَ لِإِمَامِكَ وَ أَنْقَاهُمْ جَيْباً وَ أَفْضَلَهُمْ حِلْماً مِمَّنْ يُبْطِئُ عَنِ الْغَضَبِ وَ يَسْتَرِيحُ إِلَى الْعُذْرِ وَ يَرْأَفُ بِالضُّعَفَاءِ وَ يَنْبُو عَلَى الْأَقْوِيَاءِ وَ مِمَّنْ لَا يُثِيرُهُ الْعُنْفُ وَ لَا يَقْعُدُ بِهِ الضَّعْفُ ثُمَّ الْصَقْ بِذَوِي الْمُرُوءَاتِ وَ الْأَحْسَابِ وَ أَهْلِ الْبُيُوتَاتِ الصَّالِحَةِ وَ السَّوَابِقِ الْحَسَنَةِ ثُمَّ أَهْلِ النَّجْدَةِ وَ الشَّجَاعَةِ وَ السَّخَاءِ وَ السَّمَاحَةِ فَإِنَّهُمْ جِمَاعٌ مِنَ الْكَرَمِ وَ شُعَبٌ مِنَ الْعُرْفِ ثُمَّ تَفَقَّدْ مِنْ أُمُورِهِمْ مَا يَتَفَقَّدُ الْوَالِدَانِ مِنْ وَلَدِهِمَا وَ لَا يَتَفَاقَمَنَّ فِي نَفْسِكَ شَيْءٌ قَوَّيْتَهُمْ بِهِ وَ لَا تَحْقِرَنَّ لُطْفاً تَعَاهَدْتَهُمْ بِهِ وَ إِنْ قَلَّ فَإِنَّهُ دَاعِيَةٌ لَهُمْ إِلَى بَذْلِ النَّصِيحَةِ لَكَ وَ حُسْنِ الظَّنِّ بِكَ وَ لَا تَدَعْ تَفَقُّدَ لَطِيفِ أُمُورِهِمْ اتِّكَالاً عَلَى جَسِيمِهَا فَإِنَّ لِلْيَسِيرِ مِنْ لُطْفِكَ مَوْضِعاً يَنْتَفِعُونَ بِهِ وَ لِلْجَسِيمِ مَوْقِعاً لَا يَسْتَغْنُونَ عَنْهُ وَ لْيَكُنْ آثَرُ رُءُوسِ جُنْدِكَ عِنْدَكَ مَنْ وَاسَاهُمْ فِي مَعُونَتِهِ وَ أَفْضَلَ عَلَيْهِمْ مِنْ جِدَتِهِ بِمَا يَسَعُهُمْ وَ يَسَعُ مَنْ وَرَاءَهُمْ مِنْ خُلُوفِ أَهْلِيهِمْ حَتَّى يَكُونَ هَمُّهُمْ هَمّاً وَاحِداً فِي جِهَادِ الْعَدُوِّ فَإِنَّ عَطْفَكَ عَلَيْهِمْ يَعْطِفُ قُلُوبَهُمْ عَلَيْكَ وَ إِنَّ أَفْضَلَ قُرَّةِ عَيْنِ الْوُلَاةِ اسْتِقَامَةُ الْعَدْلِ فِي الْبِلَادِ وَ ظُهُورُ مَوَدَّةِ الرَّعِيَّةِ وَ إِنَّهُ لَا تَظْهَرُ مَوَدَّتُهُمْ إِلَّا بِسَلَامَةِ صُدُورِهِمْ وَ لَا تَصِحُّ نَصِيحَتُهُمْ إِلَّا بِحِيطَتِهِمْ عَلَى وُلَاةِ الْأُمُورِ وَ قِلَّةِ اسْتِثْقَالِ دُوَلِهِمْ وَ تَرْكِ اسْتِبْطَاءِ انْقِطَاعِ مُدَّتِهِمْ فَافْسَحْ فِي آمَالِهِمْ وَ وَاصِلْ فِي حُسْنِ الثَّنَاءِ عَلَيْهِمْ وَ تَعْدِيدِ مَا أَبْلَى ذَوُو الْبَلَاءِ مِنْهُمْ فَإِنَّ آثَرَةَ الذِّكْرِ لِحُسْنِ أَفْعَالِهِمْ تَهُزُّ الشُّجَاعَ وَ تُحَرِّضُ النَّاكِلَ إِنْ شَاءَ اللَّهُ ثُمَّ اعْرِفْ لِكُلِّ امْرِئٍ مِنْهُمْ مَا أَبْلَى وَ لَا تَضُمَّنَّ بَلَاءَ امْرِئٍ إِلَى غَيْرِهِ وَ لَا تُقَصِّرَنَّ بِهِ دُونَ غَايَةِ بَلَائِهِ وَ لَا يَدْعُوَنَّكَ شَرَفُ امْرِئٍ إِلَى أَنْ تُعْظِمَ مِنْ بَلَائِهِ مَا كَانَ صَغِيراً وَ لَا ضَعَةُ امْرِئٍ إِلَى أَنْ تَسْتَصْغِرَ مِنْ بَلَائِهِ مَا كَانَ عَظِيماً وَ ارْدُدْ إِلَى اللَّهِ وَ رَسُولِهِ مَا يُضْلِعُكَ مِنَ الْخُطُوبِ وَ يَشْتَبِهُ عَلَيْكَ مِنَ الْأُمُورِ فَقَدْ قَالَ اللَّهُ تَعَالَى لِقَوْمٍ أَحَبَّ إِرْشَادَهُمْ يَا أَيُّهَا الَّذِينَ آمَنُوا أَطِيعُوا اللَّهَ وَ أَطِيعُوا الرَّسُولَ وَ أُولِي الْأَمْرِ مِنْكُمْ فَإِنْ تَنَازَعْتُمْ فِي شَيْءٍ فَرُدُّوهُ إِلَى اللَّهِ وَ الرَّسُولِ فَالرَّدُّ إِلَى اللَّهِ الْأَخْذُ بِمُحْكَمِ آيَاتِهِ وَ الرَّدُّ إِلَى الرَّسُولِ الْأَخْذُ بِسُنَّتِهِ الْجَامِعَةِ غَيْرِ الْمُفَرِّقَةِ ثُمَّ اخْتَرْ لِلْحُكْمِ بَيْنَ النَّاسِ أَفْضَلَ رَعِيَّتِكَ فِي نَفْسِكَ مِمَّنْ لَا تَضِيقُ

بِهِ الْأُمُورُ وَ لَا تُمَحِّكُهُ الْخُصُومُ وَ لَا يَتَمَادَى فِي الزَّلَّةِ وَ لَا يَحْصَرُ مِنَ الْفَيْءِ إِلَى الْحَقِّ إِذَا عَرَفَهُ وَ لَا تُشْرِفُ نَفْسُهُ عَلَى طَمَعٍ وَ لَا يَكْتَفِي بِأَدْنَى فَهْمٍ دُونَ أَقْصَاهُ وَ أَوْقَفَهُمْ فِي الشُّبُهَاتِ وَ آخَذَهُمْ بِالْحُجَجِ وَ أَقَلَّهُمْ تَبَرُّماً بِمُرَاجَعَةِ الْخَصْمِ وَ أَصْبَرَهُمْ عَلَى تَكَشُّفِ الْأُمُورِ وَ أَصْرَمَهُمْ عِنْدَ اتِّضَاحِ الْحُكْمِ مِمَّنْ لَا يَزْدَهِيهِ إِطْرَاءٌ وَ لَا يَسْتَمِيلُهُ إِغْرَاءٌ وَ أُولَئِكَ قَلِيلٌ ثُمَّ أَأْثِرْ تَعَاهُدَ قَضَائِهِ وَ افْسَحْ لَهُ فِي الْبَذْلِ مَا يُزِيلُ عِلَّتَهُ وَ تَقِلُّ مَعَهُ حَاجَتُهُ إِلَى النَّاسِ وَ أَعْطِهِ مِنَ الْمَنْزِلَةِ لَدَيْكَ مَا لَا يَطْمَعُ فِيهِ غَيْرُهُ مِنْ خَاصَّتِكَ لِيَأْمَنَ بِذَلِكَ اغْتِيَالَ الرِّجَالِ لَهُ عِنْدَكَ فَانْظُرْ فِي ذَلِكَ نَظَراً بَلِيغاً فَإِنَّ هَذَا الدِّينَ قَدْ آانَ أَسِيراً فِي أَيْدِي الْأَشْرَارِ يُعْمَلُ فِيهِ بِالْهَوَى وَ تُطْلَبُ بِهِ الدُّنْيَا ثُمَّ انْظُرْ فِي أُمُورِ عُمَّالِكَ فَاسْتَعْمِلْهُمُ اخْتِبَاراً وَ لَا تُوَلِّهِمْ مُحَابَاةً وَ أَثَرَةً فَإِنَّهُمَا جِمَاعٌ مِنْ شُعَبِ الْجَوْرِ وَ الْخِيَانَةِ وَ تَوَخَّ مِنْهُمْ أَهْلَ التَّجْرِبَةِ وَ الْحَيَاءِ مِنْ أَهْلِ الْبُيُوتَاتِ الصَّالِحَةِ وَ الْقَدَمِ فِي الْإِسْلَامِ الْمُتَقَدِّمَةِ فَإِنَّهُمْ أَأْرَمُ أَخْلَاقاً وَ أَصَحُّ أَعْرَاضاً وَ أَقَلُّ فِي الْمَطَامِعِ إِشْرَاقاً وَ أَبْلَغُ فِي عَوَاقِبِ الْأُمُورِ نَظَراً ثُمَّ أَسْبِغْ عَلَيْهِمُ الْأَرْزَاقَ فَإِنَّ ذَلِكَ قُوَّةٌ لَهُمْ عَلَى اسْتِصْلَاحِ أَنْفُسِهِمْ وَ غِنًى لَهُمْ عَنْ تَنَاوُلِ مَا تَحْتَ أَيْدِيهِمْ وَ حُجَّةٌ عَلَيْهِمْ إِنْ خَالَفُوا أَمْرَكَ أَوْ ثَلَمُوا أَمَانَتَكَ ثُمَّ تَفَقَّدْ أَعْمَالَهُمْ وَ ابْعَثِ الْعُيُونَ مِنْ أَهْلِ الصِّدْقِ وَ الْوَفَاءِ عَلَيْهِمْ فَإِنَّ تَعَاهُدَكَ فِي السِّرِّ لِأُمُورِهِمْ حَدْوَةٌ لَهُمْ عَلَى اسْتِعْمَالِ الْأَمَانَةِ وَ الرِّفْقِ بِالرَّعِيَّةِ وَ تَحَفَّظْ مِنَ الْأَعْوَانِ فَإِنْ أَحَدٌ مِنْهُمْ بَسَطَ يَدَهُ إِلَى خِيَانَةٍ اجْتَمَعَتْ بِهَا عَلَيْهِ عِنْدَكَ أَخْبَارُ عُيُونِكَ اكْتَفَيْتَ بِذَلِكَ شَاهِداً فَبَسَطْتَ عَلَيْهِ الْعُقُوبَةَ فِي بَدَنِهِ وَ أَخَذْتَهُ بِمَا أَصَابَ مِنْ عَمَلِهِ ثُمَّ نَصَبْتَهُ بِمَقَامِ الْمَذَلَّةِ وَ وَسَمْتَهُ بِالْخِيَانَةِ وَ قَلَّدْتَهُ عَارَ التُّهَمَةِ وَ تَفَقَّدْ أَمْرَ الْخَرَاجِ بِمَا يُصْلِحُ أَهْلَهُ فَإِنَّ فِي صَلَاحِهِ وَ صَلَاحِهِمْ صَلَاحاً لِمَنْ سِوَاهُمْ وَ لَا صَلَاحَ لِمَنْ سِوَاهُمْ إِلَّا بِهِمْ لِأَنَّ النَّاسَ أُلَّهُمْ عِيَالٌ عَلَى الْخَرَاجِ وَ أَهْلِهِ وَ لْيَكُنْ نَظَرُكَ فِي عِمَارَةِ الْأَرْضِ أَبْلَغَ مِنْ نَظَرِكَ فِي اسْتِجْلَابِ الْخَرَاجِ لِأَنَّ ذَلِكَ لَا يُدْرَكُ إِلَّا بِالْعِمَارَةِ وَ مَنْ طَلَبَ الْخَرَاجَ بِغَيْرِ عِمَارَةٍ أَخْرَبَ الْبِلَادَ وَ أَهْلَكَ الْعِبَادَ وَ لَمْ يَسْتَقِمْ أَمْرُهُ إِلَّا قَلِيلاً فَإِنْ شَكَوْا ثِقَلاً أَوْ عِلَّةً أَوِ انْقِطَاعَ شِرْبٍ أَوْ بَالَّةٍ أَوْ إِحَالَةَ أَرْضٍ اغْتَمَرَهَا غَرَقٌ أَوْ أَجْحَفَ بِهَا عَطَشٌ خَفَّفْتَ عَنْهُمْ بِمَا تَرْجُو أَنْ يَصْلُحَ بِهِ أَمْرُهُمْ وَ لَا يَثْقُلَنَّ عَلَيْكَ شَيْءٌ خَفَّفْتَ بِهِ الْمَئُونَةَ عَنْهُمْ فَإِنَّهُ ذُخْرٌ يَعُودُونَ بِهِ عَلَيْكَ فِي عِمَارَةِ بِلَادِكَ وَ تَزْيِينِ وِلَايَتِكَ مَعَ اسْتِجْلَابِكَ حُسْنَ ثَنَائِهِمْ وَ تَبَجُّحِكَ بِاسْتِفَاضَةِ الْعَدْلِ فِيهِمْ مُعْتَمِداً فَضْلَ قُوَّتِهِمْ بِمَا ذَخَرْتَ عِنْدَهُمْ مِنْ إِجْمَامِكَ لَهُمْ وَ الثِّقَةَ مِنْهُمْ بِمَا عَوَّدْتَهُمْ مِنْ عَدْلِكَ عَلَيْهِمْ وَ رِفْقِكَ بِهِمْ فَرُبَّمَا حَدَثَ مِنَ الْأُمُورِ مَا إِذَا عَوَّلْتَ فِيهِ عَلَيْهِمْ مِنْ بَعْدُ احْتَمَلُوهُ طَيِّبَةً أَنْفُسُهُمْ بِهِ فَإِنَّ الْعُمْرَانَ مُحْتَمِلٌ مَا حَمَّلْتَهُ وَ إِنَّمَا يُؤْتَى خَرَابُ الْأَرْضِ مِنْ إِعْوَازِ أَهْلِهَا وَ إِنَّمَا يُعْوِزُ أَهْلُهَا لِإِشْرَافِ أَنْفُسِ الْوُلَاةِ عَلَى الْجَمْعِ وَ سُوءِ ظَنِّهِمْ بِالْبَقَاءِ وَ قِلَّةِ انْتِفَاعِهِمْ بِالْعِبَرِ ثُمَّ انْظُرْ فِي حَالِ أُتَّابِكَ فَوَلِّ عَلَى أُمُورِكَ خَيْرَهُمْ وَ اخْصُصْ رَسَائِلَكَ الَّتِي تُدْخِلُ فِيهَا مَكَايِدَكَ وَ أَسْرَارَكَ بِأَجْمَعِهِمْ لِوُجُوهِ صَالِحِ الْأَخْلَاقِ مِمَّنْ لَا تُبْطِرُهُ الْكَرَامَةُ فَيَجْتَرِئَ بِهَا عَلَيْكَ فِي خِلَافِ

لَكَ بِحَضْرَةِ مَلَإٍ وَ لَا تَقْصُرْ بِهِ الْغَفْلَةُ عَنْ إِيرَادِ مُكَاتَبَاتِ عُمَّالِكَ عَلَيْكَ وَ إِصْدَارِ
جَوَابَاتِهَا عَلَى الصَّوَابِ عَنْكَ فِيمَا يَأْخُذُ لَكَ وَ يُعْطِي مِنْكَ وَ لَا يُضْعِفُ عَقْداً اعْتَقَدَهُ
لَكَ وَ لَا يَعْجِزُ عَنْ إِطْلَاقِ مَا عُقِدَ عَلَيْكَ وَ لَا يَجْهَلُ مَبْلَغَ قَدْرِ نَفْسِهِ فِي الْأُمُورِ
فَإِنَّ الْجَاهِلَ بِقَدْرِ نَفْسِهِ يَكُونُ بِقَدْرِ غَيْرِهِ أَجْهَلَ ثُمَّ لَا يَكُنْ اخْتِيَارُكَ إِيَّاهُمْ عَلَى
فِرَاسَتِكَ وَ اسْتِنَامَتِكَ وَ حُسْنِ الظَّنِّ مِنْكَ فَإِنَّ الرِّجَالَ يَتَعَرَّضُونَ لِفِرَاسَاتِ الْوُلَاةِ
بِتَصَنُّعِهِمْ وَ حُسْنِ خِدْمَتِهِمْ وَ لَيْسَ وَرَاءَ ذَلِكَ مِنَ النَّصِيحَةِ وَ الْأَمَانَةِ شَيْءٌ وَ لَكِنِ
اخْتَبِرْهُمْ بِمَا وُلُّوا لِلصَّالِحِينَ قَبْلَكَ فَاعْمِدْ لِأَحْسَنِهِمْ آانَ فِي الْعَامَّةِ أَثَراً وَ أَعْرَفِهِمْ بِالْأَمَانَةِ
وَجْهاً فَإِنَّ ذَلِكَ دَلِيلٌ عَلَى نَصِيحَتِكَ لِلَّهِ وَ لِمَنْ وُلِّيتَ أَمْرَهُ وَ اجْعَلْ لِرَأْسِ أَلِّ أَمْرٍ
مِنْ أُمُورِكَ رَأْساً مِنْهُمْ لَا يَقْهَرُهُ أَيرُهُا وَ لَا يَتَشَتَّتُ عَلَيْهِ آثِيرُهَا وَ مَهْمَا آانَ فِي أَتَّابِكَ
مِنْ عَيْبٍ فَتَغَابَيْتَ عَنْهُ أُلْزِمْتَهُ ثُمَّ اسْتَوْصِ بِالتُّجَّارِ وَ ذَوِي الصِّنَاعَاتِ وَ أَوْصِ بِهِمْ
خَيْراً الْمُقِيمِ مِنْهُمْ وَ الْمُضْطَرِبِ بِمَالِهِ وَ الْمُتَرَفِّقِ بِبَدَنِهِ فَإِنَّهُمْ مَوَادُّ الْمَنَافِعِ وَ أَسْبَابُ
الْمَرَافِقِ وَ جُلَّابُهَا مِنَ الْمَبَاعِدِ وَ الْمَطَارِحِ فِي بَرِّكَ وَ بَحْرِكَ وَ سَهْلِكَ وَ جَبَلِكَ وَ
حَيْثُ لَا يَلْتَئِمُ النَّاسُ لِمَوَاضِعِهَا وَ لَا يَجْتَرِءُونَ عَلَيْهَا فَإِنَّهُمْ سِلْمٌ لَا تُخَافُ بَائِقَتُهُ وَ
صُلْحٌ لَا تُخْشَى غَائِلَتُهُ وَ تَفَقَّدْ أُمُورَهُمْ بِحَضْرَتِكَ وَ فِي حَوَاشِي بِلَادِكَ وَ اعْلَمْ مَعَ
ذَلِكَ أَنَّ فِي آثِيرٍ مِنْهُمْ ضِيقاً فَاحِشاً وَ شُحّاً قَبِيحاً وَ احْتِكَاراً لِلْمَنَافِعِ وَ تَحَكُّماً فِي
الْبِيَاعَاتِ وَ ذَلِكَ بَابُ مَضَرَّةٍ لِلْعَامَّةِ وَ عَيْبٌ عَلَى الْوُلَاةِ فَامْنَعْ مِنَ الِاحْتِكَارِ فَإِنَّ
رَسُولَ اللَّهِ (صلى الله عليه وآله) مَنَعَ مِنْهُ وَ لْيَكُنِ الْبَيْعُ بَيْعاً سَمْحاً بِمَوَازِينِ عَدْلٍ وَ
أَسْعَارٍ لَا تُجْحِفُ بِالْفَرِيقَيْنِ مِنَ الْبَائِعِ وَ الْمُبْتَاعِ فَمَنْ قَارَفَ حُكْرَةً بَعْدَ نَهْيِكَ إِيَّاهُ
فَنَكِّلْ بِهِ وَ عَاقِبْهُ فِي غَيْرِ إِسْرَافٍ ثُمَّ اللَّهَ اللَّهَ فِي الطَّبَقَةِ السُّفْلَى مِنَ الَّذِينَ لَا حِيلَةَ لَهُمْ
مِنَ الْمَسَاآِينِ وَ الْمُحْتَاجِينَ وَ أَهْلِ الْبُؤْسَى وَ الزَّمْنَى فَإِنَّ فِي هَذِهِ الطَّبَقَةِ قَانِعاً وَ
مُعْتَرّاً وَ احْفَظِ لِلَّهِ مَا اسْتَحْفَظَكَ مِنْ حَقِّهِ فِيهِمْ وَ اجْعَلْ لَهُمْ قِسْماً مِنْ بَيْتِ مَالِكِ
وَ قِسْماً مِنْ غَلَّاتِ صَوَافِي الْإِسْلَامِ فِي أُلِّ بَلَدٍ فَإِنَّ لِلْأَقْصَى مِنْهُمْ مِثْلَ الَّذِي لِلْأَدْنَى
وَ أُلٌّ قَدِ اسْتُرْعِيتَ حَقَّهُ وَ لَا يَشْغَلَنَّكَ عَنْهُمْ بَطَرٌ فَإِنَّكَ لَا تُعْذَرُ بِتَضْيِيعِكَ التَّافِهَ
لِإِحْكَامِكَ الْكَثِيرَ الْمُهِمَّ فَلَا تُشْخِصْ هَمَّكَ عَنْهُمْ وَ لَا تُصَعِّرْ خَدَّكَ لَهُمْ وَ تَفَقَّدْ أُمُورَ
مَنْ لَا يَصِلُ إِلَيْكَ مِنْهُمْ مِمَّنْ تَقْتَحِمُهُ الْعُيُونُ وَ تَحْقِرُهُ الرِّجَالُ فَفَرِّغْ لِأُولَئِكَ ثِقَتَكَ مِنْ
أَهْلِ الْخَشْيَةِ وَ التَّوَاضُعِ فَلْيَرْفَعْ إِلَيْكَ أُمُورَهُمْ ثُمَّ اعْمَلْ فِيهِمْ بِالْإِعْذَارِ إِلَى اللَّهِ يَوْمَ تَلْقَاهُ
فَإِنَّ هَؤُلَاءِ مِنْ بَيْنِ الرَّعِيَّةِ أَحْوَجُ إِلَى الْإِنْصَافِ مِنْ غَيْرِهِمْ وَ أُلٌّ فَأَعْذِرْ إِلَى اللَّهِ فِي
تَأْدِيَةِ حَقِّهِ إِلَيْهِ وَ تَعَهَّدْ أَهْلَ الْيُتْمِ وَ ذَوِي الرِّقَّةِ فِي السِّنِّ مِمَّنْ لَا حِيلَةَ لَهُ وَ لَا يَنْصِبُ
لِلْمَسْأَلَةِ نَفْسَهُ وَ ذَلِكَ عَلَى الْوُلَاةِ ثَقِيلٌ وَ الْحَقُّ أُلُّهُ ثَقِيلٌ وَ قَدْ يُخَفِّفُهُ اللَّهُ عَلَى أَقْوَامٍ
طَلَبُوا الْعَاقِبَةَ فَصَبَّرُوا أَنْفُسَهُمْ وَ وَثِقُوا بِصِدْقِ مَوْعُودِ اللَّهِ لَهُمْ وَ اجْعَلْ لِذَوِي الْحَاجَاتِ
مِنْكَ قِسْماً تُفَرِّغُ لَهُمْ فِيهِ شَخْصَكَ وَ تَجْلِسُ لَهُمْ مَجْلِساً عَامّاً فَتَتَوَاضَعُ فِيهِ لِلَّهِ الَّذِي
خَلَقَكَ وَ تُقْعِدُ عَنْهُمْ جُنْدَكَ وَ أَعْوَانَكَ مِنْ أَحْرَاسِكَ وَ شُرَطِكَ حَتَّى يُكَلِّمَكَ

مُتَكَلِّمُهُمْ غَيْرَ مُتَتَعْتِعٍ فَإِنِّي سَمِعْتُ رَسُولَ اللَّهِ (صلى الله عليه وآله) يَقُولُ فِي غَيْرِ
مَوْطِنٍ لَنْ تُقَدَّسَ أُمَّةٌ لَا يُؤْخَذُ لِلضَّعِيفِ فِيهَا حَقُّهُ مِنَ الْقَوِيِّ غَيْرَ مُتَتَعْتِعٍ ثُمَّ احْتَمِلِ
الْخُرْقَ مِنْهُمْ وَ الْعِيَّ وَ نَحِّ عَنْهُمُ الضِّيقَ وَ الْأَنَفَ يَبْسُطِ اللَّهُ عَلَيْكَ بِذَلِكَ أَكْنَافَ
رَحْمَتِهِ وَ يُوجِبْ لَكَ ثَوَابَ طَاعَتِهِ وَ أَعْطِ مَا أَعْطَيْتَ هَنِيئاً وَ امْنَعْ فِي إِجْمَالٍ وَ إِعْذَارٍ
ثُمَّ أُمُورٌ مِنْ أُمُورِكَ لَا بُدَّ لَكَ مِنْ مُبَاشَرَتِهَا مِنْهَا إِجَابَةُ عُمَّالِكَ بِمَا يَعْيَا عَنْهُ أُتَّابُكَ وَ
مِنْهَا إِصْدَارُ حَاجَاتِ النَّاسِ يَوْمَ وُرُودِهَا عَلَيْكَ بِمَا تَحْرَجُ بِهِ صُدُورُ أَعْوَانِكَ وَ أَمْضِ
لِكُلِّ يَوْمٍ عَمَلَهُ فَإِنَّ لِكُلِّ يَوْمٍ مَا فِيهِ وَ اجْعَلْ لِنَفْسِكَ فِيمَا بَيْنَكَ وَ بَيْنَ اللَّهِ أَفْضَلَ
تِلْكَ الْمَوَاقِيتِ وَ أَجْزَلَ تِلْكَ الْأَقْسَامِ وَ إِنْ كَانَتْ كُلُّهَا لِلَّهِ إِذَا صَلَحَتْ فِيهَا النِّيَّةُ وَ
سَلِمَتْ مِنْهَا الرَّعِيَّةُ وَ لْيَكُنْ فِي خَاصَّةِ مَا تُخْلِصُ بِهِ لِلَّهِ دِينَكَ إِقَامَةُ فَرَائِضِهِ الَّتِي هِيَ
لَهُ خَاصَّةً فَأَعْطِ اللَّهَ مِنْ بَدَنِكَ فِي لَيْلِكَ وَ نَهَارِكَ وَ وَفِّ مَا تَقَرَّبْتَ بِهِ إِلَى اللَّهِ مِنْ
ذَلِكَ كَامِلًا غَيْرَ مَثْلُومٍ وَ لَا مَنْقُوصٍ بَالِغاً مِنْ بَدَنِكَ مَا بَلَغَ وَ إِذَا قُمْتَ فِي صَلَاتِكَ
لِلنَّاسِ فَلَا تَكُونَنَّ مُنَفِّراً وَ لَا مُضَيِّعاً فَإِنَّ فِي النَّاسِ مَنْ بِهِ الْعِلَّةُ وَ لَهُ الْحَاجَةُ وَ قَدْ
سَأَلْتُ رَسُولَ اللَّهِ (صلى الله عليه وآله) (حِينَ وَجَّهَنِي إِلَى الْيَمَنِ) كَيْفَ أُصَلِّي بِهِمْ فَقَالَ
صَلِّ بِهِمْ كَصَلَاةِ أَضْعَفِهِمْ وَ أَنْ بِالْمُؤْمِنِينَ رَحِيماً وَ أَمَّا بَعْدُ فَلَا تُطَوِّلَنَّ احْتِجَابَكَ
عَنْ رَعِيَّتِكَ فَإِنَّ احْتِجَابَ الْوُلَاةِ عَنِ الرَّعِيَّةِ شُعْبَةٌ مِنَ الضِّيقِ وَ قِلَّةُ عِلْمٍ بِالْأُمُورِ وَ
الِاحْتِجَابُ مِنْهُمْ يَقْطَعُ عَنْهُمْ عِلْمَ مَا احْتَجَبُوا دُونَهُ فَيَصْغُرُ عِنْدَهُمُ الْكَبِيرُ وَ يَعْظُمُ
الصَّغِيرُ وَ يَقْبُحُ الْحَسَنُ وَ يَحْسُنُ الْقَبِيحُ وَ يُشَابُ الْحَقُّ بِالْبَاطِلِ وَ إِنَّمَا الْوَالِي بَشَرٌ لَا
يَعْرِفُ مَا تَوَارَى عَنْهُ النَّاسُ بِهِ مِنَ الْأُمُورِ وَ لَيْسَتْ عَلَى الْحَقِّ سِمَاتٌ تُعْرَفُ بِهَا ضُرُوبُ
الصِّدْقِ مِنَ الْكَذِبِ وَ إِنَّمَا أَنْتَ أَحَدُ رَجُلَيْنِ إِمَّا امْرُؤٌ سَخَتْ نَفْسُكَ بِالْبَذْلِ فِي الْحَقِّ
فَفِيمَ احْتِجَابُكَ مِنْ وَاجِبِ حَقٍّ تُعْطِيهِ أَوْ فِعْلٍ كَرِيمٍ تُسْدِيهِ أَوْ مُبْتَلًى بِالْمَنْعِ فَمَا أَسْرَعَ
كَفَّ النَّاسِ عَنْ مَسْأَلَتِكَ إِذَا أَيِسُوا مِنْ بَذْلِكَ مَعَ أَنَّ أَكْثَرَ حَاجَاتِ النَّاسِ إِلَيْكَ مِمَّا لَا
مَئُونَةَ فِيهِ عَلَيْكَ مِنْ شَكَاةِ مَظْلِمَةٍ أَوْ طَلَبِ إِنْصَافٍ فِي مُعَامَلَةٍ ثُمَّ إِنَّ لِلْوَالِي خَاصَّةً
وَ بِطَانَةً فِيهِمُ اسْتِئْثَارٌ وَ تَطَاوُلٌ وَ قِلَّةُ إِنْصَافٍ فِي مُعَامَلَةٍ فَاحْسِمْ مَادَّةَ أُولَئِكَ بِقَطْعِ
أَسْبَابِ تِلْكَ الْأَحْوَالِ وَ لَا تُقْطِعَنَّ لِأَحَدٍ مِنْ حَاشِيَتِكَ وَ حَامَّتِكَ قَطِيعَةً وَ لَا يَطْمَعَنَّ
مِنْكَ فِي اعْتِقَادِ عُقْدَةٍ تَضُرُّ بِمَنْ يَلِيهَا مِنَ النَّاسِ فِي شِرْبٍ أَوْ عَمَلٍ مُشْتَرَكٍ يَحْمِلُونَ
مَئُونَتَهُ عَلَى غَيْرِهِمْ فَيَكُونُ مَهْنَأُ ذَلِكَ لَهُمْ دُونَكَ وَ عَيْبُهُ عَلَيْكَ فِي الدُّنْيَا وَ الْآخِرَةِ وَ
أَلْزِمِ الْحَقَّ مَنْ لَزِمَهُ مِنَ الْقَرِيبِ وَ الْبَعِيدِ وَ أَنْ فِي ذَلِكَ صَابِراً مُحْتَسِباً وَاقِعاً ذَلِكَ مِنْ
قَرَابَتِكَ وَ خَاصَّتِكَ حَيْثُ وَقَعَ وَ ابْتَغِ عَاقِبَتَهُ بِمَا يَثْقُلُ عَلَيْكَ مِنْهُ فَإِنَّ مَغَبَّةَ ذَلِكَ
مَحْمُودَةٌ وَ إِنْ ظَنَّتِ الرَّعِيَّةُ بِكَ حَيْفاً فَأَصْحِرْ لَهُمْ بِعُذْرِكَ وَ اعْدِلْ عَنْكَ ظُنُونَهُمْ
بِإِصْحَارِكَ فَإِنَّ فِي ذَلِكَ رِيَاضَةً مِنْكَ لِنَفْسِكَ وَ رِفْقاً بِرَعِيَّتِكَ وَ إِعْذَاراً تَبْلُغُ بِهِ حَاجَتَكَ
مِنْ تَقْوِيمِهِمْ عَلَى الْحَقِّ وَ لَا تَدْفَعَنَّ صُلْحاً دَعَاكَ إِلَيْهِ عَدُوُّكَ وَ لِلَّهِ فِيهِ رِضًا فَإِنَّ فِي
الصُّلْحِ دَعَةً لِجُنُودِكَ وَ رَاحَةً مِنْ هُمُومِكَ وَ أَمْناً لِبِلَادِكَ وَ لَكِنِ الْحَذَرَ كُلَّ الْحَذَرِ مِنْ

عَدُوِّكَ بَعْدَ صُلْحِهِ فَإِنَّ الْعَدُوَّ رُبَّمَا قَارَبَ لِيَتَغَفَّلَ فَخُذْ بِالْحَزْمِ وَ اتَّهِمْ فِي ذَلِكَ حُسْنَ الظَّنِّ وَ إِنْ عَقَدْتَ بَيْنَكَ وَ بَيْنَ عَدُوِّكَ عُقْدَةً أَوْ أَلْبَسْتَهُ مِنْكَ ذِمَّةً فَحُطْ عَهْدَكَ بِالْوَفَاءِ وَ ارْعَ ذِمَّتَكَ بِالْأَمَانَةِ وَ اجْعَلْ نَفْسَكَ جُنَّةً دُونَ مَا أَعْطَيْتَ فَإِنَّهُ لَيْسَ مِنْ فَرَائِضِ اللَّهِ شَيْءٌ النَّاسُ أَشَدُّ عَلَيْهِ اجْتِمَاعاً مَعَ تَفَرُّقِ أَهْوَائِهِمْ وَ تَشَتُّتِ آرَائِهِمْ مِنْ تَعْظِيمِ الْوَفَاءِ بِالْعُهُودِ وَ قَدْ لَزِمَ ذَلِكَ الْمُشْرِكُونَ فِيمَا بَيْنَهُمْ دُونَ الْمُسْلِمِينَ لِمَا اسْتَوْبَلُوا مِنْ عَوَاقِبِ الْغَدْرِ فَلَا تَغْدِرَنَّ بِذِمَّتِكَ وَ لَا تَخِيسَنَّ بِعَهْدِكَ وَ لَا تَخْتِلَنَّ عَدُوَّكَ فَإِنَّهُ لَا يَجْتَرِئُ عَلَى اللَّهِ إِلَّا جَاهِلٌ شَقِيٌّ وَ قَدْ جَعَلَ اللَّهُ عَهْدَهُ وَ ذِمَّتَهُ أَمْناً أَفْضَاهُ بَيْنَ الْعِبَادِ بِرَحْمَتِهِ وَ حَرِيماً يَسْكُنُونَ إِلَى مَنَعَتِهِ وَ يَسْتَفِيضُونَ إِلَى جِوَارِهِ فَلَا إِدْغَالَ وَ لَا مُدَالَسَةَ وَ لَا خِدَاعَ فِيهِ وَ لَا تَعْقِدْ عَقْداً تُجَوِّزُ فِيهِ الْعِلَلَ وَ لَا تُعَوِّلَنَّ عَلَى لَحْنِ قَوْلٍ بَعْدَ التَّأْكِيدِ وَ التَّوْثِقَةِ وَ لَا يَدْعُوَنَّكَ ضِيقُ أَمْرٍ لَزِمَكَ فِيهِ عَهْدُ اللَّهِ إِلَى طَلَبِ انْفِسَاخِهِ بِغَيْرِ الْحَقِّ فَإِنَّ صَبْرَكَ عَلَى ضِيقِ أَمْرٍ تَرْجُو انْفِرَاجَهُ وَ فَضْلَ عَاقِبَتِهِ خَيْرٌ مِنْ غَدْرٍ تَخَافُ تَبِعَتَهُ وَ أَنْ تُحِيطَ بِكَ مِنَ اللَّهِ فِيهِ طِلْبَةٌ لَا تَسْتَقْبِلُ فِيهَا دُنْيَاكَ وَ لَا آخِرَتَكَ إِيَّاكَ وَ الدِّمَاءَ وَ سَفْكَهَا بِغَيْرِ حِلِّهَا فَإِنَّهُ لَيْسَ شَيْءٌ أَدْعَى لِنِقْمَةٍ وَ لَا أَعْظَمَ لِتَبِعَةٍ وَ لَا أَحْرَى بِزَوَالِ نِعْمَةٍ وَ انْقِطَاعِ مُدَّةٍ مِنْ سَفْكِ الدِّمَاءِ بِغَيْرِ حَقِّهَا وَ اللَّهُ سُبْحَانَهُ مُبْتَدِئٌ بِالْحُكْمِ بَيْنَ الْعِبَادِ فِيمَا تَسَافَكُوا مِنَ الدِّمَاءِ يَوْمَ الْقِيَامَةِ فَلَا تُقَوِّيَنَّ سُلْطَانَكَ بِسَفْكِ دَمٍ حَرَامٍ فَإِنَّ ذَلِكَ مِمَّا يُضْعِفُهُ وَ يُوهِنُهُ بَلْ يُزِيلُهُ وَ يَنْقُلُهُ وَ لَا عُذْرَ لَكَ عِنْدَ اللَّهِ وَ لَا عِنْدِي فِي قَتْلِ الْعَمْدِ لِأَنَّ فِيهِ قَوَدَ الْبَدَنِ وَ إِنِ ابْتُلِيتَ بِخَطَإٍ وَ أَفْرَطَ عَلَيْكَ سَوْطُكَ أَوْ سَيْفُكَ أَوْ يَدُكَ بِالْعُقُوبَةِ فَإِنَّ فِي الْوَكْزَةِ فَمَا فَوْقَهَا مَقْتَلَةً فَلَا تَطْمَحَنَّ بِكَ نَخْوَةُ سُلْطَانِكَ عَنْ أَنْ تُؤَدِّيَ إِلَى أَوْلِيَاءِ الْمَقْتُولِ حَقَّهُمْ وَ إِيَّاكَ وَ الْإِعْجَابَ بِنَفْسِكَ وَ الثِّقَةَ بِمَا يُعْجِبُكَ مِنْهَا وَ حُبَّ الْإِطْرَاءِ فَإِنَّ ذَلِكَ مِنْ أَوْثَقِ فُرَصِ الشَّيْطَانِ فِي نَفْسِهِ لِيَمْحَقَ مَا يَكُونُ مِنْ إِحْسَانِ الْمُحْسِنِينَ وَ إِيَّاكَ وَ الْمَنَّ عَلَى رَعِيَّتِكَ بِإِحْسَانِكَ أَوِ التَّزَيُّدَ فِيمَا آانَ مِنْ فِعْلِكَ أَوْ أَنْ تَعِدَهُمْ فَتُتْبِعَ مَوْعِدَكَ بِخُلْفِكَ فَإِنَّ الْمَنَّ يُبْطِلُ الْإِحْسَانَ وَ التَّزَيُّدَ يَذْهَبُ بِنُورِ الْحَقِّ وَ الْخُلْفَ يُوجِبُ الْمَقْتَ عِنْدَ اللَّهِ وَ النَّاسِ قَالَ اللَّهُ تَعَالَى أَبْرَ مَقْتاً عِنْدَ اللَّهِ أَنْ تَقُولُوا مَا لَا تَفْعَلُونَ وَ إِيَّاكَ وَ الْعَجَلَةَ بِالْأُمُورِ قَبْلَ أَوَانِهَا أَوِ التَّسَقُّطَ فِيهَا عِنْدَ إِمْكَانِهَا أَوِ اللَّجَاجَةَ فِيهَا إِذَا تَنَكَّرَتْ أَوِ الْوَهْنَ عَنْهَا إِذَا اسْتَوْضَحَتْ فَضَعْ كُلَّ أَمْرٍ مَوْضِعَهُ وَ أَوْقِعْ كُلَّ أَمْرٍ مَوْقِعَهُ وَ إِيَّاكَ وَ الِاسْتِئْثَارَ بِمَا النَّاسُ فِيهِ أُسْوَةٌ وَ التَّغَابِيَ عَمَّا تُعْنَى بِهِ مِمَّا قَدْ وَضَحَ لِلْعُيُونِ فَإِنَّهُ مَأْخُوذٌ مِنْكَ لِغَيْرِكَ وَ عَمَّا قَلِيلٍ تَنْكَشِفُ عَنْكَ أَغْطِيَةُ الْأُمُورِ وَ يُنْتَصَفُ مِنْكَ لِلْمَظْلُومِ امْلِكْ حَمِيَّةَ أَنْفِكَ وَ سَوْرَةَ حَدِّكَ وَ سَطْوَةَ يَدِكَ وَ غَرْبَ لِسَانِكَ وَ احْتَرِسْ مِنْ كُلِّ ذَلِكَ بِكَفِّ الْبَادِرَةِ وَ تَأْخِيرِ السَّطْوَةِ حَتَّى يَسْكُنَ غَضَبُكَ فَتَمْلِكَ الِاخْتِيَارَ وَ لَنْ تَحْكُمَ ذَلِكَ مِنْ نَفْسِكَ حَتَّى تُكْثِرَ هُمُومَكَ بِذِكْرِ الْمَعَادِ إِلَى رَبِّكَ وَ الْوَاجِبُ عَلَيْكَ أَنْ تَتَذَكَّرَ مَا مَضَى لِمَنْ تَقَدَّمَكَ مِنْ حُكُومَةٍ عَادِلَةٍ أَوْ سُنَّةٍ فَاضِلَةٍ أَوْ أَثَرٍ عَنْ نَبِيِّنَا (صلى الله عليه وآله) أَوْ

فَرِيضَةٍ فِي كِتَابِ اللهِ فَتَقْتَدِيَ بِمَا شَاهَدْتَ مِمَّا عَمِلْنَا بِهِ فِيهَا وَ تَجْتَهِدَ لِنَفْسِكَ فِي اتِّبَاعِ مَا عَهِدْتُ إِلَيْكَ فِي عَهْدِي هَذَا وَ اسْتَوْثَقْتُ بِهِ مِنَ الْحُجَّةِ لِنَفْسِي عَلَيْكَ لِكَيْلَا تَكُونَ لَكَ عِلَّةٌ عِنْدَ تَسَرُّعِ نَفْسِكَ إِلَى هَوَاهَا وَ أَنَا أَسْأَلُ اللهَ بِسَعَةِ رَحْمَتِهِ وَ عَظِيمِ قُدْرَتِهِ عَلَى إِعْطَاءِ كُلِّ رَغْبَةٍ أَنْ يُوَفِّقَنِي وَ إِيَّاكَ لِمَا فِيهِ رِضَاهُ مِنَ الْإِقَامَةِ عَلَى الْعُذْرِ الْوَاضِحِ إِلَيْهِ وَ إِلَى خَلْقِهِ مَعَ حُسْنِ الثَّنَاءِ فِي الْعِبَادِ وَ جَمِيلِ الْأَثَرِ فِي الْبِلَادِ وَ تَمَامِ النِّعْمَةِ وَ تَضْعِيفِ الْكَرَامَةِ وَ أَنْ يَخْتِمَ لِي وَ لَكَ بِالسَّعَادَةِ وَ الشَّهَادَةِ إِنَّا إِلَيْهِ رَاجِعُونَ وَ السَّلَامُ عَلَى رَسُولِ اللهِ صَلَّى اللهُ عَلَيْهِ وَ آلِهِ وَ سَلَّمَ الطَّيِّبِينَ الطَّاهِرِينَ وَ سَلَّمَ تَسْلِيماً كَثِيراً وَ السَّلَامُ.

www.ingramcontent.com/pod-product-compliance
Lightning Source LLC
Chambersburg PA
CBHW022053020426
42335CB00012B/678